Praise for Diana Johnstone's
Queen of Chaos

"Veteran journalist Diana Johnstone captures the imperial worldview of Hillary Clinton in memorable detail. Hillary the Hawk, as U.S. Senator and Secretary of State, never saw a weapons systems she did not support nor a U.S. war practice she did not endorse. This included her hyper-aggressive launch of the war on Libya (against the opposition of Secretary of Defense Robert Gates) and the resulting sprawling chaos, violence and weapons dispersal spilling beyond Libya's war-torn society to larger regions of central Africa. Johnstone documents Hillary Clinton as 'the top salesperson for the ruling oligarchy' and 'the favorite candidate of the War Party.' That is what is at stake in November 2016."

— Ralph Nader, author of *Return to Sender: Unanswered Letters to the Presiden*

***

"In *Queen of Chaos,* Johnstone issues a Herculean call for peace. Similarly, in another work, Dr. June Terpstra warns us to Beware the Women of the Hegemon, whose policy positions are as warlike as any man's. Johnstone shows us that like Madeleine Albright, the first woman U.S. Secretary of State before her, Clinton can defend sanctions regimes, bombs, and drone attacks as well as any man. As Johnstone guides us from Honduras to Libya, it becomes clear that Hillary qualifies as a woman of the Hegemon, supporting a belligerent U.S. foreign policy on almost every Continent... Hillary Clinton stole democracy from the Haitian people. She stole their hopes, their dreams, their aspirations for themselves; she stole their human rights. Now, if Hillary Clinton would do that to them, there's no telling what she will do to us. Johnstone gives us a kind of primer on Hillary Clinton's foreign policy past: from genocide to 'We came, we saw, he died!' I think it's clear: should Hillary Clinton become Madam President, we ain't seen nothing yet."

— Cynthia McKinney, former Member of Congress

"Hillary Clinton, 'the top salesperson for the ruling oligarchy,' known in some quarters as Hitlery, has met her match in Diana Johnstone. This is a marvelous book, easy to read, by a superb writer who demonstrates that Hitlery's ambition would bring not peace and justice but World War III. This is a must read book that provides escape into reality from endless hype. The world stands on the cusp of destruction. Hillary would ensure destruction."

— Paul Craig Roberts, former Assistant Secretary of the Treasury, author *How the Economy Was Lost*

***

"Wow! No other book cuts so starkly and accurately to the heart of the current violent chaos engulfing the world, and to the significance of Hillary Rodham Clinton's decades-long love affair with power that has helped push us to this precarious moment in history. The well-researched chronology and factual details compiled by Diana Johnstone about Honduras, Rwanda, Libya, Bosnia and Kosovo, to Iraq, Syria and Ukraine, turned into bloodbaths and finally into dangerous, failed states, constitutes the harsh reality that we need to appreciate if, as decent people, we want to regain some moral conscience. But also for our simple self-preservation.

"Certainly Hillary is not the only neocon pyromaniac who likes to set a fire and then laugh when no one can put it out. But as she now vies for leadership of that cabal, more and more people will hopefully see through their Orwellian lies, effectively selling perpetual war to the US-NATO-Israel as a noble cause to bring democracy, human rights, peace and love. Self-perpetuating war may indeed make the war profiteers happy and wealthy who so prominently top the Clintons' donor list, but it is indeed as stupid as playing with fire. In putting a nuclear-armed Russia in their sights, the story cannot end well for anyone. I can assure that if you read Johnstone's book, you will want to help put out this insanity."

— Coleen Rowley, retired FBI Agent and former Minneapolis Division Legal Counsel, whistleblower and one of TIME Magazine's Persons of the Year for 2002.

***

"Diana Johnstone's wit, clarity of style and political lucidity in this book are matched only by Hilary Clinton's opportunism, meanness and self-delusion in the service of the American empire."

— Jean Bricmont, author *Humanitarian Imperialism*

"If you are still fooled by Bill and Hillary Clinton, as well as the Democratic Party, then Diana Johnstone's book will dispel the myth that either they or the party are redeemable. Hillary, like her husband, Barack Obama and the Democratic leadership, are controlled by corporate money and willing accomplices in the crimes of empire. Her appeal to gender holds no more promise for the poor, the working class or the wretched of the earth we tyrannize around the globe than Obama's appeal to race. The predatory engines of corporate capitalism and the security and surveillance state will run as smoothly under her direction as they did under her predecessor. If you doubt this, read this book."

— Chris Hedges, author of *Wages of Rebellion*

***

"Count on this witty, wise critique of U.S. 'Exceptionalism' to expose Hillary Clinton's ruthless ambition. In keeping with past pursuits to 'win,' Hillary Clinton caters to beneficiaries of systems based on greed and violence. Johnstone engages in 'slice and dice' analysis, but in describing *Queen of Chaos*, Johnstone consistently suggests alternative policies based on respect for human rights, particularly the rights of those most harmed by the menacing, destructive reach of U.S. Empire."

— Kathy Kelly, author *Other Lands Have Dreams*

***

"Diana Johnstone's *Queen of Chaos* is an excellent source of information for Hillary Clinton's political rivals But it's much more than that. It offers very perceptive accounts of US foreign policy of the last 25 years, particularly the complex and highly controversial cases of Libya, Yugoslavia, Honduras and Russia, as well as the issue of women in power. 'Is there something wrong with American women,' Johnstone asks, 'that they need Hillary Clinton as President to make them feel better?'"

— William Blum, author *Killing Hope*

Also by Diana Johnstone

Fools Crusade

The Politics of Euromissiles

Queen of Chaos

The Misadventures of Hillary Clinton

By Diana Johnstone

CounterPunch Books Petrolia, California

4/14/16

COUNTERPUNCH BOOKS

An Imprint of the Institute for the
Advancement of Journalistic Clarity

For information contact:
CounterPunch Books,
PO Box 228, Petrolia, California. 95558
1(707) 629-3683
www.counterpunch.org

Cover Design by Tiffany Wardle de Sousa.

Johnstone, Diana. Queen of Chaos:
The Misadventures of Hillary Clinton.

ISBN: 978-0-9897637-6-9
ISBN-10:0-9897637-6-5

Contents

Introduction

Baby boomer Hillary Rodham was born in 1947, one year before U.S. policy planner George F. Kennan famously wrote that: "We have about 50% of the world's wealth, but only 6.3% of its population. ... In this situation, we cannot fail to be the object of envy and resentment. Our real task in the coming period is to devise a pattern of relationships which will permit us to maintain this position of disparity."

Hillary, a Republican and a "Goldwater girl" in her youth, grew up with the viewpoint of a rich and dominant America obliged to maintain its position on top of an envious and resentful world. This was the standard attitude.

It was the result of World War II. The United States won the war in the Pacific. In Europe, the overwhelming military victor was the Soviet Union – a reality that has been obscured by Hollywood movies and repeated celebrations of the D-Day landing in Normandy, overlooking the fact that the Red Army was already pinning down and defeating the Wehrmacht on the Eastern Front. But the economic victor of World War II was overwhelmingly the United States of America. In a world largely devastated and indebted by war, the United States emerged with the huge advantage emphasized by George Kennan.

Unfortunately, since then the United States has failed to develop any great national purpose other than staying on top.

In recent years, it has become more frequent to speak of the United States as an "Empire". Yet it is an empire like no other. The United States has military bases all over the world, but their aim is more to preserve the post-World War II advantage than to expand in the ways previous empires expanded. The former European empires assumed some responsibility for the countries they conquered in order to exploit their riches more effectively. Alongside exploitation of local labor and theft of resources, previous empires built infrastructure and introduced certain beneficial measures to make their colonies run smoothly. The United States is an irresponsible empire. It devastates countries and leaves them in shambles, with no compensation. Its actions are increasingly destructive because the purpose is not in reality to build an empire, but to destroy real or potential rivals and so maintain the position of superiority gained in World War II.

The destructive nature of these wars is confirmed by the fact that on close examination, none of the recent U.S. wars have been "won" in any meaningful sense. Temporary illusions of "victory" have given way to the rise of hostile extremists. Most recently, the undeclared U.S. drone war against Islamists in Yemen led to an even more effective revolutionary uprising which seized U.S.-provided weapons and forced American officials to flee. Despite the disastrous results of one war after another in the Middle East, the War Party in Washington seems ready to plunge into yet another proxy war in Ukraine, this time against a much more powerful adversary. These are essentially "spoiler" wars, intended to diminish potential rivals. They create deepening chaos and bitter enemies, with no real benefit to anyone.

Vote For Me, I'm a Woman

Hillary Rodham Clinton has spent years trying to sell women on the idea that *their* ambition, rather than hers, will be rewarded if she is elected President of the United States.

The idea seems to be that if she "breaks the glass ceiling", American women *en masse* will pour through, occupying the upper floors, the attic, even the roof.

But do we need to "prove" that a woman can be president?

If women can be wrestlers, for which they are clearly not naturally qualified, a woman can certainly be President. There is no serious qualification for the office that a woman lacks.

Proving this fairly obvious point is not the most crucial issue at stake in the next U.S. Presidential election. There is also the little matter of whether or not to lead the country into war with a major nuclear power. Avoiding World War III is somewhat more urgent than "proving" that a woman can be President of the United States.

Throughout world history, women have been rulers. This fact has had very little effect on the daily lives of millions of women. Like Hillary herself, women rulers have most often been the daughters or wives of male rulers. On her South Asia tour in 1995, she observed, as her biographer Carl Bernstein notes, that "Pakistan, India, Bangladesh, and Sri Lanka all had governments headed by women, yet women are held in such disregard in their cultures that newborn girls are sometimes killed or abandoned." The social condition of women in a society does not depend on whether or not the country has a Queen.

Women are distinguishing themselves in many fields where genuine accomplishment is more significant than politics in creating inspiring role models. For example, in August 2014, Maryam Mirzakhani was the first woman to be awarded the Fields Medal for excellence in mathematics. This could set a positive trend.

In politics, as in other fields of power, women are often their own "glass ceiling", in the sense that they may be content to stay out of the limelight in order to help others. This is not to be despised. But for women who need a politically powerful female as a role model, history offers Cleopatra, Catherine the Great of Russia, Eleanor of Aquitaine, Queen Elizabeth the First, among many others. Many elected national leaders in today's world are women, most notably in Latin America. It's too late for the United States to take the lead by electing a women president, but don't worry, the USA is sure to catch up eventually.

Is there something wrong with American women that they need Hillary Clinton as President to make them feel better?

Certainly not. American women are creating many new ways to lead fruitful, useful and rewarding lives. And rather than making us feel better, it might make us feel much worse if the first woman President brings disaster on the world.

Let us hope that the inevitable first woman president will be a person distinguished by a profound understanding of the world and genuine human compassion, rather than by relentless personal ambition.

A Taste of Hillary Clinton in action:
Hypocrisy in Honduras

Barack Obama promised change.

Then, upon election, he chose Hillary Rodham Clinton as his Secretary of State. This was an early sign that when it came to foreign policy there would be no real change – at least, no change for the better.

The first real test of "change" in U.S. foreign policy came six months later on June 28, 2009, when armed forces overthrew the elected President of Honduras, Manuel Zelaya.

It is easy to see what real change would have meant. The United States could have vigorously condemned the coup and demanded that the legitimate President be reinstated. Considering U.S. influence in Honduras, especially its powerful military bases there, U.S. "resolve" would have given teeth to anti-coup protests in Honduras and throughout the Hemisphere.

That is not the way it happened.

Instead, we got a first sample of the way Hillary Rodham Clinton treats the world. She calls it "smart power". We can translate that as hypocrisy and manipulation.

In early June 2009, Hillary flew to Honduras for the annual meeting of the Organization of American States with one thing in mind: how to prevent the lifting of the 47-year-old ban excluding Cuba, which a large majority of the OAS now considered "an outdated artifact of the Cold War". Moreover, Venezuela, Nicaragua, Bolivia and Ecuador would go as far as to characterize the ban, for some strange reason, as "an example of U.S. bullying".

So Hillary and staff solved the problem by pouring the old wine into a new bottle. No more Cold War, no more "communist threat".

"Given what President Obama had said about moving past the stale debates of the Cold War," Hillary wrote in her memoir *Hard Choices*, "it would be hypocritical of us to continue insisting that Cuba be kept out of the OAS for the reasons it was first suspended in 1962, ostensibly its adherence to 'Marxism-Leninism' and alignment 'with the communist bloc.' It would be more credible and accurate to focus on Cuba's present-day human rights violations, which were incompatible with the OAS charter."

Hillary has a strange definition of hypocrisy. She sees nothing hypocritical in simply changing the pretext for exclusion, while never mentioning the historic reasons for U.S. hostility: the expropriation of U.S. property that liberated resources for social welfare, education and one of the best free medical systems in the world, as well as intense political pressure from the dispossessed

Cuban diaspora in the United States.

She sees nothing hypocritical in inventing a transparent device to keep Cuba out while pretending to let Cuba in: "What if we agreed to lift the suspension, but with the condition that Cuba be reseated as a member only if it made enough democratic reforms to bring it in line with the charter? And, to expose the Castro brothers' contempt for the OAS itself, why not require Cuba to formally request readmittance?"

Indeed, this proved just hypocritical enough to persuade the fence-hangers, Brazil and Chile, to go along.

Thus Hillary began her diplomatic career in Latin America, marked by rebranding hostility to any independent socio-economic policy from "anti-communism" to defense of "human rights", by transparent hypocrisy enforced by arm-twisting, and by enforcing the Monroe Doctrine in both domestic and international affairs.

During her visit to Honduras, her host, President Manuel Zelaya, annoyed her. She didn't like his white cowboy hat, she didn't like his dark black mustache, and above all, she didn't like his fondness for Hugo Chavez and Fidel Castro. But she was hypocritical about that, too. "I pulled Zelaya aside into a small room and played up his role and responsibilities as host of the conference. If he backed our compromise, he could help save not just this summit but the OAS itself. If not, he would be remembered as the leader who presided over the organization's collapse."

Hillary left Honduras satisfied at having "succeeded in replacing an outdated rationale with a modern process that would further strengthen the OAS commitment to democracy."

Shortly thereafter, President Zelaya was overthrown.

The context of that coup d'état makes the motivation clear.

Manuel Zelaya was a traitor to his class. Although a landowner from a wealthy family in the lumber industry, Zelaya had developed populist ambitions to liberate his country from its longstanding status as the ultimate banana republic. The country is divided between a small selfish wealthy class and the mass of dirt-poor inhabitants whose only prospects tend to lie in drug smuggling. Fierce competition in the narcotics trade contributes to Honduras holding the highest murder rate in the world. In addition, the U.S. Air Force base at Soto Cano has served as the organizing center of two of the most vicious "regime change" operations in history: the 1954 overthrow of reformist president Jacobo Arbenz of Guatemala, to the north of Honduras, and the illegal Contra sabotage operations against Nicaragua, the country's southern neighbor, in the 1980s. Meanwhile, in Honduras itself, the rich got richer and the poor got poorer.

Elected in 2005, Zelaya wanted to make a difference. With the apparent breeze of change blowing throughout the region, Zelaya decreed a 60% minimum wage increase amid howls of protest from private business associations. Criticizing the so-called war on drugs as a pretext for foreign intervention, Zelaya proposed instead a fresh approach to the drug problem with a focus on educating addicts and curbing demand. And he thought that Soto Cano should be transformed into an international civilian airport. In 2007, Zelaya made the first official trip by a Honduran President to Cuba in 46 years and discussed policy matters with Raul Castro. Worst of all, he joined ALBA, the *Alternativa Bolivariana para los Pueblos de Nuestra América* (subsequently renamed the "Alianza"), founded in 2004 by Cuba and Venezuela, inspired by Hugo Chavez. This rapprochement promised Honduras real economic benefits.

In 2008, Washington sent as its Ambassador to Tegucigalpa the man who had been director of Andean Affairs at the National Security Council during the failed U.S.-backed attempt to overthrow Hugo Chavez in 2002, Hugo Llorens. Born in Cuba in 1954, at the age of seven Llorens had been one of over fourteen thousand unaccompanied children shipped from the revolutionary island to the United States in Operation Peter Pan to be saved from "communist indoctrination".

In May 2009, the Democratic Civil Union of Honduras was formed by "civil society" organizations, many of them receiving "democracy promotion" grants from the U.S.-financed National Endowment for Democracy (NED), with the objective of getting rid of Zelaya. Their campaign focused on Zelaya's proposal for a referendum to voters during the upcoming November elections on whether or not to convene a convention in 2010 to revise the Constitution, ostensibly to make it more democratic via proportional representation with a recall mechanism and greater rights for ethnic minorities.

Honduras' 1982 Constitution, the country's twelfth in its 144 years of existence, had already been amended over 20 times by Congress. But the country's reactionary oligarchy chose to decry Zelaya's initiative as a criminal attempt to violate "articles written in stone" which banned any attempt to allow a president to run for more than a single four-year term. His opponents denounced the referendum as aimed solely to end the current constitutional ban on re-election and thus enable Zelaya to extend his presidency after the end of his current term.

In short, the constitutional proposal was portrayed as a way to set the stage for Zelaya to become dictator by election, like the elected "dictator" of Venezuela, Hugo Chavez. On June 23, the Civil Union issued a statement saying that they "trust the armed forces" to "defend the Constitution, the law, peace and democracy." Llorens added the weight of official U.S. support to the campaign by declaring that "one can't violate the Constitution in order to create another Constitution, because if one doesn't respect the Constitution, then we all live under the law of the jungle."

This plea for constitutional order was clearly understood by the Honduran military as a green light to violate the constitution in order to save it. In the early morning of June 28, the day of the proposed opinion survey on amending the constitution, a hundred Honduran soldiers invaded Zelaya's bedroom and whisked him off to Costa Rica without even allowing him to get dressed. Expelling the President in his pajamas was an extra touch of disrespect.

The officer in charge of the military coup, General Romeo Vasquez, was a graduate of the notorious School of the Americas in Fort Benning, Georgia, which has trained a long line of Latin American putschists and torturers. The Honduran military let it be known that they were "obligated" to remove President Zelaya from power because of the "threat" he posed with his leftist ideology and alignment with Venezuela and Cuba.[1]

Under the post-Zelaya regime, Honduras rapidly withdrew from ALBA.

As she tells it, Hillary was unprepared and unaware when she received word of the crisis from Tom Shannon, Assistant Secretary of State for Western Hemisphere Affairs. "He told me what we knew, which still wasn't much." This was odd because it emerged that Shannon and Deputy Assistant Secretary of State Craig Kelley had been in Honduras the week before, meeting with the very same civilian and military groups who later carried out the coup. They claimed subsequently that they had been there to "urge against" it. Hillary could also count on expert analysis from the notorious former U.S. ambassador to Honduras during the Iran-Contra affair, John Negroponte, whom she had reportedly hired as a special consultant. Negroponte had recently been to Tegucigalpa to urge Zelaya not to change the status of the main U.S. Air Force base at Soto Cano. Now it was Hillary's turn to employ "smart" power by never calling a coup d'état a coup d'état. Instead, what had happened was a "crisis" or the "forced exile" of the President which inspired the United States to call on "all parties" to resolve their differences "without violence".

In *Hard Choices*, Hillary implicitly endorses the *golpistas'* pretext.

"Certainly the region did not need another dictator, and many knew Zelaya well enough to believe the charges against him. But Zelaya had been elected by the Honduran people [...] I didn't see any choice but to condemn Zelaya's ouster.

"In a public statement I called on all parties in Honduras to respect the constitutional order and the rule of law and to commit themselves to resolve political disputes peacefully and through dialogue", she recalled in *Hard Choices*. The State Department went on to praise the Honduran military, which had hardly used "peaceful dialogue" to depose their President, for having acted as "the securer of public order during this process".

While Zelaya was demanding to be reinstated, Hillary sought mediation between the "two sides": the democratically elected President-in-exile in Costa Rica and the "temporary interim president" Roberto Micheletti, installed by the coup. In a sense, there were indeed "two sides". It was a quarrel between those who *had* violated the constitution and the man whom they accused of *wanting* to violate the constitution. In the end, the accusation of bad intentions won out over the plain facts of the matter – a pattern which would be repeated in Hillary's career, notably in Libya.

Meanwhile, representatives of the new Micheletti government trekked to Washington to plead their case for "saving democracy from a new Chavez" to Congress and the policy-making caste. The coup defenders enjoyed the knowledgeable guidance of top lobbyist Lanny Davis. Davis happens to have been special counsel to President Bill Clinton from 1996 to 1998, and a close friend of Hillary.

Stalling for time, Hillary "strategized on a plan to restore order in Honduras and ensure that free and fair elections could be held quickly and legitimately, which would render the question of Zelaya moot and give the Honduran people a chance to choose their own future."

Zelaya was never reinstated. From then on, Hondurans have had the chance to choose their future – as long as it looks very much like their past. "Honduras" is Spanish for "depths". Politically, the impoverished country has continued to deserve its name.

Our "bottom line", as Hillary put it, "is free, fair, and democratic elections with a peaceful transfer of power." Elections to "render the question of Zelaya moot" were held on November 29. Much of the campaigning in these "free and fair" elections was severely inhibited by a temporary Micheletti decree suspending the very same five rights spelled out in the constitution that the *golpistas* had been so eager to defend: personal liberty, freedom of expression, freedom of movement, habeas corpus, and freedom of association. Over three thousand soldiers and police were called in to "neutralize" members of a newly-formed National Resistance Front which had called for boycott of the elections in protest against the June 29 coup. The campaign was marked by intimidation, beatings, at least one death, and the occasional disappearance. Employees were told to vote or lose their jobs. Despite all the pressure, just under half the voters turned out, at 49 percent.

All's well that ends well, and the winner in the end was Porfirio "Pepe" Lobo Sosa, the National Party candidate who had been defeated by Zelaya in the previous election. The governments of Argentina, Bolivia, Brazil, Chile, Cuba, Ecuador, Guatemala, Nicaragua, Paraguay, Spain, Uruguay, and Venezuela refused to recognize the result, but Washington was content.

President Lobo described his regime as a "government of national reconciliation." Hillary Clinton praised it as a "resumption of democratic and constitutional government."

"Ever since Porfirio 'Pepe' Lobo came into office as President of Honduras in January, after a fraudulent election from which opposition candidates withdrew, he's been testing what he and the nation's elites can get away with, gradually unleashing more and more violence against the opposition", historian Dana Frank noted nine months later. "Paramilitary-style assassinations and death threats against trade unionists, *campesino* activists, and feminists active in the opposition continue unabated, with complete impunity. Last Friday night, September 17, gunmen shot and killed Juana Bustillo, a leader in the social security workers' union. Nine journalists critical of the government have been killed since Lobo took office." [2]

Despite the repression, the resistance had by then collected 1,346,876 signatures (out of a country of 7.8 million) calling for a constitutional convention to democratize Honduran society, just as the deposed populist Manuel Zelaya had proposed.

In the following elections in November 2013, voters in Honduras were once again free to choose a dismal past for their dismal future. But at first there was a glimmer of hope, as the polls for several months had shown the front-runner to be deposed President Zelaya's wife, Xiomara Castro de Zelaya, leader of a new party formed out of the post-coup resistance movement. Here was an excellent opportunity for feminist Hillary Rodham Clinton to support "breaking the glass ceiling" in Honduras – the election of a charismatic woman which would break the hold of the ruling oligarchy. It did not occur.

As the election approached, violent intimidation increased and Xiomara Castro's lead shrank.

National Party candidate Juan Orlando Hernández built his candidacy around the promise of "a soldier on every corner", as Dana Frank reported in *The Nation*. "It's well established that the country's police, judiciary and prosecutor are corrupt, interlaced with drug traffickers and organized crime. The police are directed by Juan Carlos 'El Tigre' Bonilla, an alleged death squad leader. Lacking the political will to clean this up, current President Porfirio Lobo and the Congress are instead sending in the military to take over police functions... Constitutionally, the military oversees the balloting process. In this context, prospects for a free and fair contest are grim."[3]

According to the human rights group Rights Action, in the period between May 2012 and October 2013, there were 36 murders and 24 armed attacks targeting candidates or potential candidates and their families or supporters. 59 percent of Hondurans polled expected the elections to be fraudulent. Amid accusations of fraud and intimidation, Juan Orlando Hernández was proclaimed President with 37 percent of the vote, while Xiomara Castro came in second with about 29 percent.

According to Dana Frank: "Yes, gangs are rampant in Honduras. But the truly dangerous gang is the Honduran government. And our own tax dollars are pouring into it while our top officials praise its virtues.

"This June 28 marks the fifth anniversary of the military coup that deposed democratically-elected Honduran President Manuel Zelaya. Since then, a series of corrupt administrations has unleashed open criminal control of Honduras, from top to bottom of the government. Current President Juan Orlando Hernández, who entered office in January, was himself an enthusiastic supporter of the coup...

"The Honduras police are overwhelmingly corrupt, working closely with drug traffickers and organized crime. Last August, even a Honduran government commission overseeing a clean-up of the police force admitted that 70 percent of the police are 'beyond saving.' *InSight Crime* concludes: "a series of powerful local groups, connected to political and economic elites...manage most of the underworld activities in the country. They have deeply penetrated the Honduran police." The judiciary and prosecutors are often corrupt as well: "Perpetrators of killings and other violent crimes are rarely brought to justice," reports *Human Rights Watch;* "as a result, post-coup Honduras now boasts the highest murder rate in the world, according to United Nations figures."

In the two years following the coup, spending on public housing, health, and education all dropped, while extreme poverty rose by 26.3 percent. In May 2014, the entire agency charged with children's interests was eliminated and its assets liquidated.

"In this overall scenario, children indeed die. With few jobs and without a functioning criminal justice system, truly terrifying gangs have proliferated, and drug trafficking engenders spectacular violence, including multiple massacres of children in April and May splayed all over the papers. According to *Casa Alianza*, the leading independent advocate for homeless children in Honduras, in May 2014 alone 104 young people were killed; between 2010 and 2013, 458 children 14 or younger were assassinated.

"On May 6, José Guadalupe Ruelas, the director of *Casa Alianza*, charged that police are operating operate 'social cleansing' death squads killing children." [4] Meanwhile, the ruling National Party has changed its mind about articles "written in stone". At the party's request, the Honduras Supreme Court itself violated the Constitution by simply scrapping the articles banning a presidential second term. At a meeting with businessmen in Miami, President Juan Orlando Hernández shrugged off the change, remarking that "re-election has become the general rule in many countries of the world..."

Ever since the fledgling populist Manuel Zelaya, who dared to try to improve the lot of his people, was carted off in his night shirt, the situation in Honduras has gotten steadily worse. More poverty, more crime, more murders – so many murders and so few arrests and prosecutions that it is impossible to distinguish drug related killings from political assassinations carried out by police and the military. The situation for youth is so dire that the influx of unaccompanied minors from Honduras has become an immigration problem for the United States. In the summer of 2014, kids from Honduras made up the largest contingent of some forty-seven thousand unaccompanied minors apprehended as they tried to enter the United States.

Asked on a June 17, 2014 CNN Town Hall broadcast about what to do with thousands of minors from Honduras and neighboring countries seeking asylum in the United States, Hillary acknowledged that many children are fleeing from an "exponential increase in violence". However, they "should be sent back as soon as it can be determined who the responsible adults in their family are", she said; "all of them who can should be reunited with their families".

"We have to send a clear message: just because your child gets across the border doesn't mean your child gets to say", she said. Do we need to recall that Hillary began her career as advocate for "children's rights"?

It is interesting to compare the readiness of the United States to accept thousands of unaccompanied children escaping from "communist propaganda" in the 1960s to the current unwillingness to accept children fleeing for their lives.

When a white hat appears on the horizon of a wretched place like Honduras, proclaiming his intention to try to improve conditions, couldn't the rich and powerful United States react otherwise than stigmatizing him as a potential 'dictator'? Instead of giving an advocate of change the opportunity to try, Hillary's State Department connived to help bundle him out of power. All is back to normal; however below normal that particular normal happens to be.

On the face of it, the overthrow of Manuel Zelaya was a relatively mild "regime change", as far as U.S. operations go. The real violence came later, with the unsolved murders of oppositionists and children. But like other U.S. - backed interventions in the political life of weaker countries, the result was chaos; the chaos of poverty, crime and hopelessness. On the pretext of preventing the elected President from becoming a "dictator", Hillary and her colleagues contributed to shoring up the longstanding United States dictatorship over the Southern Hemisphere. The Monroe Doctrine, proclaimed to protect the continent from outside powers, has in practice come to mean a license for the United States to protect the inhabitants from themselves and their "errors".

As we will see throughout this book, the foreign policy of Hillary Clinton amounts to the application of an enlarged Monroe Doctrine to the entire world.

Chapter 1

Riding the Military-Industrial-Financial Tiger

In April 2014, a peer-reviewed study for Princeton and Northwestern Universities concluded that the United States is not a democracy, but an "oligarchy" run by "economic elites". This has been obvious for some time to anyone paying attention, but an academic study helps clinch the argument. The report, entitled "Testing Theories of American Politics: Elites, Interest Groups, and Average Citizens", by comparing nearly 1,800 policy choices between 1981 and 2002, concluded that what the rich and powerful wanted, they got. That is, the policy choices of those above the 90th percentile of income were enacted while the wishes of average Americans, in the 50 percentile of income, were neglected. The scholars concluded that: "The central point that emerges from our research is that economic elites and organized groups representing business interests have substantial independent impacts on US government policy, while mass-based interest groups and average citizens have little or no independent influence."

"When a majority of citizens disagrees with economic elites and/or with organized interests, they generally lose. Moreover, because of the strong status quo bias built into the US political system, even when fairly large majorities of Americans favor policy change, they generally do not get it."

Only when the less affluent majority happens to want what the richest ten percent want do they have a serious chance of getting it, the study concluded.

This imbalance is not new, as the rich have always had the advantage of personal contacts and influence over the politicians who make the laws and run the executive. It has apparently been exacerbated by recent Supreme Court rulings increasing the scope of campaign donations, as well as by the extension of the presidential primary system, which is supposed to make the choice of presidential candidates "more democratic". In reality, it creates more occasions for money to play a role in candidate selection and reduces the influence of party members on both choice of candidate and definition of political program.

Every four years, the U.S. two party system essentially gives voters a choice between only two candidates, both heavily vetted by billionaires and lobbies representing major corporations and financial interests. There is the Bad Cop, the Republican Party, and the Good Cop, the Democratic Party. They play their roles, but however they appeal to the voters, the first task of anyone who aspires to be one of those two exclusive candidates is to appear as the best investment for contributors who expect to get what they paid for. When it comes to domestic legislation, no truly progressive or egalitarian policies are feasible. However much they quarrel, both parties have accepted that domestic politics must conform to the interests of financial capital, "the markets". A perfect example is health care reform: in the United States, single-payer programs, which function well in various other countries, were never even seriously considered, but automatically condemned as "socialistic", in favor of a complicated and costly scheme profitable to private insurance companies.

In short, today presidential power is very limited on the domestic scene. But the world stage offers the opportunity to wield great power – or at least to appear to wield great power.

This contrast sums up Hillary Rodham Clinton's initial experience at the White House. Her much-heralded universal health insurance plan ended as a fiasco. Aside from her own mistakes, this failure was fundamentally inherent in the effort to construct a public health system on the basis of ensuring a big profit margin for the shareholders of private insurance companies. Obamacare suffers from the same contradiction.

Due to the current relationship of forces, financial and ideological, progressive domestic reform is an exercise in powerlessness. However, the President of the United States is able to exercise enormous power abroad. It is essentially the power of destruction. But it does make an impression, notably on American voters. If Bill Clinton's administration is not remembered solely for Monica Lewinsky, it will mainly be thanks to the destructive forces Clinton let loose on Iraq, Sudan and the Balkans. Wrap those sanctions and bombing raids in a media package called "defending human rights" or "defying dictators" and domestic failures fade before the grandeur of conquering Evil abroad.

How We Got Where We Are

Starting in 1950, the United States built an economic trap for itself from which it now seems unable to escape. The trap was given a name by Dwight Eisenhower in his farewell speech as President on January 17, 1961: the military-industrial complex (MIC).

The birth of this monster can be traced to National Security Council document 68, NSC-68, submitted to President Harry S. Truman on April 14, 1950. The document was top secret then and remained so until 1975. Its main author was Paul Nitze, a prosperous and highly educated investment banker unknown to the general public. He summarized an elite consensus that in effect turned the United States decisively away from its New Deal social programs to endless military buildup. At the end of World War II, the United States was in danger of falling back into the Depression, especially since overseas trading customers were impoverished by the war. A Keynesian boost was needed, but the elite implicitly favored spending on the military over public works. To win Congressional and public support, it was therefore necessary to exaggerate the "Soviet threat". But Communism was never a serious political threat to Western Europe beyond the Soviet-occupied buffer zone in Eastern Europe. Nor was it a military threat, for, under Stalin, the Soviet Union had abandoned the doctrine of "permanent revolution" (over protests from the exiled Trotsky) and was now concentrating on reconstruction from the devastation of the war and on building defenses against the further aggression it feared from the capitalist West. NSC-68 claimed that the USSR was still "led by a fanatic faith" to "impose its absolute authority over the rest of the world". As a result, Pentagon contracts became the life-blood of the U.S. economy, affecting every Congressional district and virtually every activity (most notably in the universities) which welcomed the influx of grants, ignoring the implications of the strings attached.

Without any public discussion, NSC-68 set the future course of the United States for generations to come. The "Cold War" was already announced in 1947 in a speech in South Carolina by Bernard Baruch, who used the alleged Communist threat as an argument

3

against the wave of post-war labor demands. Baruch called for "unity" between labor and management, longer workweeks, and no-strike pledges from unions, since "today we are in the midst of a cold war".

This largely-invented and certainly overblown "Soviet threat" was used both to pump Congressional appropriations into the Pentagon and to tame the labor movement, using guilt by association with an American Communist Party which was never a threat to anything but racial segregation in the South.

It is significant that this historic turning point was accomplished by an elite, behind closed doors, which used dire warnings of an external "threat" to smother any possible democratic debate on the direction the nation might take. The media largely orchestrated this campaign, framing international news as an eternal dualistic contest between freedom and communism.

The NSC-68 Cold War dominated U.S. foreign policy without serious challenge until Mikhail Gorbachev moved to end it. The "Soviet threat" was such a valuable focus for U.S. policy that much of the ruling establishment remained wary, suspicious or outright hostile. What could we do without it?

The impulse for world peace came from Moscow. Clearly, the Soviet elite had decided that their interest lay in loosening their power system and abandoning their Eastern European buffer zone in the hope of a peaceful partnership with the West. They were led to believe that this was possible largely by the German peace movement of the early 1980s, which gave the impression that German aggressive intentions toward the East had been rejected by the post-war generation.

Western media have managed to distort that decisive Russian move for peace by reducing the end of the Cold War to a single symbol: the fall of the Berlin Wall. It was more a spectacle than an historic event. The real event happened earlier: Gorbachev's visit to the West German capital, Bonn, in June 1989, which sealed Moscow's abandonment of the German Democratic Republic. East Germany was no doubt the most sincerely socialist and economically successful of all the Eastern European Warsaw Pact members, despite widespread resentment of institutions such as the Stasi.[5] Once Moscow decided to allow German reunification, the Berlin Wall was obsolete and its "fall" in November was simply the inevitable result. To fixate on "the Fall of the Berlin Wall" creates the impression that Eastern European changes were caused principally by a popular uprising of the people against communism. This interpretation obscures the historic decisions made by the Soviet *nomenklatura*.

From Cold War To Global Leadership

The self-controlled collapse of the Soviet Union opened the prospect for a new era of international cooperation, disarmament and peace. Moscow in particular was urging Washington to agree to mutual nuclear disarmament. But by this time the military-industrial complex had its clutches on the entire nation, including its mentality. It would have taken extraordinary events or extraordinary leadership to liberate the United States economy from the MIC and direct it toward constructive domestic activities.

The moment of greatest opportunity was the presidency of Bill Clinton. But far from marking a turn toward peace, the Clinton administration opened a new phase of seemingly endless war.

It is doubtful that this was intentional or even conscious. A president with no strong foreign policy vision who reacts to unexpected events in unfamiliar places is inevitably manipulated by advisers with an agenda. In the American oligarchy, the President is a temporary chairman of the board who is there to take responsibility for actions decided in private sessions. He is there to sell policy more than to make it.

A vast power such as the MIC demands a certain degree of continuity. It cannot be bounced back and forth every four years between opposing forces. Reduction of military spending would raise the question of finding an equally profitable alternative to the incredibly lucrative possibilities of MIC contracts with government-guaranteed returns on investment.

But the MIC needs more than profits. It requires constant ideological justification for its dominance, if only to satisfy its own main actors, most notably in the military, where belief in a mission is a vital necessity. Congressmen and business leaders may be satisfied with votes and profits, but military officers and soldiers are expected to be ready to die for a cause. They and their families require some sort of inspiration. The immense military power of the Pentagon has spawned a community of "defense intellectuals", always on the lookout for "threats" and "missions" to justify the very existence of such a destructive, bloated power.

As the "communist threat" faded out, this task fell primarily to the Washington think-tanks, privately-funded policy institutes that began to proliferate in the 1970s. In the post-Gorbachev era, they became more creative and more influential. K Street and Dupont Circle are the centers of foreign policy formulation, with strong links to the op- ed pages of major newspapers. This privatization of policy-making represented an opportunity for rich donors to gain influence. The funding sources ensure that the leading think tanks have a strong right-wing bias. The think tank community has become overwhelmingly influenced by generous pro-Israel donors and active pro-Israel intellectuals.

The most notorious of the latter group are the neoconservatives, or neocons, who have become the main force defining U.S. foreign policy. The term can be considered a euphemism, since this tight network of activists is far from "conservative" in any real sense of the word. On the contrary, their ambition is to use U.S. military power to bring about vast changes in the world. They are nonpartisan; they go where the power is. In the 1970s, they nested in the office of the Democratic Senator from Washington, Henry "Scoop" Jackson, nicknamed the Senator from Boeing for his devotion to his major home-state Pentagon contractor. The flagship legislative measure won by the early neocons was the 1974 "Jackson-Vanik amendment", sponsored by Jackson in the Senate and Charles Vanik in the House of Representatives, which denied normal trade relations to Soviet bloc countries with "brain drain" restrictions on the freedom of Jewish emigration. Jackson and Richard Perle championed Ukrainian "refusenik" Anatoly (later Natan) Sharansky. Once in Israel, Sharansky became a leading ultra-nationalist politician and is currently dedicated to the emigration of French Jews. The Jackson-Vanik amendment merged main neoconservative themes which persist to this day: the assertion of U.S. power to dictate internal policies of other countries, hostility to Russia, devotion to Israel, and the use of "human rights" demands as grounds for economic sanctions or other forms of intervention.

It was in the administration of George W. Bush that the neocons gained notoriety as architects of the disastrous invasion of Iraq. The main thinker behind this war was Bush's Under Secretary of Defense for Policy, Paul Wolfowitz, whose doctrine comes down to a few simple assumptions. Perhaps the linchpin of this doctrine is the erroneous idea that "democracies don't go to war against each other", a notion that retains credibility only thanks to the subterfuge of automatically labeling our adversaries as "dictatorships". This leads to the specious conclusion that war against dictators is the way to ensure peace. Like it or not, in 1999, Serbia was quite as "democratic" as any other country in the region, and Slobodan Milosevic had been elected several times in perfectly "democratic" elections. But he was a "dictator" because the United States and NATO bombed his country. In any case, thinks to this syllogism, which has been absorbed as part of the U.S. foreign policy doctrine, Wolfowitz persuaded George W. Bush that the way to solve the Palestinian deadlock was to remove the "dictators" surrounding Israel. Thus the neighboring states would become "democracies" and as such would naturally make peace with "democratic Israel". So much for the Middle East. The other point of neocon focus is Russia and for that, the doctrine calls on the United States to prevent the rise of a great power rival in Eurasia. Russia must be held down. Inherent in all this is an apology for "preventive" war. That is, unprovoked aggressive war, waged to "prevent" the rise of a rival, or to get rid of a dictator, or to head off some supposed threat, such as (nonexistent) weapons of mass destruction.

In the Bush II era, the neocons dominated the influential American Enterprise Institute (AEI) as well as operating through think tanks of their own. Most notable of these was the Project for the New American Century (PNAC), which disbanded in 2006, as its major policy triumph, the 2003 invasion of Iraq, was turning into a disgrace. But their influence began before George W. Bush, and lives on after his presidency.

PNAC was founded early in the second Clinton administration. Its June 1997 "Statement of Principles" asks whether the United States has "the resolve to shape a new century favorable to America principles and interests?" The implication is that the United States surely has the capacity to "shape the century", and the only thing missing might be its "resolve". PNAC thus called for a foreign policy "that boldly and purposefully promotes American principles abroad", adding that "it is important to shape circumstances before crises emerge, and to meet threats before they become dire". The wars against Serbia, Iraq and Libya illustrate this principle, as all three wars were initiated to meet threats that were in reality imaginary. This is the most blatant trick in the "preventive war" doctrine: we may go to war to prevent something that never would have happened anyway, but since it didn't happen, we can claim credit for preventing it. In short, PNAC called for a doctrine of preventive war, which has indeed been adopted and applied, with the sole clear result of destroying existing regimes and to a large extent the countries that were governed by them.

The PNAC Statement of Principles concluded with four demands:

1. to increase defense spending significantly;
2. to strengthen ties to democratic allies (meaning Israel especially) and "to challenge regimes hostile to our interests and values" (meaning regime change, supposedly to shape a "democratic" world);
3. to promote the cause of political and economic freedom abroad (opening markets and intervening in the domestic affairs of targeted countries);
4. to accept responsibility for America's unique role in preserving and extending an international order friendly to our security, our prosperity and our principles.

This last point foreshadows current movements to create a Community of Democracies, composed essentially of the English-speaking world and Western Europe (plus Israel) to rival and dominate the United Nations as a more legitimate world authority by virtue of being made up of purely "democratic" states, with NATO as its global police force.

In February 1998, a PNAC offshoot calling itself the Committee for Peace and Security in the Gulf sent an Open Letter to President Clinton urging him to use U.S. military force to help "friendly" Iraqi opposition groups overthrow Saddam Hussein. Bill Clinton was busy with other matters at the time, but the policy was to be followed by his successor, using 9/11 as pretext. The signatories were a roster of prominent neocons, including Elliott Abrams, Robert Kagan, Donald

Rumsfeld, and Paul Wolfowitz.[6]

This neo-conservative line (which might better be termed "archeo-radical", since it actually reverts to a radical application of the ancient law "Might Makes Right") has won overwhelming assent from America's political class because it fills a vacuum: the vacuum of purpose for the military-industrial complex. The United States of America, essentially a vast island without enemies real or in potential, has absolutely no need to be armed to the teeth, ever-ready to destroy the planet in self "defense". Since the dissolution of the Soviet Union and the Warsaw Pact, the United States has been in a perfect position to lead a movement of negotiated worldwide disarmament, starting with nuclear weapons, a movement which the second great nuclear power, Russia, was eager to join. By shifting resources to constructive rather than destructive uses, the United States could have led a movement to combat illiteracy and disease, to improve vital global infrastructure such as hydraulic installations whose natural result would be to create conditions for solving local conflicts and promoting a peaceful world. But this would have implied dismantling the very skeleton of the current U.S. economy. Rather than putting engineers and scientists to work figuring out how to make such a dramatic shift, it has been easier for U. S. leaders to heed the siren-songs of those fast talking neocons who contrive countless pretexts for retaining and expanding the existing order of destruction.

The term "neocon" makes sense only if it refers to the new con game that has befuddled the U.S. political leadership class.

The neocons owe their ascendancy to their ability to espouse a coherent world view that satisfies the military-industrial complex, the highly influential pro-Israel lobby, and a large section of "liberal" opinion (notably in the media and entertainment industry) that eagerly adopts the worldwide defense of "human rights" as a legitimate justification for U.S. intervention in other countries. Even when the neocons have been in semi-disgrace, as in the aftermath of disastrous interventions such as the one in Iraq, this ideology has remained dominant. It offers a purpose to the militarization of American society through the MIC that would otherwise persist simply through bureaucratic inertia.

The idea that United States world leadership is "necessary" to fulfill the nation's unique global "responsibilities" provides a *raison d'être* for the endless increase in so-called "defense" spending that is intended to maintain the capacity for military intervention the world over. In the absence of the communist boogeyman, the stress is now on the necessity to promote our American "interests" and "values" worldwide, the two being considered complementary if not identical, since both revolve around the idea of "free markets". In the hothouse atmosphere of the Washington foreign policy establishment, dominated by military contracts, AIPAC, and the fear of losing the next election, the neoconservative formula offers a simple way to appeal to campaign donors as well as the least sophisticated part of the electorate. The line that America is "exceptional", a nation above all others (and above the law) echoes a traditional semi-religious notion of America as "God's country".

"As Much As Needed"

The election of Obama in 2008, following the self-dissolution of PNAC several years earlier, left a widespread impression that the neoconservative hold on U.S. foreign policy had been broken, for the most part by disillusion with the results of the war in Iraq. Yet Obama has gradually come to adopt the PNAC line, albeit with seeming reluctance. His first Secretary of State, Hillary Clinton, however, has positioned herself as their new darling.

In July 2014, billionaire Haim Saban declared in a Bloomberg TV interview that he would contribute "as much as needed" to elect Hillary Clinton in 2016. This is significant because both Saban's fortune and his zeal seem to be inexhaustible. Saban declares proudly that his greatest concern is to protect Israel through strengthening the United States-Israel relationship.[7] "I'm a one-issue guy, and my issue is Israel." If Americans in general can see no urgent use for the nation's enormous military power, the use is obvious for someone like Saban, with dual Israeli-U.S. citizenship: the strengthening of Israel's position in the Middle East.

Saban sees three ways to be influential in American politics: make donations to political parties, establish think tanks, and control media outlets. Although he lost his bid to buy the *Los Angeles Times* in hope of changing its "pro-Palestinian" line, in

2002 Saban showered seven million dollars on the Democratic National Committee, donated five million dollars to Bill Clinton's Presidential Library, and above all, founded his very own think tank, the Saban Center for Middle East Policy within the Brookings Institution, previously considered the most politically neutral of major Washington think tanks. This was accomplished by a record donation to Brookings of thirteen million dollars. The Saban Center fosters dialogue, not between Israelis and Arabs, of course, but between Israelis and American decision-makers.

While betting on the Democrats, Saban picks favorites, as illustrated by this anecdote:[8] "Obama was asked the same question Hillary was asked – 'If Iran nukes Israel, what would be your reaction?' Hillary said, 'We will obliterate them.' ... Four words, it's easy to understand. Obama said only three words. He would 'take appropriate action.' I don't know what that means." Saban's rant continued, calling Iran "a rogue state... that is a supporter of Hezbollah, which killed more Americans than any other terrorist organization", etc. In short, Hillary passed the test, but Obama flunked. Neither one of them would ever dare say what former French President Jacques Chirac replied years ago to the same question, by observing that should Iran dare attack Israel, Teheran would be wiped out by Israeli's nuclear arsenal, which was a way of pointing out the absurdity of the scenario. For pointing this out, Chirac was attacked by France's pro-Israel press, a risk no leading American politician would ever dare to take – not with moneybags like Saban waiting in the wings.

On the very eve of her own entrance into electoral politics, Hillary had learned her first lesson in risk avoidance. As first lady on a Presidential visit to Ramallah in November 1999, her polite kiss on the cheek of her hostess, Yasser Arafat's wife Suha, caused an uproar. "Shame on Hillary" headlined the *New York Post*. Right-wing Jewish leaders let it be known that this might be the kiss of death to her campaign for junior Senator from New York in 2000. As Jason Horowitz of the *New York Times* put it, this led Hillary to enroll in "political Hebrew School. Under the tutelage of the senior New York senator, Chuck Schumer, she became extremely adept at winning the trust of audiences who held an absolute pro-Israel position."[9]

In February 2007, with the Presidential race in sight, she

tripped up slightly at an AIPAC dinner by suggesting that it would be smart to "engage with Iran". The reception was cold. But she rapidly atoned during a July 2007 debate with Obama by distancing herself from his declared readiness to meet with leaders of "pariah" nations – including Iran. In a September 2007 position paper, Hillary played her trump card by expressing belief that Israel's right to exist "as a Jewish state" with "an undivided Jerusalem as its capital" must never be questioned. This extreme position outflanked even that of the previous Bush administration, and was a factor inciting Obama to turn to Malcolm Hoenlein, executive vice chairman of the Presidents of Major Jewish American Organizations, to get Hillary to take the job of Secretary of State in order to reassure the lobby. She has since earned the devotion of Haim Saban.

Saban is not the only one. On the other side of the aisle, backing Republican candidates, there is Sheldon Adelson, also with dual U.S.-Israeli citizenship, who made his billions in the gambling casinos of Las Vegas and Macao. A close pal of Benjamin Netanyahu and a backer of AIPAC, Adelson despises Obama and is as eager to buy the Presidency for a Republican as Saban is eager to elect Hillary. As things look now, the 2016 presidential race could be a contest between Haim Saban and Sheldon Adelson. In either case, the winner would be Israel.

To provide personnel and policy direction for the new president, whoever he or she may be, two veterans of the defunct PNAC, William Kristol and Robert Kagan, returned in 2009 to found the Foreign Policy Institute (FPI). Robert Kagan is the current leading neocon theorist and the husband of Secretary of State Hillary Clinton's spokeswoman, Victoria Nuland, instigator of the Ukrainian coup in early 2014. To put it simply, the main purpose of the FPI, as of earlier neocon emanations, is to keep the United States perpetually at war. They stigmatize as "isolationist" those rare politicians who openly oppose their war policy (although, as their arch-adversary Ron Paul has pointed out, the neocons and their acolytes strive to "isolate" whole countries they don't like).

The military-industrial complex has no direction of its own, no philosophy, and no values. It is simply *there*, a monster which, as a planetary public safety measure, desperately needs to be tamed and destroyed. But instead of figuring out how to get rid of it, policy intellectuals contrive things for it to do. Naturally enough, the most successful are those with a passionate cause to serve, such as unwavering allegiance to the Israeli state, especially when the money is there to finance their lobbying.

There is all that power, and, as Madeleine Albright famously said: "What's the point of having all that military might if you don't use it?" For politicians who want power, this is the tiger to ride. Politicians who want to climb aboard claim that this is an invincible force for good, when it is primarily an immense force of destruction. It has brought devastation to Vietnam, to Iraq, to Afghanistan, to Libya, and there is no limit to the chaos it may still create.

Chapter 2

Multicultural Manipulations

Our Exceptional "Values" and "Interests"

Our political leaders never cease assuring us that our foreign policy is determined by "our values" and "our interests". Whose interests exactly? "Our interests" remain unclear. As for "our values", "democracy", "freedom", "human rights" are concepts that raise more questions than they answer, if you stop to think about it. But thinking is precisely what such abstractions are intended to prevent.

Hillary Clinton regularly repeats these standard, meaningless words as if "our interests" and "our values" were divine commandments, guiding us like icebreakers through a recalcitrant world. Get out of our way... Here we come with our values and interests!

America is an exceptionally ideological country – and that is a clue to the "exceptional" nature of the United States. No society lives without an ideology, but the ideology of America's current political leaders and opinion-makers thrives in an utter fog of self-justification. For decades, so-called American Exceptionalism has been successfully exported both by Hollywood and by an extensive official propaganda machine funding "non-governmental" organizations in countless countries (NGOs). The idea that America is the "best country on earth" and the proper model for all others, has succeeded in creating cultural inferiority complexes in youth around the world. Since World War II, Western European leaders have accepted this notion to the point of having surrendered their national sovereignty to the "governance" of the European Union, a false and essentially unworkable imitation of the United States. This is an unstable situation, but it helps to confirm Washington's illusion of world domination.

We are always very good at seeing through the mass illusions of other times and other places, and especially those of the last century. Our own illusions remain as invisible as the air we breathe.

Hitler is considered insane for having believed that the Germans were "the master race". This judgment has not yet been pronounced on current leaders who proclaim that America is "the indispensable nation" and an "exception" to all the rules that apply to the rest of the world.

Because it is shared by men and women in charge of the greatest power of destruction that ever existed on earth, this ideology is the number one threat to humanity, to all forms of life on our planet. It risks unleashing the total devastation of nuclear war. None of our "interests" can do that; interests are inherently not suicidal. It is our "values" that are dangerous. It is the belief in our overwhelming superiority, the superiority of "our values", which leads us toward the destruction of ourselves and of others.

Hillary Clinton personifies the hubris of American Exceptionalism. She seems incapable of doubting that America is "the last hope of mankind". Above all, she certainly believes that the American people also believe in American Exceptionalism and want to hear it confirmed and celebrated. As long as that is what the American people want to hear, Hillary Clinton is not the only problem. She is not even the most basic problem. A more basic problem is our ideological fog.

American Globalization

If Americans were staying at home and minding their own business, belief in the country's "exceptionalism" would be nothing but a quaint ethnic trait. But the present context is globalization, and for Americans believing in the exceptional nature of the United States, globalization means Americanization of the entire world. Our interests and values must prevail everywhere.

In short, globalization means a world tied together by the universal penetration of financial markets in every sector of each national economy, thus allowing international capital to shape production, trade, and services via their own investment choices. This has radical political implications. In their efforts to attract mobile capital, nation-states are expected to lower dissuasive taxes and provide widened investment possibilities by privatization even of the most vital national activities, such as education and basic utilities. This leaves the national government without resources to ensure public welfare, to develop industry and farming, to redistribute wealth through public services. The gap between rich and poor widens radically. The powers of national governments tend to be reduced to maintaining public order. Even those may be privatized.

Globalization is also an ideological construct. It is now widely accepted as an inevitable stage of human history, as the product of communications and transport technologies that turn the world into a "global village". This notion, which ignores the enormous subjective and material gaps which still divide humanity, underlies the American assumption that "we" are justified in prying into everybody's business.

Although presented as an inexorable destiny, real "globalization" is the product of a particular relationship of forces. Promoted as "free trade", the slogan does not at all mean what the words suggest: freedom to buy and sell goods and services. In practice, it means a complex system of international agreements that facilitate the movement of investment capital in or out of countries at the expense of national regulations. In hammering out these agreements, the United States benefits from superior bargaining power thanks to its control of the dollar as world currency, the influence of its ideology, and not least by its military presence around the world. The United States has between 662 and over a thousand military bases or installations (depending on what one defines as such) spread across some 148 foreign countries, effectively controlling the armed forces of many of these nations through "aid" and "joint training programs". The United States not only succeeds in using its influence to obtain trade deals to the advantage of its own corporations and financial institutions, it also feels free to violate the spirit and letter of free trade whenever it chooses to "punish" some country or other with economic sanctions.

U.S.-led globalization is a process. It is a process intended to absorb more and more of the world into the sphere of "free market democracy".

This is indeed a new form of world conquest. It is not a matter of conquering territory by military force and creating colonies, as in past empires. It is not a matter of taking over responsibility for governing conquered territories. It is a process of creating conditions for the gradual absorption of one region after another into a single system in which free enterprise, or private capital, commands both the economy and the political process, based on the model of the present-day United States. Note that "free elections", U.S.-style, can be freely influenced by financial contributions. Our modern so-called "bourgeois" democracy began with voting rights limited to men of property. Gradually, property requirements were lowered and for a short time in the twentieth century, voting rights were equal in the United States (and still are in some other countries). But by allowing unlimited campaign contributions, the United States has reverted, not to "bourgeois" democracy, but to billionaire democracy. The advantage of this revised democracy is that if you have the money, you can buy it.

Such "democracy", if exported, looks like the easy non-violent way for our friendly financial interests to take over foreign states. A "free market democracy" can be influenced politically and economically by international finance capital. The United States government is already spending hundreds of millions of dollars to support "democracy" – usually through grants to NGOs in foreign countries by way of the National Endowment for Democracy (NED). Such grants select leaders and build careers. These efforts are supported by numerous associations and private foundations, more or less government-linked, of which the most notorious is George Soros' Open Society Foundation.

The European Union is the vanguard example of this expansion process. Under strong influence from the United States, which effectively occupied Western Europe after the defeat of Nazi Germany, six countries – France, Germany, Italy, the Netherlands, Belgium and Luxembourg – began the integration process with the 1957 Treaty of Rome. It has been expanding ever since. This expansion is closely related to, although not quite identical with, the expansion of NATO. The paradox is that the more it expands, the less democratic it becomes, as key decision-making is transferred to a central bureaucracy. "Free market democracy" is becoming an oxymoron.

Soon to be cemented by the Trans-Atlantic Free Trade Area (TAFTA), the European Union, the United States and NATO will form the core of this projected "World Community of Democracies".[10] This "international community" is designed to claim superior legitimacy on the world stage due to two factors: the supposed moral superiority of "democracy" and the armed force of NATO. Specifically, the armed "democracies", under U.S. leadership, will – as they are already doing in regard to Ukraine – take it upon themselves to intervene in any area of the world, citing human rights, R2P (the right or responsibility to protect), or some other moral pretext.

In June 2014, lavish ceremonies were held in Normandy to commemorate the 70th anniversary of D-Day, hailed as the Liberation of Europe. In 1944, arrival of U.S. Armed Forces on the continent was indeed greeted as liberation. But after seventy years of protracted military occupation and political domination, this liberation might more appropriately be celebrated as a conquest.

The European Union provides the paradigm for a world where nation states give up their sovereignty to an overriding economic governance based on the "free market" coupled with "free elections" – free, but often expensive.

Blowing Away Whistleblowers

"Security" is another pretext for ignoring sovereignty. Nations that join NATO consciously renounce their military sovereignty in order to enjoy the alleged benefits of "collective security", which means restructuring their armed forces to serve as elements in the international "tool box" under U.S. command. But another aspect of national and individual sovereignty has been inadvertently surrendered to the United States National Security Agency (NSA) as it strives to record, collect and store every last personal, political or business communication exchanged anywhere in the world. For Hillary Clinton, this intrusion is also a "security" imperative, necessary to "protect our friends and allies". On these grounds, she vigorously condemned the revelation of NSA documents by Edward Snowden.

"As an American," Hillary told Phoebe Greenwood in an interview for *The Guardian*, "I honestly believe that our acquisition of information saves lives and protects not just the United States but our friends and our allies."[11] NSA spying, in Hillary's view, is a generous public service that should be appreciated: "I think it would be shocking to most people if the United States stopped gathering the information and we basically said: Okay everybody you're on your own. We can't tell our allies in Asia what's happening, we can't share information with our allies in Europe. We're gonna stop. Well, that's just not the way the real world works."

For Hillary, "when it comes to the information competition that exists between the West and the Rest, I think it would be an abdication of responsibility not to be gathering information that we can use to protect ourselves and, as I say, our friends and allies." It follows then that Angela Merkel should be grateful to the NSA for tapping her personal cell phone.

The "real world", according to Hillary, is as dangerously divided as it ever was during the Cold War. Today, this division is between the West and the Rest, or as she imagines, between the Good and the Threatening.

"It's no surprise to me that Hillary Clinton thinks that human beings who are not formally U.S. citizens don't have any rights", said Julian Assange, who considers Hillary Clinton a "threat" to solving the problem of whistleblowers.[12]

When she was Secretary of State, Hillary Clinton described the November 2010 Wikileaks document release as "an attack on the United States and the international community" that "puts people's lives in danger" and "threatens our national security". Speaking for the Obama administration, she announced that: "We are taking aggressive steps to hold responsible those who stole this information." This was certainly the case with Chelsea Manning, who is now paying the price for having revealed, among other things, the incriminating video of a U.S. helicopter crew murdering a group of civilians (including a BBC photographer) in the streets of Baghdad and then subsequently murdering a man who stopped his car with children inside in order to come to the aid of the victims of the first attack who were lying in the street.

For all her hostility to Wikileaks, Hillary judged Edward Snowden's May 2013 revelation of NSA documents to be a "much more serious breach".[13] Since she considers worldwide spying necessary on behalf of some imaginary contest between "the West" and everybody else, foreigners need not know about it.

As for Americans, Hillary grants them the right to engage in a polite debate "about the tension between privacy and security". She considers that there are "other ways" of doing it, that such a debate was "already going on", that Snowden deserves "no credit" for stimulating the debate, and finally that it was "puzzling" for Snowden to abscond since "we have all these protections for whistleblowers."

All of this is highly questionable, at best.

In reality, previous NSA whistleblowers had played by the rules of the 1998 Intelligence Community Whistleblower Protection Act but still failed to arouse any interest in flagrant abuses of law, either among their superiors or in Congress. When one of them, decorated Air Force and Navy veteran Thomas Drake, finally gave information that was used as part of an award-winning article in the *Baltimore Sun* in 2005, his home was raided and pillaged by armed FBI agents and in 2010 he was indicted by a Baltimore grand jury for "willful retention of National Defense information" under the 1917 Espionage Act. This equates attempting to inform the American public with betraying vital information to the enemy in wartime.

Daniel Ellsberg has argued that it is no longer possible to do what he did in the 1970s when he released the "Pentagon Papers", an inside evaluation of U.S. involvement in Vietnam, because the government now silences defendants by using state secrets privilege. National security cases are tried in Alexandria, Virginia, where, as Julian Assange observed, "the jury pool is comprised of the highest density of military and government employees in all of the United States. It's not possible to have a fair trial because the U.S. government has a precedent of applying state secret privilege to prevent the defense from using material that is classified in their favor." It is only because Snowden avoided arrest that "we can talk about the issues", instead of talking about whether or not Snowden is guilty.

It was only by releasing official documents that Snowden was able to show "the complexity of what was going on. So we have proof. People did try to start a debate, using all sorts of methods, including former National Security Agency whistleblowers, and it's only primary source documents in volume that are probably capable of starting a debate about a complex issue like mass surveillance", Assange has explained.

Hillary has even managed to insinuate that Snowden may deserve the draconian Espionage Act, since she finds it "odd that he would flee to China, because Hong Kong is controlled by China", and that he had than "taken refuge in Russia, under Putin's authority". She conveniently forgot that Snowden was actually en route to Latin America and only ended up being marooned in Russia because the State Department had revoked his U.S. passport on June 22, 2013. He remained stranded in a Moscow airport for well over a month until he was granted temporary asylum by the Russian government on August 1. There was never any indication either of Russia's eagerness to receive him or of Snowden's eagerness to be in Russia.

Hillary Clinton sees the "issue" as balancing "privacy and security". What she fails to notice is that privacy *is* itself a form of security. The privacy she is concerned with is the privacy of the State. This privacy was violated by Wikileaks, which believes that the people have the right to know what their government is doing. In contrast, NSA prying violates the privacy of individuals and by doing so, is a threat to the security of all citizens.

Many citizens who say that the surveillance state doesn't matter "because I have nothing to hide" also miss another crucial point which NSA whistleblowers have been trying to make. For the moment, the vast accumulation of personal data may indeed be harmless for citizens "with nothing to hide". It may even be harmless for terrorists: an overload of information can actually be an obstacle to tracking the few dangerous individuals who might commit acts of violence. But we live in the midst of a negative social trend: wealth and power have become increasingly concentrated. As this imbalance increases, those who hold power may find it ever more tempting to suppress the inevitable protests and campaigns for change engendered by the increasing gap between the very few and the very many. Personal information can be used to frame, entrap, or eliminate anyone who might oppose a system where the concentration of power has grown to a point where ordinary people are forced to fight back. The surveillance machine becomes an important weapon in any state's arsenal of repression. Some future leader, protecting the power of the ruling .01%, might say, echoing Madeleine Albright, "What's the use of having that splendid repressive machinery if we don't use it?" Like any powerful weapon, its masters can use its very existence as an argument for its use. By the same token, its potential use is a reason for those who do not control such a weapon to demand its abolition.

Champions of state security like Hillary Clinton apparently neither know nor care that the NSA's comprehensive surveillance machine is a serious potential threat to the "civil society" they claim to cherish.

Co-opting Civil Society

On February 16, 2011, Secretary of State Hillary Clinton officiated at the inaugural session of the Strategic Dialogue with Civil Society, a new device for organizing U.S. intervention in the internal affairs of other countries. As usual, she repeated the mantra that the United States "supports democratic change" because it agrees with "our values and our interests". As a matter of "standing up for universal principles", the United States will help "our partners" take steps to "open their own political and economic systems"… so that Uncle Sam can walk right in.

This session took place in the State Department, with thousands of participants via interactive videoconferences at 50 U.S. embassies around the world. Hillary trotted out her favorite image of a three-legged stool that upholds stable societies: "a responsive, accountable government; an energetic, effective private sector economy; and then civil society, which represents everything else that happens in the space between the government and the economy, that holds the values, that represents the aspirations."

This "stool" is actually the image of the bland governance of a corporate society: a government responsive to the demands of finance capital, a capitalist economy, and private, unelected and well-funded organizations that will determine "our values". Note what is missing: a vigorous political life, scrupulously independent media, and an education system that prepares intellectually alert and critical citizens.

Hillary said she was "very pleased to announce that we are more than doubling our financial support for efforts to respond to threats to civil society, to help human rights workers who have been arrested, activists who've been intimidated, journalists who have been censored. We have launched an international fund that will provide quick assistance, such as communications gear and legal support to NGOs affected by government crackdowns."

In short, as Secretary of State, HRC presided over an intensification of U.S. interference in the domestic affairs of fifty countries. Earlier, she had instructed U.S. ambassadors "to engage with civil society as a cornerstone of our diplomacy." She named three senior State Department officials to lead working groups on governance and accountability, democracy and human rights, and empowering women. What this means is that Hillary heightened a major ongoing shift in U.S. diplomacy away from dealing with other governments, as was traditional practice, toward dealing with "civil society" *against* governments declared unfit to handle these issues to Washington's satisfaction.

Needless to say, the United States is not keen to welcome such "assistance" from foreign countries to help solve the problems of its own "civil society". For example, what to do about the high rate of infant mortality or the record the U.S. currently holds for the world's highest prison population. Or how to cure the epidemic of fatal police shootings of unarmed "suspects" and the drug-fueled violence of America's inner cities. Or, how to curb the corruption of democratic practice by billionaire campaign funding; or even such minor ills as an education system that fails to teach the majority of Americans even the most rudimentary history and geography of the world which their government is intent on reshaping.

Civil Society is a malleable concept, but this much is certain: the representatives of civil society are self-selected and do not represent anybody. Or, in the case of groups chosen by NED, they may be selected by NED itself to become "oppressed dissidents" representing genuine democracy. The State Department's emphasis on civil society implies that the genuine values of a society are not expressed by its government, whether or not that government is the product of democratic elections, but rather by volunteer associations organized outside the political process. By proclaiming U.S. support for "civil society", the United States government is very clearly attempting to co-opt whatever grievances exist in dozens of foreign countries and to posit itself as the only solution to these ills. The State Department is encouraging such groups to look toward

America, rather than to work politically for their cause within their own society.

Hillary also counts on "civil society" to aid in genocide prevention by spotting such dark tendencies and opposing them. This is a strange and sinister assignment (more later on "genocide prevention").

Active "civil society" is a matter of minorities, very often relatively privileged minorities. However sincere, these educated, Western-oriented minorities active in human rights organizations can easily be seen as the beginning of a dominant managerial class in the globalized world that the United States aspires to create and administer. The Strategic Dialogue with Civil Society is one of many means to solidify the ideological hegemony acquired by the United States since World War II. Although this ideology has aroused a growing skepticism, and even outright hostility, as a result of U.S. military aggression and intervention, it is not yet effectively opposed by any coherent rival ideology. In much of the world, Americanization still holds a strong appeal for certain privileged classes.

Any civil society is a complex of various minorities, and therefore defense of ethnic, religious or sexual minority rights is a fertile field for movements with the potential to weaken support for central governments. By their emotional impact, identity movements can destabilize governments without in any way interfering with the growing domination of finance capital in determining economic and social relations, as economically-based social movements might do. Civil society is a good breeding ground for the formation of self-selected elites eligible for recruitment to U.S.-managed globalization.

From Equality to Diversity

Over the past three decades, the economic left has been crushingly defeated in the Atlantic core of the West. The defeat was homegrown in the United Kingdom and the United States, led by Thatcher and Reagan in the 1980s. In continental Europe, it is being pursued vigorously by the European Union bureaucracy, whose directives and budgetary rules are dismantling the "European social model" in preparation for the great TAFTA wedding. Complicit elected leaders feign helplessness. In Europe, "labor" parties no longer care about labor and "socialist" parties are not at all socialist. In the United States, the Democratic Party has long since abandoned the social reformism of the New Deal. But a certain "left" does continue to exist, claiming to be both generous and progressive, but it is no longer the old social democratic left, once concerned with the fight for economic equality. Instead of equality, the new establishment left is more concerned with "diversity" and the "right to be different".

Incidentally, people *are* different. There is no reason why this should be considered a "right". It is just a fact. In a decent, fair and sensible society, people would simply *be* different and nobody would make an issue of it. But for us, the question of "identity" has become a major concern.

In many respects, the old division between right and left, between conservative and progressive (or "liberal" in the United States), has mutated into an historic compromise between economic dogma and social doctrine. On the right, the economic dogma is not conservative in any meaningful way. It does not conserve anything. It is wildly disruptive of stable existence. It states that the markets must rule, meaning of course the *financial* markets. But even political parties claiming to be "left", "liberal", "progressive", or even "socialist" in Europe, have largely come around to tailoring their programs to meet the demands of the financial market, in order to "lure investments and create jobs" (jobs that do not get created). The economic order is presumed to be logical, scientific, inevitable. Treating mainstream economics as an exact science, which it is *not*, conveys the impression that the current economic order follows the laws of nature.

For the left, the consolation prize is ideological hegemony in the more sentimental area of human relations, especially that of "human rights". Completely defeated in the area of economic policy, the left gets to define the dominant social doctrine, based on multiculturalism, concern for minorities, and anti-racism. Americans are taught to judge the governments of other countries almost exclusively by how they treat pro-Western dissidents or select minorities. Other qualities or defects, such as whether or not they feed and educate their populations, are of scant interest. The American entertainment industry creates an imaginary world celebrating this doctrine and channeling domestic revolt into artistic dead-ends. Rap music encourages young Afro-American men to defy authority, but in the real world, a young Afro-American man doesn't even need to defy authority to be shot dead by police in the street or sent to prison for life.

Since Western leaders opted for the illusion of building their prosperity on services instead of production, even the left has forgotten about the industrial working class. In the 1970s, much of the radical left began to lose interest in the working class as a revolutionary agent, since it had failed to bring about that socialist revolution that had by now withered to a dissipating mass illusion. Focus shifted instead to various identity groups that were supposed to be more effective agents of revolution: students, women, blacks, or gays. This has since evolved into a general left focus on "identity" groups of all kinds.

"Multiculturalism" expresses a view of society as a composition of identities, rather than of classes. And yet, economic classes still exist. The gap between rich and poor has been widening drastically in most of the West and especially in the United States. Political power is more than ever concentrated at the top, among the ultra-rich, the big corporations and financial institutions. There is no mainstream political force actively defending the interests of the lower classes and striving to counter the growing inequalities between classes. The Occupy Movement defined the ruling class as the top one percent, and claimed to represent the remaining 99 percent. It was eventually marginalized. The societal left is primarily concerned with respect for minorities, rather than the welfare of the majority.

In the 1990s, as the Bill Clinton administration proceeded to unravel the New Deal, multiculturalism emerged as a social ideal. It is mainly a mixture of European ideology with American reality.

Europe's political integration has turned into a showcase for economic globalization. But it began as something else. It was presented as the final renunciation of nationalism and war, primarily by sealing the reconciliation and partnership of France and Germany, two nations that had destroyed each other in a series of wars in the past. Transferring sovereignty to European institutions was justified as a necessary remedy to that nationalism that was the reason for war. Western Europe naturally became the center of anti-nationalist ideology, fed by the celebration of "multiculturalism".

The promotion of multiculturalism owes a great deal to the seemingly endless Western fixation on the long Hitlerian decade of twentieth century history. It would seem that all values were fixed forever in the years between Hitler's rise to power in 1933 and his fall in 1945, and this period must remain the decisive reference for all subsequent events. Multiculturalism is the virtuous pole of a secular Manichaeism. The evil pole is centered on the presumed ideological core of Nazism: nationalism, racism and exclusion. Influenced by the increasingly religious commemoration of the Holocaust, which tends to blur all other aspects of the Second World War, Nazi anti-Semitism is widely attributed to a more or less spontaneous "hatred of those who are different". This is highly questionable, since Hitler's anti-Semitism was above all an extreme hysterical reaction to very specific historical events: Germany's humiliating defeat in the war of 1914-1918 and the rise of Bolshevism in Russia, a series of disastrous events for Germany that Hitler, himself an heir to Austria's political anti-Semitism, attributed to the hostile machinations of international Jewry. Exhortations against "hatred of those who are different" are superfluous in ensuring that such a sequence of events will not be repeated. This is a fear of effects that overlooks causes.

Guilt over treatment of the Jews during World War II is the emotional core of a West European tendency to hold every national majority under permanent suspicion of oppressing minorities or of wanting to oppress them. Every ruler with a restive minority is suspected of contemplating genocide.

In Europe, aside from environmental issues such as opposition to genetically modified organisms, about the only cause that inspires active protest from leftists is the defense of undocumented immigrants. For some small ultra-left anarchist groups, the long-term prospect is a world without frontiers, in which everyone is free to move everywhere. National borders and nation states will disappear. These groups consider themselves radically anti-capitalist, but their ideal is identical to that of the capitalist globalists, who see more clearly: without nation states, private corporations and financial interests may rule the world unimpeded. The difference between the anarchists and the capitalist-globalists is the perception of the relationship of forces: the former ignores them, while the latter actively shapes them.

The "multicultural" ideal of globalism would turn every country into a mix of identities. Each of these identities would be spread between countries and feel more loyalty to its identity than to any State. This is not going to happen. It is not even consciously planned, but it is the inherent logic of many capitalist policies and anarchist dreams. In the short run, national loyalty will be undermined by various group loyalties and the legitimacy of majorities will then weakened by favored attention to minorities. The culmination would be a world empire, divided among geographically dispersed tribes, somewhat similar to a gigantic replica of previous empires such as the multiethnic Habsburg or Ottoman. The past has shown that such a model leads sooner or later to clashes between groups: one group accuses another of unfair domination, or perhaps the confrontation occurs as a result of differences in customs or religion. This leads, in turn, to centrifugal movements to reconstitute separate territories. But the thrust of the ideal is to make the whole world the same by turning each country into a mixture of differences.

Exporting Sexual Identity Politics

In recent decades, as labor unions and political party membership waned, single -issue identity groups grew and proliferated. Multiculturalism shifts focus from economic and legal equality to psychological attitudes whose definition is problematic and whose control is impossible.

Some aspects of U.S. advocacy of multiculturalism abroad can be seen as an export of American identity politics, especially concerning gender issues.

The main novelty has been the growth of sexual identity groups, starting with "gay liberation". Originally, gay liberation sought legal reforms to end discrimination and criminalization for sexual orientation. This amounted to a genuine civilizing advance for Western countries, even though it was not a step toward the mass social revolution some activists hoped for.

The problem with identity movements is that once equal rights have been obtained, where do you go from there? A wise choice might be the consolidation of gains and the avoidance of backlash. Instead, the success of gay liberation has favored the creation of new "identities" that can organize as pressure groups claiming to represent a particular constituency which seeks public recognition and political influence.

The most politically active identity group based on gender today is the composite known as LGBT for Lesbian, Gay, Bisexual and Transgender, and in some circles, with a Q tacked on for "Queer". There is no such thing as an LGBT individual. Nor is there an "LGBT community". Lesbians and gay men scarcely make up a single "community". Nor, for that matter, do heterosexuals. There are too many variations within any sexual orientation, and aside from sexual orientation, each and every individual also has a more comprehensive social activity and interest with which to identify (e.g., professional, political, religious, etc.). One can assume that transsexuals may have particular problems in common with, but are very different from, the Ls, the Gs and the Bs.

Nevertheless, there are organizations claiming to represent this hypothetical community which act as political pressure groups. They have successfully lobbied for legalization of gay marriage, which in France is called "marriage for everybody", but has aroused fresh controversy over its implications for surrogate child-bearing. They also campaign in favor of extra punishment for crimes motivated by "hate", which can be seen as special treatment in comparison to persons who are assaulted for some other reason aside from 'identity'. In the second decade of the 21st century, the demands of the LGBT lobby have largely displaced the demands of organized labor as the leading "progressive" or "left-wing" cause.

Unable to accomplish anything for the economic losers of this society, progressives welcome as a major victory of social progress the fact that gay men and lesbians can now enjoy marriage and divorce on the same terms as heterosexuals. This conformism masquerading as revolutionary gains credibility from the outrage it arouses among traditionalists who fail to grasp that these "advances" are more mimicry of tradition than true social innovation. Prior to the gay marriage movement, the real social innovation was acceptance that couples could live together without the permission of the State or the Church. Insistence on gay marriage seems to be a step back from innovative institutions providing security for long-term couples, whether heterosexual or same sex, as well as for adopted children.

Gay marriage is not necessarily exportable, least of all to places where marriage is still considered an institution designed to ensure the security and identity of children born to a particular couple. Gay marriage echoes an historically very recent view of marriage as the happy outcome of a love affair. Time will tell whether "gay marriage" is a universal advance or a temporary fashion in Western countries which may give way to new institutions and customs.

Sexuality is humanity's most uneasy heritage from evolution, a condition that is so necessary, so contrary to reason and so emotionally dangerous that efforts to keep it under social control are at the basis of wildly varying social customs and overriding obsessions, not least in the monotheistic religions. Sexual customs are not only highly sensitive and often ringed with taboos, but they also tend to be largely secret. It should be recalled that either the famous anthropologist Margaret Mead, or her principal critic, Derek Freeman (who contradicted what she wrote in *Growing Up In Samoa*), or perhaps both of them, were fooled by Samoan women telling them about their youthful sexual practices. Homosexuality has always existed but is treated very differently from one society to another, and the way it is actually treated may be far from obvious to outsiders. Hillary Clinton, like many others, cites former Iranian President Mahmoud Ahmadinejad as claiming that: "In Iran, we don't have homosexuals, like in your country" – a preposterous statement at face-value. What was not mentioned was that Iran is a world leader in free transgender operations. Like it or not, this was how the Islamic Republic responded to the demands of local activists. In various Muslim societies, as among the Pashtuns, a corollary of the cloistered condition of women is the custom for adult men to take boy lovers. Societies like Saudi Arabia that physically punish and even execute homosexuals are both deeply hypocritical and deeply cruel. How to oppose such barbaric practices is a complex issue which cannot be resolved by imposing Gay Pride Parades.

The United States, which began with a reputation of oppressive puritanism, is a late convert to official sexual liberation, but there is no zeal like the zeal of the convert. In the post-1968 atmosphere, the American way of dealing with sexual liberation, and particularly with gay rights, has been the political protest model, demanding that everybody "come out" and organize flashy parades. In a very short time, the United States has become a missionary for its own newly discovered universal sexual values, demanding that other countries adopt the same customs in the same way, complete with Gay Pride marches. These customs are right at home in Western countries like Germany ... but not everywhere else.

Hillary Clinton is particularly proud of her speech to the U.N. Human Rights Council arguing that "LGBT rights are human rights", although the use of that acronym seems inappropriate. It should be possible to use plain English to say that nobody should be treated cruelly because of sexual orientation.

In late 2013, when the United States was already deep into operations planned to detach Ukraine from its traditional economic partnership with Russia and to use it as a base to launch an anti-Russian offensive, Russian president Vladimir Putin was absorbed in hosting the Winter Olympics in Sochi. Although participants later expressed enthusiasm about the event, before and during the games Western media concentrated on anything they could denounce as socially backward in Russia, primarily on the alleged danger to gay athletes in Sochi. World media usually enjoy sports, but not this time. Aside from nitpicking examinations of hotel bathrooms, a scare campaign flickered in the media over the question of whether gays would be arrested in Sochi. This imaginary risk contributed to the mounting demonization of the Russian president.

The anti-Putin campaign focused on an amendment to the child protection law overwhelmingly adopted by the Duma in June 2013 that bans promotion of "non-traditional sexual relationships" in the presence of minors. The measure in no way outlaws homosexuality, but was certainly designed to outlaw "Gay Pride" marches, which are seen by many Russians as Western-sponsored provocations. The law rests on the dubious assumption that public information normalizing same-sex relationships risks seducing children, and by implicitly associating homosexuality with pedophilia, will have a negative impact on efforts to overcome prejudice against homosexuals during the present era of conservative backlash in post-communist Russia. Westerners who are genuinely concerned about the problem need to realize that while the West's insistence that Russia should hold Gay Pride Parades is surely not intended to "corrupt children", as Church leaders claim, it is indeed clearly intended to provoke dissension and embarrass Russian leaders, starting with Putin.

The Christian Orthodox Church is not the only factor in today's Russia that works against a more receptive attitude toward homosexuality. The post-Soviet collapse of Russian society in the 1990s was accompanied by a dramatic population decline. One aspect of Putin's effort to revive the nation is concern to restore a birthrate that can ensure Russia's demographic survival. Efforts from unfriendly Western powers to "promote" homosexuality can be easily interpreted as attempts to undermine the very survival of the nation. Good intentions include estimating how those intentions are perceived.

The international campaign for LGBT rights has been poisoned by the inherent double standards of the U.S. position. Criticism of Saudi Arabia when it executes a homosexual remains toothless, with no threat of boycott or sanctions, in contrast to the uproar over nonexistent problems for gays in Sochi.

As intended, blatant political exploitation of the issue to attack Russia's President causes divisions within Russia between those who defend tradition and those who yearn to make Russia resemble their ideal of the West. For the former, who currently seem to constitute a majority, this uproar confirms the impression that Western advocacy of Gay Pride marches is simply an effort to spread "decadence" as part of a multi-pronged campaign to weaken and defeat Russia. If the West were behaving in a kindly manner toward Russia, things might be different. But in the current climate, these exhortations are understood by many in Russia as acts of hostility – which indeed they are.

As gay rights activists in Russia told interviewers at the time of the Sochi games, their cause could only suffer from aggressive Western LGBT agitation which would only serve to arouse suspicion and associate gays with a belligerent West. If Washington really cared about sexual mores in Russia, a more discreet approach would be far more appropriate. Shoving gays and lesbians onto the front lines of a perilous "conflict of civilizations" is doing them no service, to put it mildly....

Times change. It is almost comic to recall that at the start of the Cold War, J. Edgar Hoover and Senator Joe McCarthy coupled homosexuality with communism as the main threats to America. Whereas the United States has become more sexually libertarian, Russia has become more conservative, more Christian, more puritanical. For decades, the West railed against Russia for its "godless communism". Now Russia is a country in which the Orthodox Christian Church has regained influence as a result of the collapse of communism. This return to religion is felt by many as the recovery of dignity and morality after the humiliation and confusion of the Yeltsin decade. Outsiders who sincerely want to contribute to the wellbeing of gays in Russia should take these factors into consideration and keep their distance from the hostile nagging of the U.S. propaganda machine.

But as for Hillary Clinton, she seems perfectly sincere in believing that world progress depends on America telling everybody how to behave, from prayer to the bedroom.

Gay rights – or rather "LGBT" rights – is now the one human rights area where the United States can claim to be "in advance" of most of the world. The issue can be used to attempt to discredit and embarrass other countries at a time when the United States is lagging behind in areas such as child mortality, income equality, life expectancy, primary education, and industrial productivity. As mentioned above, there is one area in which it does lead the world: the size of its prison population. Surely this is a more meaningful measurement of the state of "human rights" in the United States than the legality of gay marriage.

Religious Empowerment

On the West side of the Atlantic, multiculturalism is simply a term for the natural composition of an immigrant society such as the United States or Canada. As seen from the United States, promoting multiculturalism means promoting a sort of global Americanization. The United States can live comfortably with a mixture of religions precisely because the official religion of the United States is the United States itself. U.S. schools celebrate "America" every day, "one nation under God", complete with extremely conformist celebrations of the country's flag and armed forces – exercises that would be considered ominously nationalistic in Europe. Hillary Clinton herself demonstrated allegiance to this state religion by cosponsoring legislation that would make it a federal crime to burn the American flag. In immigrant societies, "multiculturalism" does not threaten the existence of the State: the unification of different identities is even part of its basic identity. For Americans, "multicultural" can mean little more than a choice between pizza, burritos, or sushi before we all rally 'round the flag.

In America, religion is largely a matter of taste. Any religion will do, and they are all considered good for you. The United States has a pragmatic attitude toward religion which has worked well for over two centuries. But it is not necessarily applicable to the whole world, least of all in places where a particular faith is believed to be an absolute truth, rather than a personal preference.

Indeed, religion in the United States is very largely a practical matter. It is also a factor of personal identity, like style. While theological concepts are vague, Americans tend to associate religious belief with morality and hold that anyone who does not believe in divine punishment must be without a conscience. There seems to be a lack of popular recognition of a rational, social or innate basis for moral conscience and this leads to public displays of religious faith by persons eager to convince others of their morality, especially those with political ambitions. What matters is to *be* religious; any religion will do. The separation between any Church and the State doesn't prevent a growing symbiosis between the State and a one-size-fits-all religiosity.

Hillary Clinton exhibits a typically American attitude toward religion. Raised as a Methodist, she says she still draws inspiration from the Bible, but evidently not from this passage of Matthew:

> "And when you pray, do not be like the hypocrites, for they love to pray standing in the synagogues and on the street corners to be seen by others. Truly I tell you, they have received their reward in full. But when you pray, go into your room, close the

door and pray to your Father, who is unseen. Then your Father, who sees what is done in secret, will reward you."

Since 1993, Hillary has made a habit of regularly praying in public, in Bible study groups, at the high-level annual Washington Prayer Breakfast or at the weekly Senate Prayer Breakfast. It seems to be forgotten in Washington that ostentatious prayer has always been considered in ages wiser than our own as a practice that should be rigorously banned from politics, for the simple reason that nothing is easier to fake than piety. Ostentatious prayers were once considered the most conspicuous sign of hypocrisy.

These Washington prayer events are power trips. They are organized by a conservative network called the Fellowship, or the Family, headed by a very ecumenical ordained Presbyterian minister, Doug Coe, born in 1928. His mission is to bring together leaders from all over the world in a fraternity of those who share the circumstance of having been "chosen by God" for their high position and seek divine guidance as to what to do with it. Hillary has described Coe as "a unique presence in Washington: a genuinely loving spiritual mentor and guide to anyone, regardless of party or faith, who wants to deepen his or her relationship to God." [14] But attending the National Prayer Breakfast is not for everybody: attendance costs over four hundred dollars and guests are carefully selected. The goal is nothing less than the Fellowship of the powerful, working together to "do God's work", whatever that may be. Maintaining power is logically the first order of business and power is what makes good works possible. Doug Coe states that "we work with power where we can, build new power where we can't."

Building on her earlier study of the conservative, Cold War period of Reinhold Niebuhr and Paul Tillich, Hillary's religion is a utilitarian self-empowerment faith with little social content. Working for the community is the stated goal, but this is primarily a way of ensuring personal salvation and there is only a limited hope of accomplishing anything in this imperfect world. As the pastor of the Methodist church she attended in Arkansas recalls, Hillary is convinced that she is "called by the Lord to be in public service at whatever level he wants me." She may well believe that she is predestined to be President.

Hillary's conspicuous faith has dulled the initial hostility of the most conservative right-wing Republicans. She joined devout Catholic Senator Rick Santorum in supporting an unsuccessful re-introduction of the Workplace Religious Freedom Act, supported by a wide range of religious groups but opposed by the ACLU. This Act would make it easier for employees to refuse to cooperate with actions contrary to their convictions, such as abortion or the sale of contraceptives.

This is a religiosity basically devoid of any coherent theology or intellectual content, largely reduced to self-empowerment, and often combined with conservative attitudes toward sexuality and reproduction. The Prayer Breakfasts are the religion of the self-selected Power Elite, individuals who got where they are by personal ambition, but who prefer to blame God.

Even American leaders who do not attend Doug Coe's prayer breakfasts use religion in much the same way: as national self-empowerment. Presidents' public prayers and reference to "our values" lift the hypocrisy of personal bigotry to national and international levels. *Gott mit uns* referred to the Christian God of the Germanic people, but "In God We Trust" is wildly ecumenical, and like the dollar, is meant for everybody.

Under the Influence

The habit of thinking in terms of ethnic identities and religious groups is supposed to be a sign of tolerance in a multicultural world. In reality, it produces quite the opposite result, and sets the stage for conflicts, since it tends inevitably to highlight differences rather than shared values and goals.

As they began their forays into rearranging territories of the former Ottoman Empire in the Balkans and the Middle East, the Clintons, with their interest in religion, had their moment of fascination with Islam. After all, they were taking the side of Muslims in Bosnia against Christian Serbs, and (they could suppose) of "moderate" Muslims in the Middle East against "dictators" like Saddam Hussein. This new involvement in a previously unknown part of the world probably encouraged Hillary to develop a particularly close relationship with a rather glamorous young Muslim woman named Huma Abedin.

Huma was born in Michigan in 1976 but her family moved to Saudi Arabia two years later where her Pakistani father, Zyed Abedin, was recruited by the Muslim World League (MWL) to work for the Institute of Muslim Minority Affairs (IMMA), an organ of Saudi foreign policy designed to influence and make use of Muslim minorities in non-Muslim countries. After Zyed died in 1993, Huma's mother Saleha Mahmood Abedin took over the leadership and the Journal of IMMA (the whole family, including Huma, was involved in working for the organization), as well as important roles in the MWL and the International Islamic Committee for Woman and Child (IICWC). She founded the Muslim Sisterhood, an organization which includes the wives of Muslim leaders, such as Naglaa Ali Mahmoud, wife of deposed Egyptian president Mohammed Morsi. In short, Huma's family was exceptionally prominent in international Islamic affairs.

In 1994, at the age of 18, Huma returned to the United States to study at George Washington University, and two years later went to work as an intern in the Clinton White House. She was soon adopted by Hillary as her closest aide and expert on the Middle East and Muslim affairs. Hillary's public statements make it clear that she was infatuated with Huma: her competence, her poise, and evidently her intimate knowledge of a world that to Hillary Rodham Clinton was exotic and even romantic. In her chic designer dresses, the striking Huma became an eye-catching appendage to the traveling Hillary show for the next fifteen years. The two women were so close that a few European newspapers went so far as to speculate on the nature of their personal relationship. But what matters is that there can be no doubt that Huma largely influenced Hillary's vision of Islam and the Middle East. It must have added a personal touch to Washington's support to the Muslim parties in the Yugoslav civil wars. The political interactions of the Middle East and of Muslim societies in general are both highly complex matters. There can be little doubt that putting such confidence in one charming young woman inevitably transformed Huma Abedin into an "agent of influence", even if by accident.

Since the entire Abedin family was so intensely involved in IMMA, it is no surprise that as one of her first initiatives as Secretary of State, Hillary Clinton created the office of U.S. Representative to Muslim Communities. On September 15, 2009, Hillary gave the oath of office to the first person to hold this post, an attractive young friend of Huma, Farah Pandith. At the swearing-in ceremony, Hillary stressed that the office would organize round tables with Muslims in Europe, promoting the "pluralistic values" of the United States, and building "strong partnerships" with Muslim communities around the world based on what we have in common "as people of faith". This seems to fit in with various U.S. initiatives to spot and foster "young leaders" in other countries, in this case young Muslims in Europe.

Serious world powers, whatever their other faults, are sufficiently attentive to their own national interests to see to it that some of their own experts are trained to understand and explain other parts of the world. As an immigrant country, the United States has militant diasporas able to overrule experts (when they exist) and influence foreign policy by appealing to members of Congress. The Israeli lobby is the extreme example of a foreign nation's heavy influence on Congress, but it is not the only one (the Cuban lobby is another notorious case in point). But when it comes to less familiar places, a few individuals may succeed in winning over most of a Congress whose members are generally too engrossed in domestic political matters to have more than a totally superficial notion of international affairs.

Naturally, Hillary Clinton, supported by Senator John McCain, has fiercely rejected suggestions that Huma Abedin could be a Saudi agent planted in the White House. But even if such suspicions are entirely unfounded, it is simply not serious for a Secretary of State to rely so heavily on a young woman with her background to interpret the Middle East.

Indeed, at a time when support to Muslims in Bosnia and in Kosovo was judged to be in U.S. geostrategic interests for various reasons, a sentimental affinity with Islam was a way to merge "interests and ideals". Having Huma at her side could enforce the illusion that Washington's pro-Muslim policy in the Balkans was building genuine friendship between America and the Islamic world.

In July 2010, Huma Abedin married Brooklyn Democratic Party politician Anthony Weiner, a left liberal colleague of Hillary

Rodham Clinton. Weiner's congressional career got off to a flying start during the Democratic Party primary when he anonymously blanketed his heavily Jewish district with leaflets linking his opponents to black leaders David Dinkins, then mayor of New York City, and Jesse Jackson. At the time of their marriage, Weiner seemed to have a promising future as a New York City mayoral hopeful. Alas, his campaign was ruined by revelations of sexual exhibitionism on Twitter.

Weiner was always an ardent champion of Israel. He supported the 2003 invasion of Iraq, and in May 2006 tried to bar entry of the Palestinian delegation to the United Nations, declaring that they "should start packing their little Palestinian terrorist bags". He even accused the pro-Israel *New York Times* of being biased against the Jewish state. Following the September 11 attacks on the Twin Towers, Weiner led congressional demands to cut off arms sales to Saudi Arabia, which he accused of having a "history of financing terrorism" and teaching children to hate Christians and Jews.

It may therefore seem paradoxical that Huma Abedin, with her strong Saudi and Muslim background, should choose to marry a Zionist Jew like Weiner. And yet, their surprising interfaith marriage actually embodies a key feature of Clinton foreign policy: the *de facto* alliance between Saudi Arabia and Israel. That alliance, like the marriage, may look strange and precarious, but it is in reality a major factor of international relations. In both these alliances, marital or geopolitical, there is certain to be much that remains invisible to the general public.

Diasporas and Discontents

As relatively recent nations built on mass immigration, the United States and Canada are inherently multicultural in ways that are out of the question for most of the world. The United States has absorbed masses of people from diverse cultures in the context of its own extremely strong unifying national ideology. As an immigrant country, the United States tells itself that it is exceptional because people chose to come here: of all the nations of the world, this is the "country of choice". As such, the United States must embody what humanity truly desires and this makes it the model that all other nations should follow.

This belief can have a dire effect on U.S. foreign policy. Rich and influential exiles have shown that they can talk Washington's leaders into believing that their people back home yearn to be Americanized, and that they only need a boost from the Pentagon to put them in charge of bright and shining new democracies. So-called civil society recruitment abroad can also be used, not to influence foreign countries, but to influence the American public. This has been the case particularly with the Middle East, where the main advocates of U.S. wars, the Israelis and their many friends in America, have managed to enlist natives of the countries targeted to justify subsequent hostilities. U.S. support to rebels in Syria certainly did not begin with the so-called "Arab Spring" uprising in early 2011. In February 2006, the Bush administration announced it would award five million dollars in grants to "accelerate the work of reformers in Syria". To get that money, a group of Syrian exiles in Europe founded the Movement for Justice and Development, described by Wikileaked U.S. cables as a group of "liberal, moderate Islamists" who were former members of the Muslim Brotherhood. Many other such dissident exiles have been funded through a variety of channels, often used in order to convince well-intentioned American citizens' groups that "the people back home" want the United States to intervene on their behalf against their "dictator".

Perhaps the most notorious of these high-flying international con men was (and still is) Ahmed Chalabi, the Shi'ite exile who befriended the leading neocons in the run-up to the 2003 invasion of Iraq, briefing the Pentagon, the State Department, Congress and the *New York Times* into believing that Saddam Hussein had weapons of mass destruction and ties with al Qaeda. Chalabi ran a profitable little trade, channeling the fantasies of various Iraqi exile and introducing the notorious "inventor" of the Iraqi WMD called "Curveball" to a grateful and generous Pentagon. Once the United States followed his advice, Chalabi was put in charge of throwing all the Sunnis out of the conquered Iraqi government; the repercussions of this act can be observed today. Over hundreds of thousands of dead bodies, Chalabi is still making money and hoping to pick up the remaining Shi'ite pieces of Iraq. French intelligence believes Chalabi was an Iranian agent, but in Washington, they loved him.

The plain fact is that Washington politicians are not very skilled at grasping the true intentions of sophisticated exiles from exotic regions. This should be one reason for caution in foreign adventures, yet it is a lesson that is clearly ignored.

Diaspora lobbies can be all the more effective in influencing members of Congress with scant knowledge of the outside world if they back up their stories with hefty campaign contributions. Even such a relatively insignificant diaspora as the Albanians managed to gain Congressional support by influencing a single important legislator. In the 1980s, Republican ex-Congressman Joe DioGuardi rediscovered his Albanian roots and created a pro-Albanian lobby that channeled campaign funds to Republican Senator Bob Dole, the 1996 Republican Party presidential candidate. Coached on Balkan history by his staff adviser Mira Baratta, the granddaughter of a Croatian fascist Ustashi, Dole in 1993 declared that "Serbs are illiterate degenerates, baby killers, butchers and rapists" who should all be "placed in Nazi-style concentration camps." (Actually, that is precisely what the Croatian Ustashi had done during World War II.) His Democratic colleague Joe Biden also shared this "identity politics" approach to the Balkans, dividing the world between "our friends" and a subhuman species. Serbian-Americans never had such an effective organized lobby, and naively expected the United States to remember that hundreds of American pilots shot down over Nazi-occupied Serbia in 1944 had been rescued by the Serbian resistance. In contrast, it was precisely those Yugoslavian national groups that had been allied with the Nazis that felt the need to sell themselves as America's best friends.

The rich Israeli lobby has managed to buy virtually the entire Congress, thanks to all-expenses-paid trips to Israel and campaign contributions (especially the tacit threat to provide generous financing to the campaign of your opponent, if you get out of line), but over the years the Chinese Nationalists, the Cuban lobby, exiled Iraqis and Iranians, and now the Ukrainian lobby have all had their moment of influence. The anti-Russian Ukrainian diaspora has been influencing Washington ever since the start of the Cold War, but now it also has power in Kiev. Immigrants and exiles with ambitions to use U.S. power to influence their countries of origin can contribute to building American hostility toward the leaders they wish to overthrow. They can also be used to replace governments Washington does not like with client regimes.

One way to mine this domestic resource for use abroad was developed at the end of the Cold War by former U.S. ambassador and leading policy-maker Morton Abramowitz, as President of the Carnegie Endowment for International Peace (1991-1997). Faced with a drastic shortage of "threats", Abramowitz devised a rationale for an active foreign policy based instead on the promotion of U.S. interests combined with American "ideals".

"American ideals and self-interest merge when the United States supports the spread of democracy around the globe – or what we prefer to call 'limited' constitutional democracy, meaning rule by a government that has been legitimized by free elections", was the conclusion of a Carnegie study directed by Abramowitz, summed up in the Endowment's 1992 publication entitled *Self-Determination in the New World Order.*

The authors of this study made no bones about the fact that the "new world order" was "a world with one superpower – the United States – in which the rule of law supplants the rule of the jungle, disputes are settled peacefully, aggression is firmly met by collective resistance, and all people are justly treated". This future "rule of law" is not to be confused with existing international law. Rather it will be developed under U.S. influence. "International law – as it always has done – will respond and adjust to the behavior of nations and the actions of multilateral institutions". A major feature of this "new world order" will be the weakening, or destruction, of national sovereignty, the basis of existing international law. The sovereignty of the single superpower cannot be seriously challenged, but for other nations, the concept of nationhood may be outdated.

The sovereign nation is being broken down from the outside by the pressures of economic globalization. It may also be undermined from the inside by domestic insurgencies. In the post-Cold War world, the Carnegie Endowment study noted that "groups within states are staking claims to independence, greater autonomy, or the overthrow of an existing government, all in the name of self-determination". In regard to these conflicts, "American interests and ideals compel a more active role", which may extend to military intervention when claims of self-determination or internal repression lead to "humanitarian calamities". In the future, the authors announced in 1992, "humanitarian interventions will become increasingly unavoidable". The United States will have the final word as to when and how to intervene. "The United States should seek to build a consensus within regional and international organizations for its position, but should not sacrifice its own judgment and principles if such a consensus fails to materialize".

In short, we are open to a coalition of the willing – as in, willing to follow us.

"Humanitarian intervention" was theorized by the Abramowitz team shortly before it was put into practice in Yugoslavia. And the people who put it into practice were precisely those members of the Abramowitz team. Seldom has reality imitated fiction quite so rapidly. The Abramowitz disciples who led the United States and NATO into war in Yugoslavia included Richard Holbrooke, Madeleine Albright, special ambassador for war crimes issues David Scheffer, State Department policy planning director Morton Halperin, and Leon Fuerth, Vice President Al Gore's foreign policy expert, who was subsequently put in charge of administering sanctions against Serbia.

It is almost as if the team had rehearsed their play at the Carnegie Endowment before producing it on the world stage. Yugoslavia was the experimental laboratory for the defense of "multiculturalism"; it actually produced the opposite effect. A multi-cultural nation was violently split into ethnically monocultural statelets (although Serbia still includes ethnic minorities who may be incited to demand further partitioning). The Western left intelligentsia abandoned its previous reluctance to support war for the illusion that force was necessary to save the precious ideal of multiculturalism in Yugoslavia.

This mistake owed a lot to the canny strategy of the Muslim party in Bosnia, which chose to play the role of total victim in the Abramowitz scenario. While both Serbian Bosnian and Muslim Bosnian armies skirmished over territorial control, and irregular militias on both sides wreaked havoc, Alija Izetbegovic kept his forces and arms deliveries out of the sight of Western media (but not of Islamic sites, which exalted his exploits), leaving the impression of a one-sided war with Serb invaders slaughtering unarmed Muslim civilians. Izetbegovic's strategy was to get the United States to do what it seemed to want to do: that is, to intervene on the Muslim side. A well-connected young American from a family close to Izetbegovic, Mohammed Sacirbey, became Bosnian ambassador to the United Nations.

On the eve of two major U.N. decisions concerning Bosnia, numerous civilians were killed by mysterious explosions in a market square in Sarajevo. While international military forensic experts concluded on both occasions that the explosions were probably Muslim "false flag" attacks, international media immediately described them as deliberate Serb atrocities. This led to sanctions against Serbia and eventually to the fairly ineffective NATO bombing of Bosnian Serb positions – the start of "humanitarian intervention".

The propaganda that identified the Muslim party in Bosnia with "multiculturalism" enjoyed extraordinary success among Western intelligentsia. Paris intellectuals formed an ephemeral political party for the European elections around the slogan "Europe lives or dies in Sarajevo". Bernard-Henri Lévy was a leading promoter of the belief that the very existence of Europe's unification was at stake in Bosnia, interpreting a struggle for political control of territory as a racist rejection of Muslims for being "different". Viewing the tragic conflict in terms of ethnic identities obscured the political causes inherited from centuries of bitter conflict involving the Ottoman and Habsburg Empires. Many in the West considered Bosnia to be "our Spain", the combat of a generation. But in this case, instead of volunteering to fight for it themselves they were ready to send NATO.

Meanwhile, the Great Powers had other things in mind. Germany was taking revenge for two World Wars. Washington had several geopolitical motives for supporting Alija Izetbegovic. One reason was to demonstrate to the world's Muslim countries that the United States could be their defender, despite constant U.S. support for Israel. Another reason to use Yugoslavia as an experimental laboratory to practice methods of using Russia's Central Asia Muslim "underbelly" to weaken and dismember the great northern Slavic state. Many in Washington thought of Yugoslavia as a miniature Soviet Union, with Serbia as a mini-Russia. Tearing apart the little one could be practice for tackling the big one.

A major drawback of intervention in foreign countries' quarrels is that those doing the intervening often do not get their facts straight, either deliberately or by accident. In reality, Bosnia had never been a "multiethnic paradise". It was the most harshly-governed republic in the Yugoslav Federation, formerly the scene of the worst interethnic slaughters during World War II, held together only by Marshal Tito's autocratic rule until his death. While the West European left assumed that Muslims must be the underdogs, as in their own countries, in Bosnia the Muslims had constituted the dominant caste for centuries since the Ottoman Turk conquest. Alija Izetbegovic was a notorious political and religious figure, supported by Pakistan and Saudi Arabia, who had written that once a country has a Muslim majority, it must be ruled by Muslim law. This led Bosnian Christians to fear belonging to a State where the Muslims might soon constitute an absolute majority. Since Izetbegovic, with U.S. political support, had installed himself permanently in what was supposed to be a rotating presidency, he quite naturally wanted to maintain control over the entire country, including the areas inhabited by Serbs, which then constituted over half the countryside. For this, his propaganda network, including professional U.S. public relations experts, dismissed as "Serb propaganda" any attempt to point out that Izetbegovic was a political Islamist and not a champion of multiculturalism. While Islamic countries supported Izetbegovic because he was their coreligionist, the West supported him because he was "multicultural". This support prolonged the civil war, costing many lives, including the victims of the Srebrenica massacre toward the end of the conflict.

Once the West had chosen sides, secular Manichaeism took over. One side was described as victim, the other side as evil incarnate. Under the influence of memories of the Holocaust, the Serbs were accused from the start of genocide, an accusation that finally stuck after the massacre at Srebrenica. But the war might never have started, had Izetbegovic not been encouraged by Washington to reject compromise. Mujahidin who came from Afghanistan to support the cause went as far as to photograph their games of "football" with the heads of decapitated Serbs, but videos of these exploits were never shown on Western television.

In 1999, based on the impression that in Bosnia, the Serbs had proved themselves to be "genocidal", the United State drew NATO into intervening on the side of the Kosovars (Albanian separatists) in the Serbian province of Kosovo. Once again, the defense of "multiculturalism" meant taking the side of one culture against another.

The defense of "multicultural" Bosnia marked a mutation in much of the far left and its historical attachment to "international solidarity". In the past, that had meant mutual support between groups sharing the same ideology and the same long-term political ideals, such as socialism or working class solidarity. No more. Since the civil war in Bosnia and the Kosovo war, most of the left has been inclined to support almost any minority in revolt against its government, regardless of the issues, and whether or not the demands were reasonable or just. Form had won over content.

Thus, the remnants of past leftist "international solidarity" were transformed into a cheering session for the Abramowitz strategy and U.S. interventionism.

The lesson was not lost on other discontented ethnic minorities around the world who might like to use U.S. support in order to gain local power, such as the Uyghurs of Northwestern China. The National Endowment for Democracy provides grants to the Uyghur American Association, whose exiled separatist leader Rebiya Kadeer issues anti-Chinese statements from her home in New York. While the United States officially hails "multi-ethnicity", ethnic minorities in China and Russia are clearly seen as weaknesses to be exploited in order to destabilize and even break apart these great nations into more manageable pieces, on the model of Yugoslavia. Divide and rule is the eternal imperial imperative.

The United States continues to show concern for the minority of its choice, in the country it chooses to destabilize.

Looking For Genocide

The most unpleasant aspect of the current official U.S. foreign policy ideology is the obsession with genocide. The subject itself is obviously disturbing. Even more so is the assumption that we Americans are living in a world full of monsters eager to "commit genocide" who can be deterred only by the threat or application of

U.S. military power.

It is important to recognize that the current U.S. obsession with genocide is neither a national defense nor a humanitarian concern. It is an ideology and its purpose is political, although this purpose may be unconscious or sublimated by those who wield the powerful ideological weapon of Holocaust memory.

An official Genocide Prevention Task Force was jointly convened in November 2007 by the United States Holocaust Memorial Museum, the American Academy of Diplomacy and the United States Institute of Peace. It was co-chaired by former Secretary of State Madeleine K. Albright and former Secretary of Defense William S. Cohen, two individuals certainly not distinguished for their peacekeeping endeavors. In December 2008, the task force released the report, "Preventing Genocide: A Blueprint for U.S. Policymakers", asserting that genocide is preventable and that progress to this end begins with leadership and political will.

The thrust of the U.S. approach is to treat genocide as if it were a sort of epidemic, apt to break out unexpectedly, with only the United States capable of preventing contagion. U.S. prevention consists of spotting "symptoms", such as "hate speech", which then need to be repressed. Genocide is seen as the result of purely subjective psychological causes, rather than situations apt to cause antagonism between groups, such as basic resource scarcities, as in the case of Darfur. This is consistent with an essentially religious approach which considers genocide a manifestation of "evil". The religious approach sees "evil" (Satan) as the cause, rather than as a description of the effects. The evil is in the intention. As Hillary Clinton said in her keynote speech at a conference entitled "Imagine the Unimaginable: Ending Genocide in the 21st Century" on July 24, 2012, "genocide is always planned."

The first and most obvious political purpose of the official U.S. anti-genocide campaign is to occupy the moral high ground. It is a way of telling the world, but much more so of telling ourselves, that genocide – the worst of all crimes, the crime that makes other forms of killing almost acceptable in comparison – is something that we Americans cannot and will never do. Genocide "is always planned" and we, surely, never plan genocide. We may make mistakes, but that is different. The Vietnamese killed by the United States number in the millions, but never can it be suggested that the U.S. committed genocide in Vietnam. Subjectively, the United States never intended to exterminate the Vietnamese. Genocide is a subjective crime. The definition of genocide always depends on intention and our intentions are always good. We meant well. We always mean well.

Firebombing Dresden and Japanese cities built of paper was not genocide either. Of course, during World War II, it would not have been difficult to find Americans expressing the desire to "kill all those Germans", and even less so to "wipe out the Japs". Such sentiments flourish in war. People rage against the enemy and want to kill them all. War does that.

So what needs to be prevented, "genocide" or war?

The U.S. anti-genocide campaign, by rating genocide as *worse than war*, and as something that *war can prevent*, actually ends up *justifying war.*

At the conference mentioned above, Hillary Clinton cited Syria as an example, complaining that Washington's virtuous effort to stop atrocities were being blocked by "a small group": Iran, Russia and China. She went on to say that: "we are also increasing our efforts to assist the opposition", before adding that if we are successful, "Assad will increase the level of violent response".

At a moment like this, one must ask whether she realizes what she is saying. She is admitting that U.S. military aid to the opposition intended to prevent violence will provoke more violence. If there is indeed a possibility of "genocide", which is doubtful, this possibility will be increased by that very assistance to the opposition Hillary is calling for, since it will increase the overall violence. Yet her speech received warm applause and a standing ovation.

"We are countering hatred with truth", Hillary proclaimed.

On the contrary. Hillary's speech, like the whole U.S. anti-genocide campaign, thrives on arousing hatred against Washington's current enemies, who are denounced as potential genocidal murderers. However, when Washington's irregular Ukrainian allies can be seen on YouTube advocating wiping out the "excess" inhabitants of Eastern Ukraine in order to take their resources, while the official Ukrainian army shells civilian areas, the alarm bells remain silent in the genocide prevention establishment in Washington.

Ironically, while eagerly looking out for "genocide" to be

committed by Serbs in Bosnia, the Clinton administration stubbornly refused to describe as "genocide" the massive slaughter that took place in Rwanda in the spring of 1994. The difference is that U.S. policy-makers were looking for a reason to intervene in Bosnia, but absolutely did not want to do so in Rwanda.

On April 6, 1994, the plane carrying the presidents of two neighboring countries, Rwandan President Juvenal Habyarimana and Burundi President Cyprien Ntaryamira, was shot down as it approached the Rwandan capital of Kigali. Responsibility for this extraordinary act of terrorism remains controversial and the crime has never been sufficiently investigated. A civil war had been going on in Rwanda ever since armed Tutsi exiles crossed the northern border from Uganda in early 1990 and began their long struggle to wrest the country back from the Hutu majority, represented by President Habyarimana. With Anglo-American support, the Tutsi invaders, under the banner of the Rwanda Patriotic Front (RPF) led by Paul Kagame, had strengthened their political and military position in the country. The dramatic assassination of two Hutu presidents set off a horrendous bloodbath, with Hutus massacring Tutsi men, women and children while the RPF made a dash to seize power in Kigali.

Boutros Boutros-Ghali, then U.N. Secretary General, frantically tried to get the great powers to send troops to stop what he almost immediately described as "genocide". He wanted to beef up the small U.N. peacekeeping force UNAMIR already in Rwanda, as it began to withdraw. The Clinton administration, however, adamantly refused to speak of "genocide" or to agree to any form of outside intervention. On April 15, a State Department cable instructed U.S. Ambassador to the United Nations Madeleine Albright to inform her colleagues that "the United States believes that the first priority of the Security Council is to instruct the Secretary General to implement an orderly withdrawal of all/all UNAMIR forces from Rwanda." U.S. officials refused to use the term "genocide", because that might oblige them to intervene, which they were determined not to do. On May 1, a Department of Defense memo urged caution, since State Department legal advisors warned that a "genocide finding" could commit the U.S. Government to "do something".

The slaughter had raged for weeks when President Bill Clinton, in a speech in Annapolis on May 26, listed Rwanda among the world's many bloody conflicts where the interests at stake did not justify the use of American military power. "We cannot solve every such outburst of civil strife or militant nationalism simply by sending in our forces", Clinton said.

There were two reasons for this refusal to intervene; one technical and the other political. The technical reason, well-documented, was that the Clinton administration did not want to foot the bill for any more international peace-keeping missions. This was made quite clear at the time to Boutros Boutros-Ghali. Madeleine Albright carried out her instructions to block any intervention on the grounds that Washington would eventually get the bill and did not want to pay it. In a January 2004 interview with PBS, Boutros-Ghali recalled that when he pled for a peacekeeping operation, even without United States participation, the Americans told him: "We don't allow you to do a peacekeeping operation even without the United States. Why? Because, one, we have to contribute 30 percent of the budget of this peacekeeping operation, and two – and let us be objective – it is true in the case that you will have problems in this peacekeeping operation, you will ask our assistance, and we will be compelled to give you this assistance." [15]

The second, political reason that the United States "stood on the sidelines" rather than support a U.N. cease-fire was related to its long-time support to the Rwandan Patriotic Front led by Kagame. The absence of any international intervention left the way open for the RPF to complete its dash to seize power in Kigali in the wake of the assassination of the president.

In the interview cited above, Boutros-Ghali was asked whether he, like "very senior people in the Clinton administration", was aware that "the RPF had made it clear that it was going to press towards Kigali".

Boutros-Ghali replied: "No, no, no. Again, this just proves the weakness of the United Nations system. The member states, to maintain a kind of pressure on the United Nations, will not give you all the information. But definitely, when a decision is taken, or when you are trying to oppose a decision, you are in a weaker position than the member states, because they know more about the situation than you. We gave information, but they never gave us any information."

Later, he added: "The control of the superpower on the United Nations is greater than everybody will be aware of. They have a control on the finance in the administration, they have the control on the Peace-Keeping Office; they have the control on the Security Council, and they have information which they will not share with others."

Washington knew that Kagame was going to seize power in Rwanda, and didn't want to allow anything to happen that would get in his way.

The United States had strongly supported Kagame all along. It gave him a year of military training at the U.S. Army Command and Staff College at Fort Leavenworth, Kansas, just before he took command of the Rwandan Patriotic Front. As a consequence of Belgian rule, the Hutus remaining in Rwanda spoke French as their international language, whereas the Tutsi exiles in the formerly British colony of Uganda were English-speaking. This gave the struggle the air of a colonial Anglophone-Francophone rivalry. In Brussels, capital of the European Union and of NATO, in the spring of 1994 the Tutsis were all considered heroes and martyrs and the French were despised for having backed the Hutu losers. Moreover, it was enough to hold a private conversation with American personnel to grasp that they were genuinely enraptured with the Tutsis, in a candidly racist fashion, admiring them as tall, beautiful and intelligent, and especially appreciative of the "aristocratically" liberated Tutsi women. It was as if the racist prejudice against black Africans in general had at long last found its redemption in an excessive admiration of the Tutsis. And besides, they spoke English. In January 1996, Kagame's Rwanda adopted English as an official national language.

The Tutsis were a minority in Rwanda and could not expect to win the elections promised under the auspices of foreign powers in the attempt to negotiate a peaceful end to the civil war. The RPF needed a military victory to gain power and it used the April 6 attack on the presidential plane to break the truce and press for military victory. At the same time, desperate and enraged Hutus went berserk and plunged into a ghastly slaughter of those they took to be supporters of the advancing RPF.

And yet, after his military victory, Paul Kagame was unbeatable. In August 2010 he won a second seven-year term as president with 93% of the vote, and a 95% turnout.

As usual, when the United States takes sides, a bloody conflict is described by mainstream media as a one-sided killing spree. The reality is far worse. The RPF had been killing Hutu civilians for quite some time and they went on doing so, not only in April of 1994 but for years afterwards. And not only in Rwanda but even more so in the neighboring Republic of Congo, where the death toll is much higher than that of Tutsis slaughtered by Hutus. The truth here is that if "genocide" is the appropriate term, it was a mutual genocide with horrible massacres on both sides.

There can be no doubt that it was the worst bloodbath of this generation. Still, is the term "genocide" really helpful? Who is to know whether the Hutus who wielded knives against defenseless Tutsis really intended to "exterminate" them all, or whether they acted in some sort of insane impulse born of fear and revenge? Was this madness really "planned in advance"? Allegations by the Kagame side of a deliberate Hutu plan to commit genocide have never been satisfactorily proved. The corpses were there, the crimes are unquestionable, and the horror is real. But what goes on in people's minds in such cases is unfathomable.

Moreover, if the subsequent mass killing across the border in the Democratic Republic of Congo does not qualify as "genocide", this could be because less emotional motives can be discerned. In May 2001, former U.S. Congresswoman Cynthia McKinney accused the Clinton administration, the Kagame regime in Rwanda, and the Ugandan state of using the pretext of clearing "guilty" Hutu refugees out of eastern Congo in order to engage in the large scale pillage of natural resources for the benefit of U.S. and European companies. The illegally looted resources include tropical timber, gold, cobalt, diamonds, zinc, uranium and especially the world's largest deposits of coltan, a mineral essential for the computer industry. [16]

It is not easy to draw a moral from such a human catastrophe. But this much can be said: the usual context for such massive slaughter is war – especially civil war. The sphere of civil war creates not only hatred but fear of one's neighbors, a fear that leads to blind gestures made to remove the source of that fear. One can see similar behavior even in animals: it is fear, much more than hatred, which motivates such murderous reactions. If this is so, then campaigns against "hatred" are irrelevant. What is necessary is to avoid situations where fear reaches such a fevered pitch that blind, indiscriminate killing is the result.

If this is the case, then the United States approach to "combating genocide" is counterproductive. The fact that the superpower takes sides can help push desperate people over the edge, whereas the prospect of a genuinely unbiased power prepared to judge with wisdom and equanimity might have a calming effect. Unfortunately, such a power does not exist. The United States manipulates the United Nations and has managed to take control of the International Criminal Court. It will not itself abide by the decisions of the ICC, which destroys the very appearance of the Court's impartiality toward those involved.

Taking their cue from Samantha Power's *A Problem From Hell*, even the Clinton administration officials responsible for the fact that Washington "stood on the sidelines" as the blood flowed in Rwanda, now try to use that fact to argue for future interventions. They are so dreadfully sorry now! And their heartfelt regret proves that the United States must be the great humanitarian sentinel looking out to spot genocide on the horizon in order to prevent it from happening again.

Actually, it pretty much proves the opposite. The Rwanda episode shows that for all the talk about "ideals", the United States sides with its "interests" in the crunch and will use its information advantage to keep others in the dark until the crisis is past. The absence of international action in response to the Rwandan catastrophe was due primarily to the fact that everything depended on one single superpower, with its control of the U.N. budget, U.N. personnel, and the knowledge of what was happening on the ground. This unipolar world, which Samantha Power defends passionately as the proper result of America's unique virtue, is a major cause of deepening chaos. It doesn't work and it can't work.

The U.S. approach is always Manichaean. It is a dualistic approach to conflicts, which consists of taking sides and then identifying the "bad" side as potentially "genocidal", even before people are killed. This was definitely the case in Yugoslavia, where an International

Tribunal was established with the declared intent of judging Serbian leaders for "genocide" before any remotely "genocidal" crime had been committed. In the absence of any evidence of intention, the Srebrenica massacre was judged "genocide" by that Tribunal thanks to a rather odd sociological argument: Bosnian Muslim society is "patriarchal", and by killing off only the menfolk, the Serbs ensured that Muslim women and children, although spared, would never return to Srebrenica, thus committing genocide in a single town. This reasoning broadly extended the meaning of "genocide", but satisfied the American sponsors of the Tribunal who wanted the label of "genocidal" to stick to the Serbs, thereby giving an advantage to the Muslim side which they supported in both Bosnia and Kosovo.

A massacre is a massacre. There are bodies, there is forensic evidence, and there is material proof. Murdering prisoners or civilians in time of war is wrong, whatever the label. A massacre is called "genocide" only because of the assumption of an intention for which, in the case of Yugoslavia, there was never any evidence. Calling a massacre "genocide" is not dependent on the number of victims; the number of victims at Srebrenica was tiny compared to the number of Vietnamese killed by the United States. But a massacre labeled "genocide" is understood to be much worse than any ordinary massacre because it implies the *intention* to kill everybody in a particular human group. The word is a moral multiplier.

It is also a political term. Once a leader is accused of "genocide", there can be no negotiations, no diplomacy, no attempt to find a peaceful solution to the conflict which is the background of the alleged crime. The guilty party can only be indicted or killed.

A glance at the way the United States has used the term "genocide" in the last two decades suggests that the current search for potential genocide, supposedly for prevention, is in fact a search for internal conflicts which can be labeled "potentially genocidal" in countries targeted for regime change. The "threat of genocide" can justify destabilizing measures: propaganda campaigns, boycotts, sanctions, the threat and even the use of military forces, with the possibility of armed intervention if the relationship of forces is favorable.

There is no end to these double standards. The United States sets itself up as uniquely capable of identifying and combating what it calls genocide, thereby ruling out the very possibility of a coordinated international effort to prevent ethnic conflicts from degenerating into mass slaughter. In the case of the civil war in Syria, Hillary Clinton claimed that well-intentioned U.S. efforts at intervention were thwarted by a "small group" which included Russia and China. There was no real threat of genocide, and moreover, Russia was more than cooperative in the effort to get rid of Syria's chemical weapons. On the other hand, when real slaughter was going on in Rwanda, a "small group", consisting of the United States and Britain, did indeed block any effort at international intervention in order to make sure that "their side" won. Their team did indeed win and the crocodile tears keep flowing, twenty years on, simply to justify future interventions.

Chapter 3

The Taming By the Shrew

For a woman to get ahead in the United States foreign policy establishment, it helps to be as aggressive as the policies themselves. Tough women are proof that there are no soft spots in America's approach to the world. Indeed, in recent years, aggressive women in key positions have become a trend.

A precursor of this trend was Jeane Kirkpatrick, President Reagan's ambassador to the United Nations from 1981 to 1985. Kirkpatrick's career provided the same lesson as that of her contemporary, Margaret Thatcher: women in power are no more tender-hearted than men. Given what it takes to succeed in "a man's world", they may go out of their way to act even tougher. An early neoconservative, Kirkpatrick was credited in Washington with the doctrine that it was perfectly all right for the United States to support regimes that were "authoritarian", usually referring to U.S.-sponsored Latin American military dictatorships, while Washington must oppose "totalitarian" regimes, meaning communist states. As a member of the Committee on the Present Danger, she helped stoke the national paranoia that keeps the arms industry flourishing. Focused on imaginary threats and perils, Kirkpatrick was openly contemptuous of human rights and cared little for the supposed United States mission to spread democracy. The collapse of the Soviet Union rendered the Kirkpatrick line obsolete.

During the Bill Clinton administration, foreign policy focus shifted to human rights. America's "values" and "interests" demanded intervention to protect and save the victims of human rights violations. The concern and indignation of a woman seemed particularly appropriate and convincing for this position. Ignoring legal and political complexities, the disintegration of Yugoslavia was treated by Western media and governments primarily as a human rights crisis, in which one party was the violator and other parties were victims. CNN's correspondent Christiane Amanpour, particularly close to the State Department, led the way in using one-sided reports to demand U.S. intervention against the Serbs. The model was so successful that it became the standard for the Obama presidency, applied to Libya, Syria and the Ukraine, with women in the forefront.

In the Clinton co-presidency, Hillary's domain was domestic policy, in particular the design of a vast health care reform initiative. When that failed, she reverted to her original public service field of children's law, writing a book about care for children (*It Takes a Village*), under the influence of New Age gurus. For a while, she reportedly sought refuge in New Age self-empowerment, gaining spiritual strength through religion and mystical experience. The trouble with such subjective self-empowerment is that it may produce more self-confidence than is justified when facing particularly difficult encounters with complex reality.

After the debacle of her health reform project and the damage done to her image from endless Republican probing both into her past as an Arkansas lawyer and her dealings with White House staff, she was sent on a tour of South Asia and Africa. Her main interest continued to be women and children. In September 1995, Hillary led the U.S. delegation to the United Nations Fourth World Conference on Women held in Beijing. In China, Hillary made a favorable impression with a dramatic speech denouncing abuse of women and girls: "It is a violation of human rights when babies are denied food, or drowned, or suffocated, or their spines broken, simply because they are girls. It is a violation of human rights when women and girls are sold into the slavery of prostitution. It is a violation of human rights when women are doused with gasoline, set on fire and burned to death because their marriage dowries are deemed too small..."

Hillary, in semi-disgrace back home, was now suddenly hailed as a heroine. The *New York Times* praised the speech as her "finest moment in public life". The political lesson was strong and clear: when in trouble on the home front, a politician can compensate abroad, especially by defending "human rights".

Up until then, Hillary's interests and expertise were limited to children's rights, education and health care. Those were traditionally feminine fields, vitally important to be sure, but not yet "presidential", because they were too far from the traditional center of male power: war.

War is the citadel that women must conquer for full equality.

It is considered an advancement for women to be able to join the military, and not just in clerical jobs, but also in combat, doing the real killing. Glorifying this particular path toward "breaking the glass ceiling" is potentially useful to the War State.

The way to make war acceptable and even popular is to show that it is good for women and children: war protects them. Who better to get this message across than women? A mutual interest brought together neocons who want war and women who want to break glass ceilings. If neocons need women to make war look good, highly ambitious women need war to advance their careers.

Hillary strongly urged Bill Clinton to choose her friend Madeleine Albright to replace Warren Christopher as Secretary of State for his second term. Hillary and Madeleine were both Wellesley graduates, and Hillary argued that the job of Secretary of State should go to a woman. Unlike Hillary, Madeleine, who had already served as Clinton's ambassador to the United Nations, did indeed have a background in foreign policy. Her father, Josef Korbel, a former Czech ambassador to Yugoslavia, immigrated with his family first to Britain to escape World War II and later to the United States, where he founded the School of International Studies at the University of Denver. One of his students was Condoleezza Rice. Like many East European immigrants, Korbel saw U.S. power as a force to be used to settle issues in the rest of the world. In 1959, Madeleine married into the U.S. press aristocracy as the bride of Joseph Medill Patterson Albright, grandson of the founder of the New York *Daily News* and great grandson of the owner of the *Chicago Tribune*. During her 23-year marriage, she worked for Zbigniew Brzezinski while he was National Security Advisor during the mid-1970s and taught international relations at Georgetown University. At age 59, as she prepared to take office as Secretary of State, she announced: "It's conceivable that I'm of Jewish background." While claiming to be "shocked" at the news of her family's hidden identity, being a Holocaust survivor bestows incomparable moral authority today. "Albright liked to say, 'My mindset is Munich.' She was the rare official in the Clinton team who lobbied relentlessly for NATO bombing and who laced her public condemnations of Serb 'extermination' and expulsion with Holocaust references," according to Samantha Power. [17]

Mad For War

A salient trait of the new school of women diplomats is that they are strikingly undiplomatic. Indeed, Madeleine Albright's greatest diplomatic success was to obstruct diplomacy. When European allies expressed reluctance to bomb the Serbs without at least a stab at diplomacy, her manipulation of a special conference held in the Rambouillet chateau outside Paris in February and March of 1999 made sure that there could be no negotiated solution to the crisis in the Serbian province of Kosovo. NATO would have its pretext to bomb what was left of Yugoslavia (Serbia and Montenegro – the latter subsequently seceded peacefully under Western pressure).

The Kosovo problem was basically an ethnic minority issue that was no more intractable than many other similar problems on the planet. Albanians were a recognized minority in Yugoslavia, but a majority in the southern Serbian province of Kosovo, bordering Albania. As is often the case, the problem was aggravated by conflicting versions of a shared history (each side accusing the other of past abuses), but was no more acute or unsolvable than dozens of others. There were voices on both sides in favor of the sort of compromise that the United States officially stated to be its goal: a large measure of autonomy for Kosovo within Serbia. Jan Oberg of the Swedish Transnational Foundation for Peace and Future Research was meeting with both sides in search of a compromise at the time. Serbia's most distinguished novelist, Dobrica Cosic, who had served for a short time as President of Yugoslavia, went so far as to call for a negotiated independence for Kosovo.

Meanwhile, in Paris, another President's wife, Danielle Mitterrand, was discretely using her influence to seek a peaceful agreement. Danielle, who had been a liaison agent for the French Resistance as a teenager, was hosting meetings of leading Serbian and Kosovo Albanian intellectuals to discuss possible solutions. All that was needed was for the Great Powers to actively promote such genuine efforts at diplomacy and the war and its destruction could have been avoided.

In the winter of 1998-99, there were Organization for Security and Cooperation in Europe (OSCE) monitors in Kosovo who saw clearly that incidents of violence were being deliberately provoked by armed Kosovo Liberation Army (KLA) killers in order to goad Serbian police into retaliation that the media would describe as "ethnic cleansing" or "the threat of genocide". To please Washington, the Polish foreign minister Bronislaw Geremek used his temporary chairmanship of the OSCE to put the Kosovo mission under the command of U.S. agent William Walker, a veteran of dubious operations in Central American. Walker provided vital aid to the KLA project, notably by publicly denouncing a police action against the KLA in the village of Racak as a "massacre of civilians, a crime against humanity". With few exceptions, Western media eagerly helped inflate Walker's sensationalist accusations into the *casus belli* NATO needed.

As Secretary of State, Madeleine Albright's role was to prevent diplomacy from producing a peaceful solution that would get in the way of NATO's first "humanitarian war". Bombing Yugoslavia provided the opportunity to transform a formally defensive alliance into an offensive force prepared to act outside its treaty area. On its fiftieth anniversary, NATO took its first steps toward becoming a planetary police force under U.S. command.

The United Nations had to be kept out of this. As U.S. Ambassador to the United Nations, Madeleine Albright had seen to it that Boutros Boutros-Ghali was deprived of a second term as U.N. Secretary General. As substitute, Washington chose Ghanaian diplomat Kofi Annan, whose wife Nane Lagergren was from an aristocratic Swedish family, the niece of Raoul Wallenberg, famous for having rescued thousands of Hungarian Jews during World War II. In 1995, as Assistant United Nations Secretary General for Peacekeeping Operations, Annan enabled the United States to go ahead and bomb the Bosnian Serbs. For that reason, according to Richard Holbrooke, Kofi Anna "won the job" of U.S. Secretary General, replacing the less manageable Boutros-Ghali.[18]

Having got him the job, Madeleine Albright tended to treat Annan like hired help, calling at all hours to give him orders. Eventually, Annan complained that she "never quite understood" that he was supposed to work for all the other members of the United Nations. As she prepared for Rambouillet, Albright grew alarmed by reports that Annan was thinking of appointing a group of negotiators to deal with Belgrade. To head that off, she called him twice, telling him: "Kofi, we don't need negotiators running all over the place". She followed up, calling Annan again "to make sure he doesn't have negotiators proliferating."

In reality, U.S. agencies were making deals behind the scenes with the most radical element of the Albanian nationalists in Kosovo, whose assassination targets were mostly Serbs but also included Albanians whose jobs, such as postman, branded them as "collaborators with the Serbs".

While Madeleine Albright took the public lead, her old mentor from the Carnegie Endowment for International Peace, Morton Abramowitz, was in the background, in the role of advisor to the Albanian delegation at Rambouillet.

Madeleine Albright's job was to steer "peace negotiations" toward a deadlock which could be blamed on the Serbs. In Rambouillet, Albright was assisted by her close aide James Rubin, who would go on to marry mainstream media's star advocate of war against Serbs, CNN's fiercely pro-interventionist war correspondent Christiane Amanpour. Belgrade's delegation, including members of all Kosovo's ethnic groups, expressed readiness to compromise. The two sides, Yugoslav and Kosovo Albanian, were kept separate and fed ultimatums by the U.S. delegation. In a surprise move, the Americans pulled off a coup in the Kosovo Albanian delegation, replacing Professor Ibrahim Rugova, who had been extra-legally elected "Kosovar President" in 1992, with the 30-year-old KLA leader, Hashim Thaci, alias "the Snake". In February, Rubin and Thaci met and "got together over a lunch of lamb chops and red wine at the ornate residence of the U.S. ambassador" to Paris and have been chums ever since.[19] Thaci was wanted by Yugoslav police for various crimes; moreover, only a year earlier the KLA had been labeled a "terrorist" organization by special U.S. envoy Robert Gelbard. According to the *Wall Street Journal*: "Throughout the Kosovo crisis, Mr. Rubin personally wooed Hashim Thaci, the ambitious leader of the Kosovo Liberation Army." Rubin went so far as to "jokingly promise that he would speak to Hollywood friends about getting Mr. Thaci a movie role." Coddled by Rubin and Albright, Thaci followed U.S. instructions, reassured that he would gain control of Kosovo as a result.

Fifteen years later, Thaci is still in charge of "independent

Kosovo", a U.S. satellite, best known for its illegal trafficking of drugs, prostitutes and human organs. Crime, ethnic cleansing and murders have gone unpunished ever since, despite (or because of) the presence of NATO forces. Today, the principal cultural attraction in Pristina is a giant gilded kitsch statue of Bill Clinton. A smiling Hillary has posed in front of it, photographed by her daughter Chelsea.

The closed meeting in a French chateau ended with the so-called "Rambouillet Accords", which were not accords at all, since Belgrade refused to sign onto a deal that included an addendum which would have permitted U.S. forces to occupy all of Yugoslavia with total impunity at the expense of the host country. Even Henry Kissinger described the false agreement as "a terrible diplomatic document", "a provocation, an excuse to start bombing". Off the record, Madeleine Albright told reporters that: "we intentionally set the bar too high for the Serbs to comply. They need some bombing, and that's what they are going to get." [20]

When the NATO bombs started falling, OSCE monitors had been hastily evacuated by their U.S. chief. Thus there were almost no foreign witnesses to what was actually happening in Kosovo during the war. Wild reports circulated of massive killings, which proved false. The stream of Albanians who crossed nearby borders to wait out the bombing in Albanian-inhabited regions of Albania or Macedonia was described as "ethnic cleansing" or even genocide, although as soon as the bombing was over, the refugees rushed back to Kosovo, bringing other Albanians with them to take over housing abandoned by terrified Serbs.

Madeleine Albright had reportedly convinced Clinton, against the better judgment of the Pentagon, that Milosevic would back down after a little light bombing. When it didn't happen that way, with Serbian civilians wearing "target" badges and massing on Belgrade bridges to keep them from being bombed, the anti-Serb propaganda escalated dramatically. Tony Blair proclaimed the war to be "a battle between good and evil; between civilization and barbarity; between democracy and dictatorship". The Serbs were guilty, Blair claimed, of "hideous racial genocide". Albright claimed that Milosevic was creating "a horror of biblical proportions" in his "desire to exterminate a group of people." On April 7, 1999, she told

CNN's Larry King: "It has reminiscences of the kinds of things that people saw during World War II where there really is a desire to exterminate a group of people or use them as pawns."

This was pure war propaganda. There was no "extermination" and no threat of extermination, but a conflict between a government and an armed secessionist group supported by neighboring Albania. The refugee exodus was dramatized by Western media as the tragic cause of the war, when it was actually the result. Albanian refugees fleeing the violence obliged Western media with invented tales of rape and murder. Reporters searched Albanian refugee camps for "somebody who has been raped and speaks English". Nobody was interested in the people getting killed by NATO bombs. Nobody cared about the little Serbian town of Varvarin, of no military significance whatsoever, yet targeted by NATO. Air strikes against people gathered on Holy Trinity Day killed at random the town priest and the mayor's daughter, 15-year-old student Sanja Milenkovic, the pride of the town for having won a mathematics prize. Schools, hospitals, and bridges were struck in an effort to turn the population against their president. A bus full of Albanians returning to Kosovo was also massacred by NATO bombs. The infrastructure that people had spent a generation building from scratch, after the devastation of two World Wars, was leveled.

In Washington, the "Kosovo war" was called "Madeleine's war" and she seemed proud of it. Perhaps it soothed some male consciences to put the blame for this shameful masquerade on an emotional woman. Madeleine gave a feminine veneer to a strategic enterprise largely planned and carried out by men. Perhaps this was supposed to strengthen the "humanitarian" pretense.

Aside from starting the first of NATO's aggressive wars, Albright's greatest legacy was a few remarks which cast serious doubt on her humanitarian commitment. The most famous was her reply to question about sanctions against Iraq broadcast by "60 Minutes" on May 12, 1996, when she was still U.S. Ambassador to the United Nations. Noting reports that "half a million children have died" as a result of sanctions, "more children than died in Hiroshima", interviewer Lesley Stahl then asked, "is the price worth it?" Madeleine replied that "we think the price is worth it."

Madeleine Albright's other famous remark was her rhetorical

question to General Colin Powell in favor of using military force: "What's the point of having this superb military, Colin, if we can't use it?"

Killing Diplomacy

The presence of women at high levels in the State Department could be seen merely as the result of women's well-deserved success in significant careers. But the roles played by these women express hostile aspects of U.S. policy more eloquently than men could ever manage in the same positions. Each in her own way uses her personality to sharpen the aggressive edge of U.S. foreign policy and to make reaching any diplomatic understanding with others more difficult. There was a time when feminists claimed that women in powerful positions would make a tremendous contribution toward world peace. America's tough women are squandering expectations, dating back to Aristophanes' "Lysistrata", that women could be mobilized against war.

The snarls of Madeleine Albright, the gloating lectures of Hillary Clinton, the insults of Susan Rice, the tough talk of Victoria Nuland, the eloquent temper tantrums of Samantha Power and even the arrogant ignorance of State Department press spokeswomen tell a different story.

These harpies all work for Democratic administrations claiming great devotion to the cause of human rights, but they have made it clear that this devotion, far from stemming from kindness and gentleness, functions primarily as a motive for punishing alleged offenders. The Obama administration intensified the use of women to whip the rest of the world into line in a U.S.-produced and directed production of "The Taming *By* the Shrew" on the world stage. Washington's foreign policy women specialize in haranguing foreign leaders or diplomats as if they were badly behaved children. Their bullying behavior displays an assurance that, because they are women, they can get away with rudeness that most men in their position would feel obliged to avoid. [21]

As U.S. Ambassador to the United Nations, before she became President Obama's National Security Adviser, Susan Rice showed no concern for the niceties of diplomatic usage. She advocated rejoining the U.N. Human Rights Council largely as a way to fight against "the anti-Israel crap" coming from defenders of the Palestinians. Protégée as well as successor to Madeleine Albright, Rice often sounds the same tone. Just as Madeleine sponsored creation of the breakaway failed State of Kosovo, Susan is credited with a large role in creating another breakaway failed State, South Sudan. Susan Rice acknowledges that she is seen as "brusque, aggressive and abrasive", but doesn't care. "Of course people don't say that to my face," Susan Rice joked at a U.N. Correspondents Association ball, "because they know I'd kick their butts." While acting as "unfeminine" as possible, Ms. Rice was implicitly taking advantage of a feminine privilege – women's certainty that the men they insult are still too civilized to "kick their butts" in return.

Susan Rice was succeeded as Ambassador to the United Nations in Obama's second term by Samantha Power, whose style is totally different, although their policy positions are usually the same. During the 2008 presidential election campaign, Power was obliged to resign from the Obama support team for publicly calling Hillary Clinton a "monster," who would stop at nothing to be elected. However, all was apparently forgiven. As a member of Obama's National Security Council, Samantha Power joined Hillary and Susan Rice in urging Obama to bomb Libya.

Samantha Power has enjoyed a carefully crafted career. Her biographies usually state that her career began as a "freelance journalist in Bosnia", where she witnessed horrors that transformed her into a crusader against genocide. But that is somewhat disingenuous.

Born in Ireland in 1970, Samantha Power went straight from Yale to a junior fellowship with the Carnegie Endowment for International Peace, working on the staff of the President, former Ambassador Morton Abramowitz. That was when Abramowitz was developing his theory that the United States would be obliged to intervene in foreign countries on behalf of beleaguered minorities (see Chapter 4). Samantha Power was an eager apprentice.

One of her colleagues at Carnegie recalls Samantha as zealously ambitious and ingratiating, and already focused on Bosnia as a career opportunity. Ready to do whatever she could in order to get where the action was, [22] at the age of 22, Samantha joined the swarm of freelance reporters heading to the big story in Bosnia, but unlike others, her Carnegie connections assured her the promise of publication in big-time mainstream magazines. At only 25, she was taken on by the International Crisis Group as a political analyst monitoring the implementation of the Dayton Accords. Later, her travels to Kosovo and Cambodia were financed by George Soros' Open Society Institute.

Since the very start of the conflict in Bosnia-Herzegovina, the word "genocide" had been bandied about by supporters of the Muslim party as a way to stigmatize the Serb adversary in what was a three-way civil war between the ethnic communities that lived there: Muslims, Serbs and Croats. The Yugoslav Army units stationed there broke up at the start of the civil war, with the two largest groups, Serbs and Muslims, forming separate hostile local armies. Serbia was then falsely accused of "invading" Bosnia. Meanwhile, the Croatian Army did in fact cross the border from Croatia to annex an ethnically pure Croat region in southwestern Herzegovina, most notable for the thriving tourist business at the site of alleged mystical visitations by the Virgin Mary in the town of Medjugorje. Nobody complained about this "violation of the sovereignty and territorial integrity" of Bosnia-Herzegovina.

This is just a sample of the extremely selective coverage of the complex Bosnian conflict. Journalistic careers could be made by finding what editors wanted, and they usually wanted the worst: rape, ethnic cleansing, genocide – perpetrated by Serbs.

For example, the use of Muslim humanitarian organizations as cover to smuggle weapons to the Muslim Army, and massacres perpetrated by foreign volunteer Mujihideen, were kept out of sight. Once it was clear that the United States was on the side of the Muslims, agents of Izetbegovic could feel confident that they could get away with "false flag" attacks designed to incriminate their Serb adversaries.

In July 1995, toward the end of the war in Bosnia, the term "genocide" finally stuck to the massive revenge killing of Muslim men following the Serb takeover of Srebrenica. Neither Samantha Power nor any other Western reporter "witnessed the horrors" of genocide, since in fact there were no witnesses and no photographic evidence: there were only verbal reports, well after the fact. But the fact of having "been in Bosnia" lent an air of authenticity to her subsequent best-selling book, *A Problem from Hell: America and the Age of Genocide.* Enthusiastically acclaimed by the establishment, this best-seller was above all an impassioned argument in favor of U.S. military intervention "to stop genocide" – a dramatic and eloquent popularized version of the dry political theory first elaborated by Abramowitz. Samantha Power has gone even farther and maintains that the United States should intervene militarily in any situation it deems a potential genocide. In short, hers is an argument for preventive war.

With a flair for drama, a knack for Irish blarney, literary talent and a forceful personality, Samantha Power has managed to drape herself in a tragic *gravitas* which has enabled this ambitious young woman to jump the career queue and successfully pose as the very embodiment of Moral Conscience.

There is, after all, nothing extraordinary in being opposed to genocide. Who is for it? But Samantha Power's specialty is to want to *do something* about it. Or rather, she wants the United States military to do something about it, and that makes her a valuable asset to the War Party. The whole power establishment, starting with Morton Abramowitz, plus *The New Republic*, the International Crisis Group, the Pulitzer Prize Committee, Harvard, President Obama and the long list of prominent figures who endorse the later editions of *A Problem From Hell* have combined to make this striking and talented young woman the very symbol of Humanitarian Intervention. It is brilliant casting.

Looks also count, and Samantha Power's long mane of red hair makes her a dramatic figure in the U.N. Security Council when she leaves her seat to go over and upbraid the startled Russian delegation. However, it did not take long before her histrionics had reduced her to a laughing stock in their eyes. Whether just plain rude, like Susan Rice, or melodramatic, like Samantha Power, self-righteous tirades serve only to derail reasonable discussion and prevent diplomacy from finding solutions to avoid war.

"Smart Power" in Action

In *Hard Choices*, her own version of her stint as Secretary of State, Hillary writes that her foreign policy philosophy embraced "a concept known as smart power". For her, she explains, "smart power meant choosing the right combination of tools – diplomatic, economic, military, political, legal and cultural – for each situation."

In fact, that doesn't mean much of anything. The term was used by Democrats primarily to distinguish themselves from the George W. Bush administration, which had relied on unilateral "hard" power (military force), while neglecting what Joseph Nye called "soft" power (which means everything else, especially propaganda and various forms of pressure on allies, or "multilateralism"). Smart power actually means the use of both.

The term especially came into fashion with a 2004 article by Suzanne Nossel in *Foreign Affairs* entitled "Smart Power: Reclaiming Liberal Internationalism". Nossel wrote that "progressive policymakers should turn to the great mainstay of twentieth-century U.S. foreign policy: liberal internationalism, which posits that a global system of stable liberal democracies would be less prone to war. Washington, the theory goes, should thus offer assertive leadership – diplomatic, economic, and not least, military – to advance a broad array of goals: self-determination, human rights, free trade, the rule of law, economic development and the quarantine and elimination of dictators and weapons of mass destruction (WMD). Unlike conservatives, who rely on military power as the main tool of statecraft, liberal internationalists see trade, diplomacy, foreign aid, and the spread of American values as equally important."

When the cheering dies down, we can observe that this is a recipe for massive intervention in the affairs of other countries, including breaking up states we don't like, such as Sudan or Yugoslavia ("self-determination"), insisting on maintaining those we do like, such as Ukraine or Georgia ("the rule of law"), sanctioning and bombing offenders ("spreading American values"), and above all, regime change ("elimination of dictators"). The notion that "a global system of stable liberal democracies would be less prone to war" is based on the totally unproven assumption that wars are caused by differences in political systems rather than by competition for resources, territorial disputes, or any number of other conflicts that may arise. It rules out coexistence between systems; the underlying implication is that our particular cause for going to war is to make every country resemble ours. Finally, there is no evidence whatsoever that "democratic" states are necessarily less warlike than any other kind – the contrary might even be true.

"Smart power" simply means using every conceivable means to advance U.S. world hegemony. In its arsenal, the most important "soft power" concept is surely human rights. This is an area in which Suzanne Nossel is a specialist.

Born in 1969, Nossel has headed both Human Rights Watch and the U.S. branch of Amnesty International. In January 2009, Hillary brought her back to the State Department (where she had worked for Richard Holbrooke) to be Deputy Assistant Secretary for International Organizations, responsible for multilateral human rights, humanitarian affairs, women's issues, public diplomacy, press and Congressional relations. This occurred just as the U.S. had rejoined the U.N. Human Rights Council, after a long boycott, with the intention of distracting it from criticizing Israel by turning the focus instead on the sins of countries Washington doesn't like, or on new issues, notably LGTB rights. Ms Nossel has won international recognition for working for the rights of lesbian, gay, bisexual and transgender people, thereby cementing the position of the United States as the vanguard of human rights against the world's many traditional societies, especially regimes that U.S. "smart power" wishes to embarrass, isolate, or outright overthrow. Nossel has played a role in getting the Human Rights Council to act on false reports of impending massacres in Libya, leading to NATO bombing and the subsequent destruction of that country.

In January 2012, Nossel left Hillary Clinton's State Department to render another service to "smart power", this time as executive director of Amnesty International, in a year marked by a major campaign of support for Pussy Riot. This is perhaps the strangest aspect of American soft power projection in recent years: the ostentatious U.S. support given to groups of young women practicing organized provocation against traditional moral, religious or behavioral standards.

Once upon a time there was an organization called Amnesty International that was dedicated to defending prisoners of conscience all over the world. Its actions were marked by two principles that contributed to its success: neutrality and discretion. In the context of the Cold War, the early AI made a point of balancing its campaigns between prisoners from each of three ideological regions: the capitalist West, the communist East and the developing South. The campaigns remained discreet and avoided ideological polemics, with focus instead on the legal and physical conditions of all captives. Their aim was not to use the prisoners as an excuse to rant against an "enemy" government, but to persuade governments to cease persecuting non-violent dissidents. It strove successfully to exercise a universal civilizing influence.

Since the end of the Cold War, the work of Amnesty International has become more complicated and more difficult. Back in the early days, most of the "prisoners of conscience" were held either in the Soviet bloc or in the US satellite dictatorships in Latin America, and this fact facilitated symmetry without undue offense to the U.S superpower. But especially since the Bush administration's reaction to September 11, 2001, the United States has increasingly become the world's most notorious jailer and this has brought conflicting pressures to bear upon an organization whose core is Anglo-American. While it has protested against such flagrant abuses as Guantanamo and the cruel jailing of Bradley Chelsea Manning, such punctual criticism is heavily outweighed by blanket denunciations of governments targeted for regime change by the United States. In the case of U.S.-backed "color revolutions", human rights organizations such as AI and Human Rights Watch are enlisted not to defend specific political prisoners, but rather to brand whole governments as "human rights offenders".

Suzanne Nossel's year at the head of Amnesty International was a milestone in the U.S. takeover of the organization. In its new phase, Amnesty, like Human Rights Watch and other Western "humanitarian" organizations, has ceased to make any distinction between genuine prisoners of conscience and semi-professional provocateurs, whose actions have no purpose other than to get them into trouble with the authorities, in order to accuse the targeted governments of being repressive. In its effort to weaken and overthrow Yugoslav president Slobodan Milosevic, the Clinton administration systematically used the techniques advocated by the Massachusetts-based theorist of nonviolent action, Gene Sharp. U.S. officials in Budapest coached a Serbian youth group calling itself "Otpor" (resistance) in these techniques, credited with destabilizing Milosevic at the time of the 2000 elections, which he lost. Born in 1928, Gene Sharp was inspired by the civil disobedience of anti-militarist and liberation movements to systematize disruptive actions which have paradoxically become part of the U.S. "soft power" arsenal. Otpor was the pioneer of the so-called "color revolutions" supported by the United States. The simple theme of these campaigns is typically that the current leader "must go", with little concern for what comes after. Aimed primarily at public opinion, effectiveness depends on a sympathetic media eager to give publicity to provocative actions, actions which would be considered disorderly conduct anywhere else in the world, but are celebrated in this case as the heroic defiance of tyranny.

Neither the quality nor the context of such dissidence seems to matter. Nobody stops to seriously ponder on how to deal with provocateurs that deliberately break the law in order to be arrested. Should the law be suspended especially for them? Should some other action be taken? Arresting them is taking the bait, but not arresting them would arouse indignation from citizens who dislike such exhibitionism. It is a real dilemma.

On February 21, 2012, five young women, scantily-clad in bright colors and wearing balaclavas to cover their faces, barged into the Cathedral of Christ the Savior in central Moscow and took their place in front of the High Altar. They began to shout obscenities, calling the Patriarch of the Russian Orthodox Church a "bitch" and inserting scatological language into liturgical phrases. The women were accompanied by technicians who filmed the performance and later, the words uttered by the performers were revised to refer to President Putin. Offended worshippers on the spot heard the anti-Christian obscenities, not any "political" message.

Although the women fled the scene, in March three women of the Pussy Riot group were arrested: Nadezhda Tolokonnikova, Maria Alyokhina and Yekaterina Samutsevich. On July 30, 2012, the three women went on trial for group "hooliganism" (violation of public order). This was used as an occasion for a massive display of U.S. soft power, mobilizing NGOs, the media and international celebrities. No other government on earth could have been this effective in making pop stars out of agitators.

Aroused by deceptive newspaper articles claiming that the women were being put on a "show trial" for merely "singing a song in a church", a whole galaxy of Western pop stars, from Paul McCartney to Madonna to Björk, rushed to the defense of their (supposed) fellow artists, now imperiled by the "dictator" Putin. Singers who earn millions of dollars can easily be persuaded that they have a moral obligation to say a few words to "save the world" from something evil or another.

Pussy Riot was a recent offshoot of a group of anarchist provocateurs called Voyna (war). Nadezhda Tolokonnikova's partner (and the father of her child) was a leader of the collective, which had a history of public actions that would get people into trouble anywhere in the world: public fornication in the Timiryazev Museum in Moscow (Tolokonnikova took part while visibly pregnant), throwing live cats at employees of a McDonald's restaurant in Moscow, firebombings and attacks on police cars, and - maybe the oddest stunt of them all - a woman stealing a chicken from a supermarket by stuffing it up her vagina. All of it was filmed for the internet.

Strangely enough, although they were frequently associated with anti-Putin slogans, none of these peculiar actions had got the group into trouble with the law. It was the Church that brought suit against them, not the State, although the group claimed that its target and tormenter was Vladimir Putin.

Amnesty International awarded "prisoner of conscience" status to the three Pussy Rioters and devoted extraordinary attention to the Pussy Riot case, treating it as a major human rights campaign. No comparable attention was devoted to the harsh treatment of Bradley/Chelsea Manning, the threat of U.S. prosecution against Julian Assange, the repeated murder by U.S. police of black suspects, the world-record prison population in the United States, or Guantanamo Bay.

The tone of the Amnesty International's Pussy Riot campaign was as far as possible from a diplomatic appeal intended to persuade authorities to free the women in question. Rather, it was precisely a tone of provocation.

For instance:

"Masha, Nadia and Maria, who are being detained for their peaceful performance of a protest song in a cathedral, **could very well be carted off to a labor camp in Siberia where they will be at risk of rape and other abuses.**" (The stress is from the original texts, widely distributed by the organizations cited.)

"Pussy Riot's crime? Singing a protest song in a church. "Amnesty International is mounting a strong global response to help keep Pussy Riot's case front and center. **Help us send a truckload of colorful ski masks to President Putin in protest.** Today's verdict is emblematic of increased efforts by President Putin and his cronies to stifle free speech in Russia. That's why we're sending President Putin as many colorful masks, called *balaclavas*, as we can. **Donate $20 or more to send a mask to Putin.** ... It is clear that Russian authorities are trying to silence these women and instill fear in other activists -- don't let them succeed."

This was a tone that could only make it more, not less, politically difficult for President Putin to grant Pussy Riot a presidential amnesty. Nevertheless he did so, prior to the Sochi games. Released, the young women pursued their anti-Putin campaign in Western countries.

Amnesty International, like other Western media, have constantly simplified the case in terms designed to suggest that Russia is returning to 1930s Stalinism. The French tabloid *Libération* splashed across its front-page a photo of the three women, "To the GULAG for a song".

Avaaz, the on-line protest organizer, went farther.

"Russia is steadily slipping into the grip of a new autocracy ...Now, our best chance to prove to Putin that there is a price to pay for this repression lies with Europe.

"**The European Parliament is calling for an assets freeze and travel ban on Putin's powerful inner circle who are accused of multiple crimes**. ... if we can push the Europeans to act, it will not only hit Putin's circle hard, as many bank and have homes in Europe, but also counter his anti-Western propaganda, showing him that the whole world is willing to stand up for a free Russia."

Well before the Ukraine crisis, America's "soft power" instruments were at work preparing Western public opinion to punish Putin. On September 26, 2012, I was among millions who received this "personal message" from Suzanne Nossel, saying that "Amnesty International is working directly with the lawyers and family members of Pussy Riot to shine a spotlight on this case in a big way....Stand with us", she exhorted, "Refuse silence" (as if there were any chance of that).

In between appeals for money, Suzanne Nossel got to the point:

"Russia's treatment of Pussy Riot reveals a chokehold on freedoms and an unwillingness to respect human rights that must be addressed.

"Beyond the clampdown within Russia's borders, President Putin continues to support ally Syria, despite mounting evidence of crimes against humanity committed by the Syrian government.

"We need to turn up the volume."

Avaaz also revealed what the real issue was:

"What happens in Russia matters to us all. Russia has blocked international coordination on Syria and other urgent global issues, and a Russian autocracy threatens the world we all want, wherever we are."

Pussy Riot was a sexy way to arouse opinion against Russia for very different reasons, starting with the U.S. effort to change the regime in Syria.

At a so-called "Friends of Syria" (meaning supporters of Syrian rebels) meeting in Geneva on July 6, 2012, Hillary Clinton lashed out against Russia and China for blocking US-sponsored Syrian regime change initiatives in the United Nations. "I do not believe that Russia and China are paying any price at all -- nothing at all -- for standing up on behalf of the Assad regime. The only way that will change is if every nation represented here directly and urgently makes it clear that Russia and China will pay a price," Clinton warned.

So here is "smart power" in action. Hillary says Russia "must pay a price" and that "human rights" NGOs need to get to work to exact that price in the area of public relations. Western media enthusiastically went along with this gambit.

Avaaz concluded: "Let's join together now to show Putin that the world will hold him to account and push for change until Russia is set free."

Now think about this. "We", the signers of Avaaz petitions, aspire to "show Putin" that despite being legally elected President of Russia, the outside world is going to "push for change until Russia is set free." Set free by and for whom? Pussy Riot? When did they, when could they, win an election? So how is Russia to be "set free"? By a no-fly zone? By U.S. drones?

Russia must "pay a price" for obstructing U.S. designs on Syria. Was Pussy Riot part of the price to be paid?

The chorus of Western media, pop stars and other assorted self-styled humanitarians all echoed the allegation that the Pussy Riot women were jailed "by Putin" because of an innocent song they sang against him in a church. But where is the evidence that they were arrested by Putin? It seems they were arrested by police on a complaint by the Orthodox Church, which did not appreciate their hijinks on the high altar. Churches tend to consider that their space is reserved for their own rites and ceremonies. The Catholic Cathedral in Cologne called the police to arrest Pussy Riot copy cats. It was not the first time the Pussy Riot group had invaded an Orthodox church. This time the offended ecclesiastics were fed up. The group had demonstrated "against Putin" several times previously without being arrested. So where is the proof that they were "jailed by Putin" as part of a "crackdown on dissent"?

Putin is on record, and on video, as saying he thinks the women should not be harshly punished for their stunt. But, hey, Russia has a judicial system. The law is the law. Once the women were arrested on a complaint by the church, the wheels turned, a trial was held; they were convicted and sentenced by a judge on the basis of complaints by offended Christians. It is an interesting detail that the witnesses at their trial heard no mention of Putin – they were simply offended by the cavorting and the dirty words uttered by the masked performers. YouTube videos show that the "song", if that is what it was, and the anti-Putin lyrics, if one can call them that, were added later to the video put on line by the group.

So why was this "a crackdown by Putin"? Because, once the West labels a disobedient leader of a foreign state a "dictator", his state no longer has a judicial system of its own, free elections, independent media, freedom of expression, contented citizens – no, none of that, because in the collective groupthink of the West, every "dictator" is Hitler/Stalin combined, and every ill or accident in his country is never anything but the direct result of his own wicked will.

Of course, it would be absurd to imagine that citizens of Russia, or any other country, are all contented with their leaders, even if they elected them by an overwhelming majority. Even democratic countries offer only a limited choice of presidential candidates to their voters. But after centuries of Tsarist autocracy, invasion by Mongols, Napoleon, and Hitler, Bolshevik revolution, Communist single-party dictatorship, and then the economic and social collapse of the Yeltsin years, Russia has nevertheless now largely adopted its own version of Western capitalist democracy, complete with respect for religion.

And here is an oddity: the West, which used to aim its intercontinental ballistic missiles at "atheistic communism", does not seem at all satisfied that the Orthodox Christian Church has re-emerged as a respected component of Russian society. And yet, like it or not, there is nothing surprising that after the collapse of a communist ideology which had in many ways been a sort of state religion, many people in Russia returned to their traditional Christian faith.

The Pussy Riot case appears to send a message that the Western criterion for a free society has changed. It is no longer freedom to practice a religion, but freedom to practice various forms of sexual exhibitionism. Now, it can be argued that this may be an important improvement, but since it has taken the Christian West two thousand years to arrive at this level of wisdom, it should be a little bit patient with other societies who lag a decade or so behind.

The Pussy Riot uproar took place on Hillary's beat, with Hillary's backstage encouragement. Appropriately, Suzanne Nossel ran the Amnesty International campaign as a model of "smart power", aimed at turning public opinion against Vladimir Putin. The portrayal of the Russian President as a persecutor of innocent girls who merely "sang a song in a church" dominated U.S.-Russian relations during Hillary Clinton's last year as Secretary of State. Later, when asked which women in the world "inspired" her, Hillary cited Pussy Riot. On April 7, 2014, after the two imprisoned women, Tolokonnikova and Alyokhina, had been released early by Putin and were visiting New York, Hillary distributed a photo of herself with the two Rioters, with the tweet message: "Great to meet the strong & brave young women from #PussyRiot, who refuse to let their voices be silenced in #Russia."

Hillary makes much of the fact that she is "a woman of faith" – any faith, in fact. Hillary expressed perfect understanding of Muslims who rioted against U.S. embassies all over the Middle East because of a vulgar video made in Hollywood that slandered the Prophet. "As a person of faith myself, I understand how hurtful it can be when your beliefs are insulted." But never did she utter a murmur of understanding for Orthodox Christians offended by the obscene antics of Pussy Riot in their place of worship.

This can only be seen as yet another example of the official United States readiness to ally with the worst elements in any society they aim to undermine.

Moral Chaos

Another group of exhibitionist women on the front lines of U.S.-led culture wars is the Ukrainian group "Femen", which shares with Pussy Riot an exhibitionist hatred of Putin, if not indeed of Russia. They claim to be the "new feminism", attacking patriarchy in three forms: sexual exploitation of women, dictatorship and religion.

The message against "sexual exploitation of women" is particularly blurred, since the group itself uses the women's exposed breasts to attract media attention, just like any sexist advertiser. Indeed, bare breasts are their trademark, and it naturally leads them to select members according to the "sexist" criteria used to hire show girls at the Crazy Horse night club.

As for "dictators", you guessed it: they focus mainly on a "dictator" who is not a dictator but an elected head of state, the President of Russia, Vladimir Putin.

Their religious targets tend to be Christian or Muslim. The women waste little time on theoretical discussions. Their attacks on religion seem to be based primarily on aspects of sexual mores.

In August 2012, Femen leader Inna Shevchenko, after chopping down a giant wooden cross in Kiev, fled alleged death threats in Ukraine and demanded political asylum in France, which was granted with uncommon speed. Moreover, her group was rapidly granted headquarters in a social center in the middle of the most heavily Muslim neighborhood in Paris. The women proceeded to make their presence known to their neighbors by marching bare-breasted through the narrow streets, shouting obscenities in English, to the wonderment of the locals. If this was intended to provoke "sexist" reactions from the Arab and African Muslim men in the street, it failed.

Installed in Paris, Inna Shevchenko's group recruited French women to train for actions against the Catholic Church. Their militants disrupted a conservative demonstration of families opposed to gay marriage by spraying baby carriages containing babies. On December 20, as singers practiced a chorale in the Church of the Madeleine in Paris, a Femen acted out the "abortion of Jesus" in front of the altar, using a piece of calf liver as a fetus, shouted "Christmas is cancelled", urinated on the steps of the altar, and left the Church.

Ordinary French postage stamps bear the portrait of "Marianne", symbol of the Republic, but the face changes regularly, frequently using the image of a famous actress. In the summer of 2013 a new stamp was unveiled, chosen by President François Hollande, with Inna Shevchenko as Marianne. The artist, Olivier Ciappa, explained that Inna "perfectly represents my values of *liberté, égalité* and *fraternité*". It is paradoxical that this new "symbol of French values" speaks only English in her role as militant.

While Vladimir Putin was in France for D-Day celebrations in 2014, a Femen accompanied by photographers managed to enter Madame Tussaud's wax gallery and "assassinate" the figure of the Russian president with a knife.

Femen have also announced that they are close to the Ukrainian far-right nationalist party Svoboda and they were present in support of the right-wing attack on federalist activists in Odessa on May 2, 2014, when at least 38 people were burned to death in the subsequent inferno.

Being a Femen is a full-time job, involving physical training and discipline. The group is said to be financed by "businessmen". One of them is Jed Sunden, an American who showed up in Ukraine after the Soviet Union fell apart to found the capital's main English-language newspaper, the *Kyiv Post* (it was later sold to another foreign businessman). The main editorial line of the newspaper was to play up the anti-Russian feeling of Western Ukrainians that has been stimulated for centuries by Western Empires to weaken Russia.

Women Against Women

For much of the world, the fact that Western governments welcome Pussy Riot and Femen as heroines, if not martyrs and role models, can only confirm a growing belief that the liberal West is sinking into total decadence. Even in the West, there is a growing rejection of the values of the Enlightenment, of liberal society and individualism. When "freedom" is reduced to meaning vulgar exhibitionism it will find few ardent defenders. In reality, these exhibitionist groups are a *reductio ad absurdum* of both feminism and freedom, discrediting both and strengthening the very traditional attitudes they pretend to attack. These performances can only confirm the most misogynist notions of "liberated women" as hysterical banshees. It is hard to understand what their Western backers intend to gain from this agitation, other than to sharpen the "conflict of civilizations". If Femen have contributed to any trend, it is the return to conservative tradition. Groups of Muslim women have responded by reaffirming their attachment to the veil as true "liberation". Even in Western countries, hundreds of young people are converting to Islam and heading to the Middle East to join a fanatical Holy War in revolt against a West that flaunts its decadence.

Millions of women in the world are struggling for the most basic rights. What can they think of Western human rights organizations that spend millions to promote a few privileged women performing mere temper tantrums in public? Not only women, but all those who have serious reasons to rebel against genuine injustice suffer from the spotlight focused on these carefully choreographed and secretly financed "protests". In the United States, while Pussy Riot was exalted, the Occupy Wall Street movement was crushed. One represents a few individuals; the other represents the "99 percent". Western powers nurse their claim to be the sponsors of world freedom by extolling Pussy Riot and Femen, while genuine social protest is increasingly spied on, repressed, marginalized and ignored. America's dominance of popular images creates a parallel universe which mimes "our values", values which increasingly resemble a vast insane asylum and contribute to a deepening moral chaos.

Chapter 4

Yugoslavia: the Clinton War Cycle

It all began in Yugoslavia.

Although the failure of the war in Afghanistan is increasingly acknowledged, the disaster of the Libyan war is hard to ignore and the catastrophe of the 2003 invasion of Iraq is now notorious, the war that began this deadly cycle, the 1999 bombing of Yugoslavia, known as "the Kosovo war", is still widely considered to have been a success. It is cited as the good example of "humanitarian war" and used as an argument in favor of still more armed interventions. As long as the historic significance of that war remains largely unrecognized, it can be considered a perfect crime: it worked and the culprits got away with it.

The Kosovo war marked the end of a pause following the end of the Cold War and the great truce sought by Mikhail Gorbachev and the Soviet elite who fancied that the moment had come to make peace in the world. That pause was the moment when American policy makers, surprised, skeptical and even frustrated by the sudden disappearance of their "enemy number one", tried to catch their breath. What would happen to the military-industrial complex, all those juicy Pentagon contracts, those military bases all over the world, and those prestigious organic intellectuals busily dissecting the permanent threat of the communist "Empire of Evil"? President Reagan was happy with his success, but it left much of the U.S. foreign policy establishment in a temporary limbo.

Gorbachev seemed to dream of a sort of historic compromise between the two systems that had opposed each other during the Cold War. In Europe, people imagined a gentle social-democratic world, combining the social of socialism with the democracy of the West. Two decades later, both principles are wounded, perhaps mortally. Social measures turned out to be revocable once the capitalist world was no longer in competition with communism for workers' loyalty. Without the social aspect, democracy, especially in the United States, was reduced to a casino for billionaires. Without the Soviet adversary, there was no powerful obstacle to what the first President Bush called the "new world order", otherwise known as "globalization".

The pause was over when the Clinton administration seized the opportunity to save NATO from the risk of obsolescence by transforming it into an international police force. The preservation and strengthening of NATO was necessary to maintain Washington's post-World War II control of Western Europe. NATO was also the nucleus of an expandable instrument of U.S. military domination. The opportunity for its use was provided by the crisis in Yugoslavia. The Clintons certainly did not create this crisis, but it was the Clinton presidency that managed to spin the NATO bombing campaign in the spring of 1999 as something entirely new: a totally "humanitarian" war.

In the 1980s, compliance with IMF demands concerning debt had fed tensions between the governments of the Republics that made up the Yugoslav federation. The Republics corresponded roughly, but unevenly, to the ethnic identities in this multicultural nation. Yugoslavia's internal difficulties were first internationalized when the Federal Republic of Germany, fresh from having achieved its longstanding goal of taking over East Germany, aggressively championed the unilateral secession of Croatia and Slovenia from Yugoslavia. Both were former provinces of the Austro-Hungarian Empire that had been merged with the Kingdom of Serbia at the end of the First World War to become Yugoslavia, land of the Southern Slavs. Breaking up Yugoslavia was an historic revenge of the Germanic world over the Slavic, as well as a way to ensure German influence over desirable Mediterranean coastal real estate. France and Great Britain, historic allies of Serbia who had originally sponsored the creation of Yugoslavia, more or less reluctantly aligned themselves with German anti-Serb policy for the sake of European unity under pressure from a coordinated propaganda campaign. Serbia's other historic ally, Russia, staggering under the U.S.-backed presidency of Boris Yeltsin, was too weak and too confused to matter.

A massive Western media campaign, begun in Germany and soon fueled by the biased press releases of hired public relations firms, played on far-fetched analogies to portray Serbia as a fledgling Nazi Germany and its president Slobodan Milosevic as a new Hitler. Milosevic's uncertain efforts to hold Yugoslavia together, or at least to protect the rights of Serbs living in parts of Yugoslavia outside the Serbian Republic, were absurdly likened to the Third Reich's campaign to conquer Europe. The conflicting territorial claims that resulted from the non-negotiated secession of Republics composing the Yugoslav Federation were portrayed as naked Serb aggression. When the civil war spread from Croatia to tri-national Bosnia-Herzegovina, temporary prisoner camps set up by the Bosnian Serbs were compared to Nazi concentration camps by Western media, while similar camps set up by Bosnian Muslims and Croats were ignored.

The success of the analogy with the Second World war in demonizing the Serbs was all the more remarkable in that the breakup of Yugoslavia was in some ways a continuation of the two World Wars, when Serbia had been a victim of German invasion. The Croatian secession was largely engineered by successors of the fascist Ustasha movement which had massacred Serbs in order to carve an ethnically-pure independent Croatian State out of Yugoslavia in Nazi-dominated Europe. The leader of the Muslim party in power in Sarajevo, Alija Izetbegovic, had been a Nazi sympathizer in his youth.

Fifty years after the Nazi defeat, a generation was in power that had been raised on a mythical simplification of World War II, with little or no knowledge of the historic origins of conflict in the Balkans. The reversal of wartime roles passed unnoticed. A generation that had known peace seemed almost eager for the drama of "living in exciting times" and the challenge of condemning "new Nazis". The Hitler analogy dictated the response: the "free world" must be ready to use force against the threat, so as not to repeat "Munich". That analogy always serves to rule out any search for compromise, stigmatized in advance as giving a green light to "dictators".

Yet this was a case of a purely local conflict where unbiased international mediation might well have been effective in working out a compromise to avoid bloodshed. Rather than attempting to mediate, or urging unbiased United Nations mediation, the Clinton administration (which took office in January 1993) rapidly chose sides. An initial territorial compromise between leaders of the Muslim, Serb and Croat communities in Bosnia-Hercegovina, sponsored by the European Community [23], which would have avoided civil war, fell apart when it was rejected by Alija Izetbegovic, after the U.S. ambassador told him he could get a better deal without it.

The Bosnian war ended in 1995 on terms quite similar to the deal rejected by Izetbegovic in 1993. Twenty years later, all that remains from two years of slaughter is bitter resentment, grief, hatred and distrust – emotions that block reconciliation and maintain the dependency of enemy-brothers on their respective foreign sponsors.

Hillary Goes to War

When voters elected Bill Clinton president of the United States in 1992, they were also electing his wife. Bill announced the fact himself, but after the failure of her health reform plan, Hillary's only political success was her excellent performance in the role of a faithful wife who "stands by her man". Her brave defense of her frivolous husband was widely appreciated, but as a qualification for the highest office in the land, it seems a bit skimpy. Having played a part in wars in the former Yugoslavia might seem more presidential.

During the 2008 Democratic Party primaries, Hillary evoked the foreign policy experience she had gained as First Lady by repeatedly regaling audiences with an exciting account of her trip to the Bosnian city of Tuzla in 1996:

"I certainly do remember that trip to Bosnia," she told audiences. "There was a saying around the White House that if a place was too small, too poor, or too dangerous, the president couldn't go, so send the First Lady. I remember landing under sniper fire. There was supposed to be some kind of a greeting ceremony at the airport, but instead we just ran with our heads down to get into the vehicles to get to our base."

As word got around of what she was telling audiences, Hillary's story was rapidly denied by numerous eyewitnesses to the event, as well as by television footage showing Ms. Clinton arriving in Tuzla with her daughter Chelsea and being greeted by little children offering flowers.

Cornered by the *Philadelphia Daily News* editorial board during an interview in late March, 2008, Hillary Clinton was forced to acknowledge that there were no snipers, but eased her way out:

"I think that, a minor blip, you know, if I said something that, you know, I say a lot of things – millions of words a day – so if I misspoke it was just a misstatement," she said.

She never had to dodge sniper fire, but she does know how to dodge embarrassing questions. The fact that she utters "millions of words per day" is supposed to give her a generous quota of possible "misstatements", or to put it more simply, lies.

The claim to have run from snipers was historically absurd and morally pretentious, in addition to being blatantly false. Four months before her visit, the hostilities in Bosnia had been decisively brought to a halt by the Dayton peace accords, signed on November 21, 1995. She could not fail to know that. Indeed, far from being sent to a place that was "too dangerous" for the President, the visit by the First Lady and her daughter was intended precisely to emphasize that the White House had not lost interest in Bosnia even though peace had been restored. Hillary's spokesman Howard Wolfson had also added to the "misstatements" by claiming that she was "on the front lines" of "a potential combat zone". Aside from the fact that there could be no "front lines" or "combat zone" when the war was over, Tuzla had never been either one. Tuzla was a largely Muslim-inhabited industrial center which had been selected as a U.S. military base, probably in part because it was a particularly safe environment.

Lying about Bosnia was nothing unusual, but this was a particularly silly, self-aggrandizing lie. Hillary evidently assumed that a brush with gunfire would be considered by the masses as adding to her qualifications to become Commander in Chief. It also showed a persistent tendency to view conflicts as occasions to display personal toughness, instead of as challenges calling for intelligent understanding of political complexities. Hillary's claim to have braved sniper fire is not so far removed from Sarah Palin's claim to understand Russia because she could see it from Alaska.

Hillary's recorded statements concerning the former Yugoslavia revealed the same tendency to play to the galleries in matters of foreign policy that would mark her subsequent term as Secretary of State.

The Holocaust Pretext

In her star-struck biography of the First Lady, *Hillary's Choice*, Gail Sheehy reported Hillary's plea in favor of bombing Yugoslavia in 1999 as a major point in her favor. According to Sheehy's book, Hillary convinced her reluctant husband to unleash the 78-day NATO bombing campaign against the Serbs with the argument that: "You can't let this ethnic cleansing go on at the end of the century that has seen the Holocaust."

This line is theatrical and totally irrelevant to the conflict in the Balkans. As a matter of fact, there was no "ethnic cleansing" going on in Kosovo at that time. It was the NATO bombing that soon led people to flee in all directions – a reaction that NATO leaders interpreted as the very "ethnic cleansing" they claimed to prevent by bombing. But Hillary's remark illustrates the fact that Yugoslavia marks the start of using reference to the Holocaust as the most emotionally-potent argument in favor of war.

It was not always so. At the end of World War II, both the long-suffering survivors and those who discovered the horrors of the Nazi concentration camps wanted only to draw the conclusion that this was yet another powerful reason never again to go to war. But as time passed, by the strange chemistry of the Zeitgeist, the memory of the Holocaust has now become the strongest rhetorical argument *for* war. It is a sort of imaginary revisionism of past history that gets in the way of facing the present. Hillary's sentence is a way of saying, "I would have said no to Hitler at Munich", or "I would have bombed Auschwitz". The history of World War II, and even world history itself, has been totally overshadowed in recent decades by the tragedy of the Holocaust to such an extent that even Western heads of State may find themselves acting out the dramas of the past instead of facing the realities of the present. The conflict in Kosovo was so obscure, so unfamiliar to Americans and so distorted by deception and self-deception [24], that the easiest way to think of it was by analogy with a conflict everyone knew about, or thought they knew about. The moral reward seemed immense, especially in consideration of the low cost, since it entailed bombing a country with inadequate air defenses, with no great risk to our side.

It is worth noting that Hillary urged Bill to bomb the Serbs via telephone, while she was in North Africa, touring Egypt, Tunisia and Morocco. Her guide on that trip was her new assistant, Huma Abedin, the young daughter of Muslim scholars and her trusted expert on the Muslim world. Many secular Arab nationalists in North Africa sympathized with the Serbs, due to past good relations with Yugoslavia during the days of the Non-Aligned Movement. However, Hillary had become an apprentice in learning to appreciate the fundamentalist Muslim outlook, and the Muslims of Bosnia and Kosovo enjoyed widespread, even fanatical support, in the Islamic world at this point. Did Huma assure Hillary that Muslims everywhere would applaud the Clinton administration for bombing Serbs?

Nevertheless, there are strong reasons to doubt that Hillary's moralistic urging was the sole cause of the NATO bombing of what remained of the former Yugoslavia in 1999. Strategists were concerned with less sentimental geopolitical reasons, briefly alluded to above. But there is much less reason to doubt that Hillary did indeed urge Bill to bomb. And there is no reason at all to doubt that she boasted of this to her awed biographer, as a way of proving her "resolve" to use U.S. military power on a "humanitarian" mission. It fits her chosen image as "tough and caring".

Crime Pays

What was really at stake in Kosovo?

The Holocaust analogy favors regarding every ethnic conflict in dualistic terms, with diabolical racists on one side who plan genocide against angelic victims on the other. The world is rarely like that. In reality, there were human beings on both sides of the Kosovo conflict, with their reasons and their faults. The Serbs and Albanians in Kosovo were sharply divided by language and customs, making coexistence difficult. The Serbs were, in their own estimation, "state builders", yearning for modern institutions. The Albanians were still attached to their medieval code of honor, and cared little for "law and order". There were prominent individuals on both sides willing to compromise. Why not let them work things out? Indeed, why not help them work it out? At least they knew each other and understood what was at stake.

But when strangers barge in, they not only change the relationship of forces: they change the story. The Americans picked a small group of armed "Kosovars" engaged in criminal activities that called themselves the Kosovo Liberation Army (KLA) to be "the good guys", and gave official approval to a version of the story that flattered their protégés. As a result, the official Western story of Kosovo is a tissue of lies.

Incidentally, calling themselves "Kosovars" was a public relations device used by ethnic Albanian separatists, making it sound as if there were a country called Kosovo whose indigenous inhabitants were Kosovars, implying that the Serbs didn't really belong there. The word Kosovo comes from the Serbian expression "*kosovo polje*" meaning field of blackbirds, with "Kosovo" meaning "of blackbirds". It is an historic Serbian heartland where the Albanian-speaking population had grown sharply in recent decades, due to immigration from neighboring Albania and having the highest birthrate in Europe. The "Kosovars" were Albanian nationalists who waved the Albanian flag, strongly supported by their cousins just across the border in Albania.

The general public in the West readily believed that the Kosovo war was a humanitarian rescue operation and a successful one as well, since it cost no lives on *our* side. Thus the first geopolitical purpose of this little war was achieved: it served as an advertisement for war itself. The operation proved that a strong propaganda campaign with an emphasis on alleged "victims of potential genocide" could successfully flout the United Nations peacekeeping system established at the end of World War II. NATO simply proceeded without Security Council authorization, in blatant violation of international law, and the influence of its leading members led to the creation of a special International Tribunal, with the United Nations stamp of approval, whose main task was to prosecute Serbians for war crimes. Thus, the main object of the "Kosovo war" was to put the United States and NATO above the law, where they remain to this day.

The bombing campaign lasted from March 24 to June 10, destroying much of Serbia's infrastructure and industry, as well as killing, wounding and demoralizing countless civilians. Casualty figures remain uncertain, but a study published by the medical journal *The Lancet* estimated that 12,000 deaths in the total population could be attributed to the war in one way or another.

During the bombing, spokesmen for the participating NATO powers accused the Serbs of slaughtering innocent Kosovars by the tens to hundreds of thousands, and the Western media eagerly spread false stories of mass rape and mass graves. German propaganda floated a report on "Operation Horseshoe", an action designed to empty the province of its entire Albanian population. All of this was invented. After the war, international investigators found no evidence of the alleged atrocities. But negative reports of "no massacres" can never undo earlier reports of "genocidal massacres" trumpeted during the bombing campaign. War propaganda makes its real impression at the moment when people are interested. Refutations come when people have lost interest. The same old lies continue to be repeated to this day.

Despite the bitterness of the combat between Serbs defending their country and KLA separatists (who were supported both by NATO air strikes and by forces infiltrated across the mountains from neighboring Albania), investigators found evidence of somewhere between two to four thousand deaths in Kosovo during the war, counting all sides and all manner of fatalities. There may have been more, but in any case, it was not enough to enable the NATO-backed International Criminal Tribunal for Former Yugoslavia (ICTY) to indict Yugoslav president Slobodan Milosevic for "genocide", as planned. To compensate, it finally accused him instead of crimes in Bosnia that he could not have committed, and had actually tried in vain to forestall. He died in a Dutch prison in March 2006, apparently from medical neglect, before having completed his defense. Meanwhile, crimes committed by the KLA during the conflict were ignored by the media and by ICTY. A request to examine crimes by the NATO aggressors was, of course, rejected as groundless.

Yugoslavia had no air defenses capable of repelling NATO's deluge of bombs and missiles. Nevertheless, the bombing failed completely to defeat or to even seriously damage the Serbian army, which had remained virtually intact and prepared to repel a land invasion. Putting U.S. "boots on the ground" in Serbia against well-trained Serbian soldiers defending their homeland would have spoiled the fun by causing American casualties. But the heavy damage to Serbia's civilian infrastructure, bridges, factories, schools and hospitals, and the threats of total destruction relayed by international mediators, induced President Milosevic to consent to withdraw Yugoslav forces from Kosovo and allow international forces led by NATO to occupy the province. The conditions for this withdrawal were spelled out in a June 9, 1999 agreement reached in the Macedonian town of Kumanovo and formalized as U.N. Security Council Resolution 1244. This agreement allowed foreign forces to enter Kosovo as "KFOR" (Kosovo forces). In return, it gave certain guarantees to Yugoslavia and Serbia which the United States and NATO failed to respect.

Resolution 1244 stipulated that Kosovo would enjoy "substantial self-government" and "substantial autonomy within the Federal Republic of Yugoslavia", taking into account "the principles of sovereignty and territorial integrity of the Federal Republic of Yugoslavia". It also called for demilitarization of the KLA.

This was in reality a *conditional* surrender. The Americans almost immediately undertook to treat it as an *unconditional* surrender. Serb forces withdrew as agreed, but the commitment to allow Serbian forces to man key border points, which would have prevented the uncontrolled influx of Albanians from Albania into Kosovo, was not respected. Russian forces, which were supposed to participate in the occupation of Kosovo, were pushed aside and finally out.

On June 30, 1999, ten days after the cease fire agreement, Chris Hedges reported to the *New York Times* that the KLA had taken sweeping control of Kosovo, "establishing a network of self-appointed ministries and local councils, seizing businesses and apartments, and collecting taxes and customs payments in the absence of a strong international police presence." Despite a peace agreement that called for an administration appointed by the United Nations and the fact that the KLA militants had no legal standing, "they have created a fait accompli."

The chief U.N. administrator for Kosovo, French humanitarian interventionist Bernard Kouchner, shrugged and said: "It is always like this after wars of liberation."

The KLA, instead of being demilitarized, as promised in Resolution 1244, was gradually transformed into a police force and then into an army allied to NATO. Washington's chosen client, KLA leader Hashim Thaci, was installed in power for a long time to come. Ibrahim Rugova, the leader whom Kosovo Albanians had chosen for themselves in 1992 and who had been willing to seek compromise with Milosevic, was marginalized by the KLA and died of lung cancer in 2006.

Immediately after moving their occupation forces into Kosovo, the United States set about building a thousand-acre U.S. military base, Camp Bondsteel, on stolen farmland. There was nothing in any international agreement authorizing this huge U.S. base, which is still there.

A genuine "ethnic cleansing" of non-Albanians took place under NATO occupation. But Albanians themselves were also victims of Hashim Thaci's takeover. On June 25, a front page article in the *New York Times* entitled "Kosovo's Rebels Accused of Executions in the Ranks" reported that senior KLA commanders "carried out assassinations, arrests and purges within their ranks to thwart potential rivals", according to rebel army members and Western diplomats. "The campaign, in which as many as half a dozen top rebel commanders were shot dead, was directed by Hashim Thaci and two of his lieutenants, Azem Syla and Xhabit Haliti." In his takeover, Thaci appointed Syla as Kosovo's "defense minister".

"Thaci was involved, along with Haliti, in arms smuggling from Switzerland in the years before the 1998 uprising", the *New York Times* continued. "Violence has long swirled around Thaci, whose *nom de guerre* was Snake." In June 1997, a Kosovar Albanian reporter, Ali Uka, was found dead in the apartment he shared with Thaci, his face disfigured by repeated stabbings with a screwdriver and the butt end of a broken bottle, the newspaper added.

A famous photo taken on July 29, 1999, shows Madeleine Albright being fondly embraced by the photogenic Hashim Thaci as part of her welcome to Pristina. Yes sir, that's my baby.

That very day, the *Wall Street Journal* speculated that: "In coming years, the risk is that the guerillas will turn against the North Atlantic Treaty Organization if their demands for an independent Kosovo remain unfulfilled. But U.S. officials say the courting of Mr. Thaci is one guarantee against that danger."

Indeed. That is because Thaci was sure to get what he wanted.

In March 2004, when tens of thousands of ethnic Albanians rampaged against Serbian Orthodox churches and monasteries, the main Western response was to show understanding for their vandalism by attributing it to "impatience" at not achieving full independence. Negotiations with Belgrade to decide the future of Kosovo according to Resolution 1244 got nowhere. In the knowledge that they enjoyed full support from the United States, the Albanians had no motivation to make even the slightest concession. When Hashim Thaci's KLA regime unilaterally declared Kosovo's independence in February 2008, in blatant defiance of the Resolution 1244 pledge to respect "the principles of sovereignty and territorial integrity", the United States and most (but not all) EU Member States quickly gave their approval. (Spain, Slovakia, Romania, Greece and Cyprus declined to recognize the independence of Kosovo.)

A Criminal State

Although Kosovo declared its independence from Serbia in February 2008, it was still far from independent. Not only was a chunk of its territory transformed into a massive U.S. military base, but the country was still occupied by foreign KFOR troops protecting the remaining Serb enclaves, and its administration was still under the supervision of the U.N. Mission in Kosovo (UNMIK). By this time, it was obvious to all the occupiers that one principal attribute of a sovereign state was drastically missing in Kosovo: a justice system capable of enforcing the law. When the Serbs left, they took law and order with them.

The main obstacle to law and order in Kosovo first became obvious when the International Criminal Tribunal for former Yugoslavia (ICTY) attempted to put the notorious KLA clan leader Ramush Haradinaj on trial. While prime minister of Kosovo, Haradinaj was indicted in February 2005 on 37 counts of atrocities, including murder, torture and rape, committed against Serbs and suspected Albanian sympathizers in 1998. Prosecution witnesses refused to testify, citing fear of retribution. Acquitted in April 2008, Haradinaj was retried on a prosecution appeal and acquitted a second time in November 2012 for lack of credible witness testimony. Whenever a KLA big shot went on trial, witnesses for the prosecution melted away – murdered, retracted, disappeared, suicided. And every indictment of an important KLA figure would lead to street demonstrations in Pristina with the complaint that Kosovo was being "slandered".

The obstacle to law and order in Kosovo comes down to one word: *omerta*. The Albanian population is so disciplined, or so intimidated, that conviction of their criminal clan leaders is virtually impossible. Moreover, according to Albanian custom, justice is a personal or family matter, not a matter fit for public accusation and legal institution. Cooperation with police often takes the form of bribing them.

This was all far enough away from the United States not to bother American officials, who still seemed fond of their clients. But many Europeans were disturbed by the activities of this little criminal statelet on their doorstep. Therefore, on December 9, 2008, the European Union launched its most ambitious civilian operation abroad, the E.U. mission for justice in Kosovo, known as EULEX. The mission also involved the United States, Turkey, Switzerland and Norway, as well as other E.U. Member States.

It has not been a great success. True, in three years, EULEX handed down just over two hundred verdicts in criminal cases involving organized crime, corruption, trafficking of women and drugs, and murder. But this must be considered disappointing for a mission with nearly three thousand employees and many more crimes to investigate. Crowds continue to demonstrate against any indictment of one of "their own", and prosecution witnesses continue to evaporate. Instead of having cured local corruption, EULEX members find themselves accused of having been corrupted themselves.

The biggest scandal implicating Kosovo's KLA leaders concerns profiteering from the illegal traffic of human organs. The accusation has been tossed around like a hot potato between the ICTY, the Council of Europe and EULEX. It began in 2008, when the former ICTY prosecutor Carla Del Ponte published a book of memoirs in Italian entitled "The Hunt", alleging that because NATO collaborated with the KLA during the war, investigations into KLA crimes were "nipped in the bud". In particular, she wrote that she was not allowed to pursue an inquiry into the alleged KLA sales of human organs extracted from civilian prisoners (killed in the process). Witnesses had reported that the prisoners were held in a "yellow house" across the border in Albania.

When asked about the "yellow house" by a Serb reporter, the first UNMIK chief, French "humanitarian intervention" advocate Bernard Kouchner, snorted in loud fake laughter and told the reporter that he should have his head examined.[25]

However, on January 25, 2011, the Council of Europe endorsed a report from its Parliamentary Assembly, made up of elected representatives from 47 countries, by Swiss prosecutor Dick Marty, which indeed confirmed the existence of "credible, convergent indications" of illegal trade in human organs going back over a decade. The victims included Albanian civilians who opposed the KLA, as well as a small number of Serb prisoners, killed for this purpose. However, as the report lacked any judicial weight, Marty called for the case to be tried in a legitimate court.

Meanwhile, police uncovered an active organ trafficking ring operating in the Medicus clinic in Pristina. On October 15, 2010, a EULEX court indicted several people, including a former Kosovo government Health Secretary, for non-lethal kidney transplants. The organ traffic was allegedly organized to benefit Israeli patients. Other prosecutions followed, but no legal action was taken concerning transplants from prisoners held in Albania at the end of the war.

EULEX passed the hot potato on to John Clint Williamson, an American prosecutor who had worked as an ICTY trial attorney and as an expert at the trials of Khmer Rouge leaders in Cambodia. On July 29, 2014, in Brussels, Williamson issued a progress report of the EU Special Investigative Task Force confirming Marty's allegations. Williamson accused "senior officials" of the KLA of "unlawful killings, abductions, enforced disappearances, illegal detentions in camps in Kosovo and Albania, sexual violence, other forms of inhumane treatment, forced displacements of individuals from their homes and communities, and desecration and destruction of churches and other religious sites." Williamson said that these crimes "were conducted in an organized fashion and were sanctioned by certain individuals in the top levels of the KLA leadership" and "resulted in the ethnic cleansing of large portions of the Serb and Roma population from those areas in Kosovo south of the Ibar River, with the exception of a few scattered minority enclaves".

But Williamson saw little chance that the perpetrators of the lethal organ transplants would ever be prosecuted. "Fifteen years down the line, we have solid information that these things happened, but no physical evidence. There are no bodies, no names of victims", Williamson told *The Guardian*.

Otherwise, this disclosure was almost entirely ignored by mainstream media. Information about the ghastly crime of cutting open prisoners to steal their organs has seeped out in such small doses, over such a long period of time, that the whole affair is likely to fade away almost unnoticed.

Referring to the impact of "witness intimidation", Williamson's report said that: "There is probably no single thing that poses more of a threat to rule of law in Kosovo and of its progress toward a European future than this pervasive practice."

In July 2011, *Der Spiegel* interviewed an unidentified German policeman who had worked in Kosovo for over ten years, and who said that "we have achieved almost nothing" because of the traditional clan structure. Nobody dares be a whistleblower. "The only thing that's clear is that Kosovo is firmly in the grip of organized crime", he said. "Kosovo is a country in which centuries-old traditions live on, and blood feuds are part of the culture. We Central Europeans have not been able to convince the Kosovars of the benefits of adopting a new legal and value system like the one we have in the West."

Wasn't that perhaps precisely the main problem that the Serbs had with Kosovo?

However, unlike the multinational EULEX, the Serb police spoke Albanian, understood the Albanians, and could probably do a better job of combating crime than strangers from some thirty countries who are forced to rely on Albanian interpreters vetted by the very same gangsters under suspicion.

Liberated from Serbia, Kosovo's economic situation is worse than ever. It is an impoverished backwater where many people suffer from disappointment that "independence" has not brought about an anticipated golden age. Without employment, education or security, more and more Kosovars are trying desperately to emigrate to

E.U. countries. Seven years after Kosovo declared independence, Hungary, Austria and Germany moved to speed up procedures for rejecting the growing flood of fake "asylum seekers" who flee Kosovo in search of some way to make a living. Nevertheless, some Albanian nationalists still aspire to create what they call "Natural Albania" by acquiring more pieces of southern Serbia, a swath of Montenegro, a piece of Greece and about half of Macedonia. Resentment is growing at the European Union's wavering effort to introduce legal order from outside.

Kosovo is neither fully independent nor a real state. It remains under foreign occupation, has no functioning judiciary branch of its own, and its economy is dependent on crime. Instead of ensuring regional peace, Kosovo has whetted the appetite of frustrated Albanian nationalists for still more territory to be carved out of neighboring countries. Money from the Gulf States promotes Islamic extremism, and threats persist against the remaining Serbian monasteries, even when they are official United Nations Heritage Sites. Kosovo is a small, but still boiling, pot.

The Kosovo Experiment

During the 1993-2000 Clinton Presidency, Yugoslavia was used by the foreign policy establishment as an experimental laboratory to test techniques of U.S. control, subversion and regime change that would subsequently be practiced elsewhere. Viewing Yugoslavia as a mini-USSR, with Serbia in the role of Russia, breaking up Yugoslavia and subsequently Serbia itself (by detaching Kosovo) was a rehearsal for the process we have recently seen unfolding in Ukraine, with Russia as the target.

The same techniques are recognizable:

Hitlerization. The aggression begins as a propaganda war, waged by mainstream media organically linked to leading government policy makers and think tanks. In the first stage, the targeted country virtually disappears under the shadow of its leader, labeled a "dictator" (even if fairly elected), who is portrayed as the embodiment of evil on earth and "must go". Personalities as diverse as Slobodan Milošević, Saddam Hussein, Moammar Gaddafi, Bachar al-Assad and now Vladimir Putin have been cast in the role of the new Hitler.

Sanctions. Economic sanctions against the Hitler of the day serve to stigmatize the evil one, destabilize relations and rally internal allies who still hesitate to have recourse to arms but are willing to go along with the supposedly "peaceful" method of making him change his ways. When sanctions fail, public opinion has been prepared to consider military force "necessary".

Local clients. The United States has a long record of supporting the worst elements in the targeted state, forces that will stop at nothing. In Serbia, the United States gave political and military support to ruthless criminals. In Muslim countries, the U.S. has supported and armed Islamic fanatics. In Ukraine, the anti-Russian campaign relies on unrepentant Nazi militias to rule the streets.

Human Rights NGOs. So-called Non-Governmental Organizations, in reality closely linked to or even financed directly by the U.S. government (most notably the National Endowment for Democracy and its subsidiaries), play a central role in claiming to incarnate a genuine democracy which is being strangled by the targeted "Hitler" when police intervene against the disorder provoked by "genuine democrats". Scenarios adapted by political scientist Gene Sharp from the experiences of revolutionary or progressive movements are used as the training manual for actions designed to win sympathy by provoking state repression, with no political content beyond opposition to the present ruler. The agitation of the "Otpor" youth group in Serbia, trained by U.S. specialists in Budapest, was the model adapted later for subsequent "color revolutions".

Sabotaging diplomacy. To prepare the Kosovo war, Secretary of State Madeleine Albright stage-managed false negotiations between the Yugoslav government and Albanian nationalists from Kosovo at the Rambouillet chateau, keeping them apart, replacing professor Ibrahim Rugova as the head of the Albanian delegation with her criminal client Hashim Thaci, and introducing an ultimatum (total military occupation of Serbia) that obliged the Serbs to refuse and thus take blame for "refusing to negotiate". It has become customary for U.S. representatives in the United Nations to sabotage negotiations by moralizing tirades, insults and lies.

Criminalization. In regard to the Yugoslav conflict, the overwhelming influence of the United States enabled Washington to initiate the practice of using international tribunals to treat the enemy as common criminals rather than as political adversaries. The concept of "joint criminal enterprise", used in U.S. criminal law against mafia gangs, was imported into the *ad hoc* International Criminal Tribunal for former Yugoslavia to apply to the Serbs, with the implication that the mere defense of Serbian interests was criminal. Subsequently, the United States has succeeded in influencing the International Criminal Court (to which the United States itself does not adhere) to indict enemies such as Moammar Gaddafi on the basis of unsubstantiated accusations. This procedure helps to rule out peace negotiations, since it is claimed that one cannot negotiate with an indicted criminal.

Scare Word "Genocide". Whenever the United States takes sides in an ethnic or political conflict somewhere, the usual procedure is to accuse the other side of planning to commit "genocide". This rules out consideration that both sides may be fighting for specific territorial or political gains which, if properly understood, might be mediated.

Media and propaganda. The key to the whole system of aggression is the U.S. mastery of a vast propaganda machine, centered on mainstream media. Background music is provided by the entertainment industry, Hollywood in particular, which churns out glorifications of the use of violence to smash an enemy. Video games are a powerful new factor in normalizing killer instincts. Fact and fiction blend together in the visual imagination of endless battles between Good and Evil, packaged and sold to the American public.

Bombing. This is the final argument, the sword of Damocles hanging over every dispute.

For the Pentagon, NATO, the CIA, the NED, mainstream media, and the U.S. foreign policy establishment, the Kosovo War was an excellent learning experience, a training ground, a preparation for future adventures. It was the war to start wars.

For the Clintons, Kosovo was a distraction from personal scandals and an opportunity to step onto the big stage of world affairs. Bill Clinton is worshiped in Kosovo as the founding father of this little U.S. protectorate wrested from Serbia. A ten-foot high gilded statue of the Arkansas benefactor waves from Bill Clinton Boulevard, with a clothing boutique named "Hillary" nearby. While the United States is increasingly hated around the world for its military interventions and constant bullying, this intervention has created an enclave of fanatic pro-Americans. On her visit to Pristina in 2010, Secretary of State Hillary Clinton was able to bask in adulation. It says a lot about U.S. decline in the eyes of the world that Kosovo and Albania are today the most enthusiastically pro-American places on earth. It is nothing to be proud of.

Chapter 5

Libya: a War of Her Own

As mounting chaos engulfed the Middle East and Ukraine in 2014, a visibly disoriented President Obama characterized his foreign policy caution by a caveat: "Don't do stupid shit." In an interview with Jeffrey Goldberg for *The Atlantic*, Hillary Clinton stepped up to the plate to show she had sterner presidential fiber: "Great nations need organizing principles, and 'Don't do stupid stuff' is not an organizing principle."

She did not make clear what her "organizing principles" would be, but one of her favorite principles has been the "right", or "responsibility" to protect, shortened to the catchy English tag "R2P". This principle has turned out to be a *dis*organizing principle, used to destroy whatever order may have existed in the "protected" region. In the wake of the Kosovo war, Washington strongly promoted R2P as a potential principle of the United Nations, to be invoked in any future Kosovo-type situation as the perfect excuse to undermine the principle of national sovereignty.

R2P was the principle behind Hillary's very own war, the 2011 assault on Libya, which turned out to be some of the most "stupid shit" ever dumped on a defenseless country.

The pretext for this war was the series of mass protest demonstrations that began in Tunisia on December 18, 2010, labeled "the Arab spring" by the media. This label turned out to be unduly optimistic, implying that the whole region was blossoming into something bright, happy and of course democratic, in the Western sense.

Most of the leaders targeted by the Arab Spring protests were longtime "friends" of the West and clients of the United States. Washington, Paris and London were embarrassed. But there was one striking exception: In February 2011, crowds in the eastern Libyan city of Benghazi demonstrated against the country's leader Moammar Gaddafi. Eureka! Here was an opportunity to put R2P into practice against a man who had been solidly detested by the West ever since he took power over forty years ago.

Colonel Gaddafi first came on the scene in 1969 as a sincere revolutionary in a revolutionary period. He was a Bedouin who had become an army officer in a country that hardly existed.

Once a thriving grain producer for the Roman Empire, the region first known as "Africa" declined into a distant backwater for well over a thousand years, made up of sand, Arabized Berber tribes, a few cities and the impressive ruins of a rich past. After centuries under the Ottoman Empire, the region was conquered by Italy in the first part of the twentieth century, and divided between Cyrenaica in the East and Tripolitania in the West. In 1934, Italy gave the colony the official name of Libya. By losing World War II, Italy also lost its colonies and in 1951, the United Nations recognized the British-sponsored Emir of Cyrenaica, Idris al-Mahdi as-Senussi, who had led armed anti-Italian resistance, as King Idris the first of Libya. The United States took over Italy's air base near Tripoli and renamed it the Wheelus Air Base. Major oil resources were discovered in 1959 and King Idris followed the common pattern of keeping the oil wealth for himself and his entourage.

As a young officer inspired by the Arab nationalism of Egyptian president Gamel Abdel Nasser, Moammer Gaddafi led a bloodless coup against King Idris in 1969. When the king was deposed, the United States was compelled to give up Wheelus Air Base. Gaddafi undertook to build an original system called the Libyan Arab Jamahiriya based on a hybrid of moderate Muslim morality, welfare state socialism, direct democracy and local customs. The opposition loyal to King Idris and his traditional Islam were repressed, while great strides were made in education, women's rights and social welfare. The General People's Congress chose the government, while Gaddafi retained power as a sort of spiritual Guide.

The early Gaddafi lavished support on foreign revolutionaries: the Palestine Liberation Organization, the Irish Republican Army, the African National Congress, and the Polisario Front in the Western Sahara. This largesse won him the lasting gratitude of Nelson Mandela, but also a wide range of bitter enemies. As his revolutionary protégés came to terms with their enemies, the Libyan leader apparently felt left behind, and finally gave up similar support in his effort to make peace with the West.

As the Nasserian dream of Arab unity faded, Gaddafi turned

away from the Arab world, which he openly condemned as hypocritical, corrupt and treacherous. He redirected his generous ambitions of anti-imperialist unity toward Africa, redefining Libya as African rather than Arab, and financing major projects to help develop the continent and provide it with financial independence.

On the memorable date of the ninth day of the ninth month in 1999, African leaders assembled in the central Libyan coastal city of Sirte, Gaddafi's home town, and formally replaced the Organization of African Unity (UAO) with the African Union (AU). The "Sirte Declaration", issued on that occasion, claimed to have been inspired by Colonel Gaddafi's vision of "a strong and united Africa, capable of meeting global challenges and shouldering its responsibility to harness the human and natural resources of the continent in order to improve the living conditions of its peoples."

In Ethiopia in February 2009, Gaddafi was elected chairman of the 53-nation African Union, pledging that he would "continue to insist that our sovereign countries work to achieve the United States of Africa." He envisioned "a single African military force, a single currency and a single passport for Africans to move freely around the continent".

During Gaddafi's reign, the old fishing town of Sirte was greatly modernized and beautified as the potential capital of an eventual United Africa. At the end of NATO's war to "save Benghazi", Sirte was in ruins.

Gaddafi's reputation in the West was so bad that it was easy to blame him for any unsolved crime. The prime example is the explosion that brought down Pan Am Flight 103 over Lockerbie, Scotland, on December 21, 1988, killing 270 people. Initial – and persisting – suspicions attributed the attack to a terrorist group hired for the task by Iran, as revenge for the downing of an Iranian civilian airliner by a U.S. Navy cruiser over the Persian Gulf the previous July.[26] The United States had never even apologized for having shot down a regularly-scheduled Iran Air flight from Tehran to Dubai on July 3, 1988, killing 290 civilians. Blaming Gaddafi because "he does that sort of thing" was no doubt less embarrassing to Washington than calling attention to Iran's revenge scenario.

The United States accused two Libyans of planting a time bomb in a suitcase that was transferred from a flight from Malta at Frankfurt and London airports before it exploded over Scotland. Evidence emerged after the trial that the Swiss timing device discovered by U.S. agents at the crash scene was a demonstration model which could not have been sold to Libya, as alleged by the prosecution, and must have been planted by the agents who "found" it. In the hope of getting the West to lift sanctions punishing Libya for Lockerbie, Gaddafi finally agreed to let two accused Libyans be put on trial by a special Scottish court meeting in the Netherlands. Under heavy U.S. pressure for a conviction, one Libyan was found guilty and the other was acquitted. Interviewed by the author in Tripoli in 2007, lawyers for the convicted Libyan believed that evidence of a frame-up was so compelling that the pending appeal would lead to a second acquittal. Suffering from cancer, the convicted man, Abdelbaset al-Megrahi, was persuaded to drop his appeal in order to be allowed to go home and spend his last days with his family. Thus the appeal court avoided having to deal with the evidence showing that U.S. agents had framed the Libyans.[27]

Even though he maintained Libya's innocence, Gaddafi paid compensation to the Lockerbie victims, ostentatiously gave up "weapons of mass destruction" (which perhaps never quite existed), and made every effort to overcome his bad reputation and normalize relations with the West. These concessions were made largely to satisfy the desire of much of the Libyan elite to finally belong to a "normal" country. His most politically ambitious son, Saif al Islam Gaddafi, studied in London and was pressing for Westernization and democratic reforms. This appeared to be the natural direction that Libya's evolution would take.

By 2011, Gaddafi had done what he could to make peace with enemies who evidently no longer considered him a threat. He was doing business with the United States and Europe, and receiving high-level diplomatic visits. He had even secretly given money to the campaign fund of French president Nicolas Sarkozy, possibly in order to induce Sarkozy to help solve the "Bulgarian Nurses Affair" – the last scandal that was damaging to Libya's reputation in the West.

Five Bulgarian nurses and a Palestinian doctor had been sentenced to death for poisoning over 400 children found to be infected with the HIV virus in the El Fatih children's hospital in

Benghazi. Disclosure of this baffling epidemic in 1999 caused an understandable public outcry and demand for the perpetrators to be found and punished. Suspicion turned to nurses recruited by a Bulgarian state-owned company, Expomed, to work in Benghazi for better wages than they would get in Bulgaria. This led to their arrests and conviction.

In Europe it was taken for granted that the charges were trumped up and false, and the assumption was that this was another criminal act by Moammer Gaddafi. Thus, when I was in Tripoli in 2007 to attend a conference on the International Criminal Court, I was surprised to learn that even Westernized jurists, critical of Gaddafi, believed that the Bulgarian nurses were guilty. This assumption seemed to be based primarily on analogy with other cases, unfamiliar to most Westerners, where Americans or Europeans had used Africans as unsuspecting guinea pigs in medical experiments.

Clearly, the Libyan public firmly believed in the nurses' guilt. This meant that it was politically difficult to release them and allow them to go home, as European governments demanded. But Saif al-Islam, who had publicly criticized the trial of the nurses, evidently wanted to put an end to the medical workers' ordeal and hasten Libya's acceptance by the West. The problem was to do so without enraging public opinion in Libya.

The solution was a scenario involving French President Sarkozy and above all, his estranged wife, Cecilia, who made a highly publicized trip to Libya in July 2007 to "rescue" the nurses from the Dictator. This show was accompanied by payments of nine and a half million euros from the European Union to "improve conditions in the Benghazi hospital". Shortly afterwards, Gaddafi paid a visit to Paris, greatly annoying his hosts by camping on the presidential palace lawn in his Bedouin tent. This was intended to impress folks back home in Libya that their Guide was now *persona grata* in Europe. Moammar Gaddafi was no longer an active demon, but he was still seen as wildly eccentric.

Then came the Arab spring.

Opposition to Gaddafi was endemic in Benghazi, the center of traditional support for King Idris and for radical Islamists. Just as he was adored in his native city of Sirte, he was hated in Benghazi. Taking their cue from the Tunisian and Egyptian uprisings, anti-

Gaddafi militants decided to stage their own "day of rage" against the regime on February 17, 2011. The day was chosen in commemoration of fourteen people who died on the same day in 2006 in clashes between police and demonstrators protesting against disrespectful cartoons of the Prophet Mohammed.

Riots spread, but what spread much farther, and more dangerously, were hugely exaggerated and downright false reports of what was happening.

Libya, with the highest living standard on the African continent, did not suffer the dire economic problems that led a young Tunisian to set fire to himself, setting off the "Arab spring", nor the mass poverty of Egypt. The Benghazi revolt was political and religious, and nothing new.

As the crisis unfolded, Gaddafi's claims that he was combating Islamic extremism, including al Qaeda, in Benghazi, were dismissed in the West as far-fetched. And yet, on April 15, 1998, Libya had been the first government to denounce Osama bin Laden to Interpol for the murder of a top German expert on the Arab world and his wife in Sirte in 1994. Gaddafi was always in a life and death struggle against Islamic extremists for the future of Libya, and of Africa itself. His complaint to Interpol was ignored. In this case, as in others, Western powers found themselves more or less *de facto* on the side of the Islamic extremists.

The flamboyant French agitator, Bernard-Henri Lévy, rushed to Benghazi to champion the "revolution", whisking a senior Libyan official, Mahmoud el Jibril, off to Paris to convince French President Nicolas Sarkozy to go to war in Libya. Jibril had been in charge of economic liberalization and privatization in the Libyan government, before defecting to become a leader of the National Transitional Council that used the Benghazi troubles to declare itself the new legitimate government of Libya. With a Ph.D. in political science from the University of Pittsburgh, Jibril was presentable in the West as leader of a "democratic revolution". The ardently pro-Israel Bernard-Henri Lévy openly boasted of intervening in Libyan affairs "as a Jew", giving the impression that he thought getting rid of Gaddafi would be good for Israel. Before the television cameras, BHL scornfully denied reports that Islamists were among the Benghazi protesters. He had been there, he said, insisting there were no

Islamists, but only citizens yearning for Western democracy.

No Islamists? On February 22, Muslim Brotherhood leader Sheikh Yussef al Qaradawi issued a fatwa calling for the murder of Gaddafi by his own soldiers: "Whoever in the Libyan army is able to shoot a bullet at Gaddafi should do so", he told Al Jazeera television.

The United States had used Gaddafi's opening to the West to cultivate relations with high ranking officials such as Mustafa Abdul Jalil. As Minister of Justice, Jalil had twice confirmed the death sentence for the Bulgarian nurses, but he nevertheless quickly won Western support as the head of the National Transitional Council. The defection of several highly-placed members of the Gaddafi regime, such as Jalil and Jibril, gave the impression that the Benghazi riots could be used by an organized pro-West faction to carry out a fairly neat "palace coup", with a little military help from their U.S. and European friends. Reality was not so simple.

Libyan internal political conflicts became invisible as soon as the uprising against Gaddafi in Benghazi was classified as a human rights issue, an effort to stop a "dictator who was killing his own people". Gaddafi's orders to rebels to lay down their arms were mistranslated as a threat to wipe out the entire population of Benghazi and denounced as an imminent genocide. In reality, Gaddafi offered amnesty to rebels who laid down their arms and the possibility of withdrawal to Egypt.

Much later, Amnesty International confirmed that in clashes with armed rebels in Benghazi, no more than 110 people were killed on all sides, far fewer than in the Cairo protests. But at the time, the version of events that prevailed was based on emotional claims made by the Secretary-General of the Libyan League for Human Rights (LLHR), Dr. Sliman Bouchuiguir, at a meeting of pro-Western NGOs in Geneva on February 21. A letter calling for action against Libya, made of totally unproven assertions asserted as "facts" by Dr. Bouchuiguir, an expert on oil politics with close ties to the United States, was signed by seventy NGOs and sent to President Obama, E.U. High Representative Catherine Ashton, and the U.N. Secretary-General Ban-Ki Moon.

The letter called on the United Nations and the "international community" to "take immediate action to halt the mass atrocities now being perpetrated by the Libyan government against its own people". Without demanding evidence, the NGOs signed onto Dr. Bouchuiguir's claims by "unidentified witnesses" that "a mixture of special commandos, foreign mercenaries and regime loyalists have attacked demonstrators with knives, assault rifles and heavy-caliber weapons." The alarmist letter went on: "Snipers are shooting peaceful protesters. Artillery and helicopter gunships have been used against crowds of demonstrators. Thugs armed with hammers and swords attacked families in their homes. Hospital officials report numerous victims shot in the head and chest, and one struck on the head by an anti-aircraft missile. Tanks are reported to be on the streets and crushing innocent bystanders. Witnesses report that mercenaries are shooting indiscriminately from helicopters and from the top of roofs. Women and children were seen jumping off Giuliana Bridge in Benghazi to escape. Many of them were killed by the impact of hitting the water, while others were drowned."

Listing just about every conceivable atrocity as widespread and systematic, the letter appealed to the newly fashionable "Responsibility to Protect" (R2P) doctrine which authorizes "collective action, through the Security Council... including Chapter VII." In short, military action.

Signatories included Carl Gershman, president of the National Endowment for Democracy, Hillel C. Neuer of the pro-Israel United Nations Watch, and others whose main stock in trade is harsh criticism of governments outside the U.S/E.U./Israeli sphere of influence.

Without investigation, mainstream media spread the sensational accusations that Gaddafi was using African mercenaries and jet plane attacks on civilians to "kill his own people". No visual or documentary proof of the air attacks ever emerged, and reliable witnesses on the spot denied they ever existed. The accusation of employing "African mercenaries" was even more sinister. It was not only false; it was the tip of the racist iceberg that underlay the whole anti-Gaddafi operation. The deplorable fact is that Gaddafi's turn toward Africa alienated an important sector of the Libyan population who did not want to identify with Africa, and who believed that Libya would be better off following the model of oil-rich Gulf emirates, like Qatar, whose wealth is monopolized by an Arab elite while labor is performed by ill-paid, semi-enslaved foreign workers with no civil rights. They were enraged by Gaddafi's proposals to distribute the country's oil wealth among the entire population. It was no accident that Qatar's popular television channel Al Jazeera led the media attack on Gaddafi, and Qatari soldiers took part secretly in operations on the ground.

Gaddafi's Libya was seen as an Eldorado by its sub-Saharan neighbor countries. Libya's own black population, as well as immigrant African workers, were treated decently. Gaddafi had also made agreements with European governments to prevent Libya from being a passage for clandestine African immigration to Europe. This accord was vehemently condemned by European leftists whose main humanitarian cause is now open borders and defense of undocumented workers. However, stopping African mass migration toward Europe was consistent with Gaddafi's long-range policy of financing development so as to enable Africans to stay and prosper in their own countries. Now that he is gone, illegal immigration across the Mediterranean is increasingly out of control.

Gaddafi was a hero to most of black Africa. The "black mercenary" tale was a way of twisting this reality into something malign, and also a way of covering up the grim fact that the anti-Gaddafi rebellion was marked by genuine pogroms against blacks. Whether they were Libyan citizens or "guest workers", whole towns were emptied of their black inhabitants and thousands were compelled into exile. By destroying Gaddafi's plans for financing independent African development, and by its brutal treatment of black people, the anti-Gaddafi revolt was a major blow to black Africa.

Hillary Clinton, who claims that her first youthful political awakening came from listening to Martin Luther King, Jr. denounce racism, eagerly supported using U.S. military force to support an uprising that was racist at its core and devastating to the black people of the region. On March 24 she proclaimed: "When the Libyan people sought to realize their democratic aspirations, they were met by extreme violence from their own government." This is the sort of ordinary falsehood at which Hillary is adept, based on the confidence that Americans will easily swallow a totally meaningless cliché such as "the Libyan people's democratic aspirations".

Three days later, when asked about the bombing of Libya on "Meet the Press", she replied: "...let's be fair here. They didn't attack us, but what they were doing and Gaddafi's history and the potential for the disruption and instability was very much in our interests ... and seen by our European friends and our Arab partners as very vital to their interests."

In short, bombing the hell out of a sovereign country that did us no harm is perfectly okay if we consider it to be in our "interests", or in the "interests" of our "European friends" and our "Arab partners". Not only that, but bombing a country, arming rebels and overthrowing its government is the way to prevent "disruption" and "instability". And this woman longs to become President of the United States.

In an interview four months later with independent French investigative journalist Julien Teil, Dr. Bouchuiguir, by then the new Libyan ambassador to Switzerland, acknowledged candidly that there was never any proof of the charges he made in Geneva. Pressed by Teil to provide evidence, Dr. Bouchuiguir answered frankly, "There was no evidence." He did not seem at all embarrassed, perhaps because he is a man who can count on his connections. What mattered was that on the basis of his claims, the official representatives of the Libyan Arab Jamahiriya were expelled from U.N. bodies and Libya was sanctioned without being able to defend itself. Libyan embassies were shut down in Western countries. Indeed, when the Libyan government mandated former Nicaraguan foreign minister Miguel D'Escoto Brockman, a Catholic priest, to present its brief to the United Nations on March 31, he was blocked by U.S. Ambassador Susan Rice on the grounds of an inadequate visa. No defense was allowed for the accused.

The Western human rights community is a network of organizations that thrive on leveling accusations against the countries that Western donors want to embarrass. They readily endorse each other's reports, apparently on the principle "I scratch your back and you scratch mine".

Dr. Sliman Bouchuiguir had friends in Washington. His thesis at George Washington University was published in 1979 as a book, *The Use of Oil as a Political Weapon: A Case Study of the 1973 Arab Oil Embargo*. His thesis advisor was Bernard Reich, a political scientist who has worked for the U.S. Defense Intelligence College, the United States Air Force Special Operations School, the Marine Corps War

College, and the Shiloah Center at Tel Aviv University and has written extensively on Israel and the Arab world. It is reasonable to assume that Bouchuiguir's work was in harmony with Reich's own devotion to the U.S.-Israeli partnership in managing Middle East policy. In short, he was not so much a humanitarian as a strategic theorist, subscribing to the Washington view that economic warfare is necessary to prevent rival powers from becoming threats.

There was significant overlap between Dr. Bouchuiguir's Libyan League for Human Rights (LLHR) and the National Transitional Council that rapidly declared itself the legitimate government of the country. LLHR members included Mahmoud Jibril, mentioned earlier, and Ali Tarhouni, a Washington protégé who was put in charge of oil and finances and given the task of privatizing Libya's oil resources and handing them over to the NATO "liberators".

At the end of February, on the basis of Dr. Bouchuiguir's accusations, the U.N. Security Council imposed sanctions on the Gaddafi family and forwarded charges against them to the International Criminal Court (ICC). Hillary Clinton herself went to the U.N. Human Rights Council in Geneva to announce that: "It is time for Gaddafi to go."

"Regime change" was in the air from the start; it was always the not-so-hidden agenda behind the "no-fly zone" U. N. Resolution. The Russians and Chinese abstained from the vote, rather than defeating it with their veto, and thereby gave the Americans the rope with which to hang themselves. The outcome of the Libyan operation served to discredit R2P for most of the world.

On March 17, the U.N. Security Council took its fateful decision authorizing a "no-fly zone" over Libya. Hillary was delighted that the resolution included the expression "all necessary measures", which supposedly meant measures to protect civilian lives. The phrase actually meant use of NATO military force, and she boasts that twisting Security Council arms in order to get those words into the resolution was her own diplomatic accomplishment. "Gaddafi must go", she declared again, leaving no doubt that regime change was on her agenda. Gaddafi, she claimed, was "a ruthless dictator that has no conscience and will destroy anyone or anything in his way. If Gaddafi does not go, he will just make trouble. That is just his nature. There are some creatures that are like that."

Hillary was finally about to have a war of her own.

Well, not entirely her own. There were numerous accomplices. But she was very proud to have played a decisive role in orchestrating the massacre.

Hillary's fingerprints are all over the Libyan crime. To start with, in the divided Obama administration, she was enthusiastically in favor of going after Gaddafi, along with Susan Rice and Samantha Power, who all cited the need to "stop" an imaginary "genocide". Defense Secretary Robert Gates and Admiral Mike Mullen, Chairman of the Joint Chiefs of Staff, were opposed to taking action. The reluctance of the Pentagon (and possibly Obama himself) to launch yet another war in the Middle East explains why Washington chose to "lead from behind", and let France appear to start the war. Nevertheless, the war relied heavily on U.S. logistics, fire power, and espionage.

Hillary brags of having used American clout to put together a "coalition of the willing" to get rid of the Libyan leader. On March 12, the Arab League voted to request a no-fly zone in Libya. As Hillary saw it, "their active participation in any military operation would provide legitimacy in the region".

Quite simply, Hillary needed the Arabs for cover. "After Iraq and Afghanistan, we weren't going to risk looking like we'd launched another Western intervention in a Muslim country." With Bernard-Henri Lévy and the Arab League out in front, the United States could lead from behind.

Arab participation was supposed to show that Gaddafi was rejected even by his peers. This would perhaps make the murderous operation look virtuous, consensual and democratic. But what peers! A gang of treacherous scheming autocrats who hated Gaddafi's guts for all the wrong reasons. And Gaddafi hated them so much that he had in effect turned his back on the Arab world to join Africa.

In *Hard Choices*, Hillary described Gaddafi as "one of the most eccentric, cruel, and unpredictable autocrats in the world. He cut a bizarre and sometimes chilling figure on the world stage, with his colorful outfits, Amazonian bodyguards, and over-the-top rhetoric." That is what you get in a multicultural world: colorful costumes, strange rhetoric. But Gaddafi's rhetoric could sometimes be revealing, as in his remarkable speech to the Arab League summit held in Damascus in March 2008. [28]

Gaddafi began his speech by ironically reminding the Arab leaders of their own hypocritical betrayal of the Palestinian cause. He then told them that if they wanted to contest Iranian ownership of islands in the Persian Gulf, they should frankly refer the issue to the International Court of Justice and accept its ruling. Then he turned to the U.S. invasion of Iraq.

"What is the reason for the invasion and destruction of Iraq? ... Let our American friends answer this question: Why Iraq? What is the reason? Is Bin Laden an Iraqi? No, he is not. Were those who attacked New York Iraqis? No, they were not. Were those who attacked the Pentagon Iraqis? No, they were not. Were there WMDs in Iraq? No, there were not.

"Even if Iraq did have WMDs, Pakistan and India have nuclear bombs. And so do China, Russia, Britain, France and America. Should all these countries be destroyed? Fine, let's destroy all the countries that have WMDs."

In Iraq, Gaddafi continued, an entire Arab leadership was executed by hanging. "Yet we all sat on the sidelines, laughing." Saddam Hussein was a prisoner of war, the president of an Arab country and a member of the Arab League, and when he was hanged the Arab leaders did nothing. "I'm not talking about the policies of Saddam Hussein, or the disagreements we had with him. We all had political disagreements with him. And we have such disagreements among ourselves here. We share nothing beyond this hall."

Then he warned: "Any one of you might be next. Yes. America fought alongside Saddam Hussein against Khomeini. He was their friend. Cheney was a friend of Saddam Hussein. Rumsfeld, the US defense secretary at the time Iraq was destroyed, was a close friend of Saddam Hussein. Ultimately, they sold him out and hanged him. You are friends of America – let's say that 'we' are, not 'you'. But one of these days, America may hang any of us."

And he concluded: "We are the enemies of one another, I'm sad to say. We all hate one another, we deceive one another, we gloat at the misfortune of one another and we conspire against one another."

In *Hard Choices*, Hillary boasts in detail of her great achievement in lining up Arab leaders to go to war to oust Gaddafi. In reality, it was a feat similar to getting children to eat ice cream. Indeed, the Arab leaders that Hillary boasts of having united in order to attack Libya all hated Gaddafi with a passion, and not out of love for democracy, but because Gaddafi had told them what they really were.

To let us know just how hard her job was, in *Hard Choices*, Hillary recounts an "exceptionally complicated" aspect of her Arab coalition building. At this crucial moment, the Emirate of Bahrain, home base for the U.S. Navy in the Persian Gulf, was actively repressing a truly peaceful "Arab Spring" protest movement of its own. On March 15, Saudi Arabia sent troops into Bahrain to help quell the popular uprising. Dear me! Washington's main Arab allies were actually doing the same thing that we were going to bomb Libya for doing! And they were doing it in plain sight, for all to see.

"At that very moment we were deep into diplomatic negotiations to build an international coalition to protect Libyan civilians from an impending massacre", and were counting on the Gulf Arab states to play key roles, she recalled.

Hillary saw clearly that: "Our values and conscience demanded that the United States condemn the violence against civilians we were seeing in Bahrain", but on the other hand, "Arab leadership in the air campaign" against Libya was "crucial". Hillary was faced with a moral dilemma: or rather, the appearance of a moral dilemma. But empty words would take care of this problem.

Hillary drafted a statement (with help from her spokeswoman, Victoria Nuland, who will later emerge from the shadows in her own right): "Violence is not and cannot be the answer. A political process is." But in Bahrain, violence continued to be the answer and no political process was ever allowed – as the American moralists fully expected. However, Hillary "felt comfortable that we had not sacrificed our values or credibility"

Now that the "values" were safely stashed away, the bombing could begin. "Soon the Arab jets were flying over Libya", she rejoiced.

Enlisting Arabs for the anti-Gaddafi lynch mob was no great accomplishment. It was a useful device to hide the fact that other far more democratic leaders, notably in Africa and Latin America, were offering to mediate the Libyan crisis.

As the military assault on Libya got underway, Hillary's role became more crucial: blocking all efforts to negotiate peace. Like her friend Madeleine Albright, Hillary used the State Department to prevent diplomacy from functioning. Ironically, while some at the Pentagon did seek a negotiated solution, Hillary at the State Department sabotaged negotiations.

Gaddafi was willing to compromise even before the NATO assault began. As early as March 10, an African Union mediation committee headed by South African president Jacob Zuma had drafted a peace accord, including a democratic transition of power, which Gaddafi was ready to discuss with the opposition. But, as former South African president Thabo Mbeki said later, the U.N. Security Council rejected this peace plan "with absolute contempt".

Independent investigation, mediation, negotiation – such were the steps that the United Nations should have taken, if it were still able to act as a peace-keeping organization. If in the early twentieth century, the United States killed the League of Nations by failing to join it, in this century, Washington is killing the United Nations through its deadly embrace. Mediation is what the United Nations should be promoting in crisis situations, but under the overwhelming influence of the United States, the organization has evolved into a rubber stamp for Washington's bellicose actions. Calls for peaceful mediation from leaders such as Venezuela's democratically- elected President Hugo Chavez were denounced as "support for dictators", as if only a country bearing the Washington label of "pure democracy" had the right to ask not to be bombed.

On March 18, Gaddafi called for a cease-fire. The next day, as French bombers began to strike Libya, Gaddafi's offer was dismissed by Hillary as "some talk from Tripoli of a cease-fire". In Paris, she justified the attacks by claiming that "Colonel Gaddafi continues to defy the world" by attacking civilians.

In reality, throughout the assault on Libya, efforts were being made to establish the truth and bring an end to the destruction. Gaddafi's son, Seif al Islam Gaddafi, was in contact with American officials, pleading with them to send a fact-finding mission to see for themselves what was happening. The Pentagon had its own informants who denied the melodramatic reports spread as pretext for violent regime change.[29]

Only one day after the NATO bombing began, the Libyan leadership was asking for a 72-hour cease-fire in order to work out terms of a settlement. They offered to withdraw all Libyan forces from Benghazi and Misrata – the two rebel-held cities – under the monitor of the African Union. Gaddafi stated that he was willing to retire and accept a transitional government, but on two conditions: that Libya be allowed to retain forces to resist al Qaeda, and that his family and those loyal to him would be protected. Retired U.S. Navy Admiral Charles Kubic, then working as a business consultant in Libya, was informed of these conditions and passed them through the military hierarchy to U.S. Army General Carter Ham, head of U.S. Africa Command (AFRICOM). The terms sounded reasonable to the military men, and General Ham began secret negotiations. But two days later, General Ham was given an order to "stand down" from "outside the Pentagon". Sources inside the military consider that this order to cut off peace negotiations could only have come from Hillary Clinton's State Department. [30]

In a telephone conversation in May, Seif al Islam Gaddafi told Democratic Congressman Dennis Kucinich that the accusations of potential genocide were being used like the false reports of "weapons of mass destruction" in Iraq. He warned the Americans that the armed rebels were not "freedom fighters" but jihadists, gangsters and terrorists.

In August, Kucinich wrote to Mr. Obama and Mrs. Clinton, informing them that he had been contacted by an intermediary in Libya who indicated that President Moammar Gaddafi was "willing to negotiate an end to the conflict under conditions which would seem to favor Administration policy". He received no answer.

Gaddafi had ruled for forty years and was visibly tired. Gaddafi's Jamahiriya was a peculiar experiment precisely because it was a type of modernization that was meant to fit the peculiarities of a sparsely-inhabited desert country imbued with Muslim traditions. It included a form of direct democracy, and a General People's Congress, which could (and did) reject proposals coming directly from Gaddafi. Moammar Gaddafi was indeed a "Guide" and not a dictator; his guidance was often rejected by the government, perhaps increasingly so. The Jamahiriya was a product of the revolutionary Zeitgeist at the end of the Vietnam War. It was characterized by a radical redistribution of wealth that dramatically raised the standard of living for the general population, but irritated elites who wanted a greater share of the oil spoils for themselves. Given the radical change in the Zeitgeist, without the 2011 NATO onslaught, Libya would have evolved, probably in the direction of Western capitalism, under the influence of its foreign-educated elites. But instead of evolution, the United States increasingly prefers what it calls "revolution", which in the case of Libya was actually a counter-revolution. It was a drastic regression, conceived to undo and reverse the social benefits of Gaddafi's revolution and turn the place over to the usual suspects: local pawns and Western players, not only oil companies but also the big construction firm Bechtel and AFRICOM, the new U.S. African command designed to police Africa. But even this failed.

A U.S.-backed "revolution" can only be destructive, a way to get rid of what is in place. We smash it all, and count on "our guys" to rise to the top of the wreck, with a little help from mercenaries and Special Forces. And if this fails, U.S. leaders shrug and insist they meant well. If the natives can't put together what we broke, then that's their problem.

Libya's armed forces were in fact weak, since Gaddafi distrusted a strong military that he feared might try to take power in a coup. Had he been as universally hated as his enemies claimed, a genuine popular revolt representing a majority of Libyans could have easily forced his resignation. But in the midst of the NATO bombing, on July first, about a million people – around a fifth of the country's population – turned out in Tripoli to demonstrate their support for their Guide. Gaddafi was a genuine populist, still supported by many ordinary Libyans. They had no bombers on their side, and they lost. The jealous elite, who hated his populism, had the bombers on their side, but they did not really win either. The winner was chaos.

"We came..."

An unknown number of civilians had been killed by NATO missiles and bombs, including Gaddafi's youngest son, Saif al-Arab Gaddafi, 29, on a visit home from his studies at Munich technical university. Along with three of Moammer Gaddafi's baby grandchildren, he died in a May 30 air strike on his home in a residential area of Tripoli. Saif had been a target before, when he was four years old, and was wounded in a U.S. bombing raid on his family in 1986. Following that raid, the Bishop of Tripoli, Mgr. Martinelli made an appeal: "I ask, please, a gesture of humanity toward Colonel Gaddafi, who has protected the Christians of Libya. He is a great friend." The Colonel would be missed. In mid-February 2015, twenty-one Coptic Christians who had come from Egypt to work in Libya were beheaded by Islamist fanatics.

On October 18, 2011, Hillary Rodham Clinton arrived in Tripoli for her first official visit to a country which she did not understand and which she was rapidly transforming into something no one would recognize.

While waiting for Secretary of State Clinton to arrive, a "senior State Department official" (unidentified, as is the custom) told reporters that the Americans would be talking to the Libyans on how to "integrate Libya fully into the 21st-century world economy in transparent ways where Libya's oil wealth is used for the benefit of all of Libya's citizens". A rich joke, considering that Gaddafi's insistence on spreading Libya's oil wealth among the citizenry, by providing free education, housing and health care, was surely a central reason that leaders of the United States, Qatar and the Arab League sought regime change. The United States, it was announced, was planning to help the Libyans learn English, as if the language were unknown to them.

Hillary Clinton, as usual, had not come to Libya to learn about the country, but to tell people what to do. "Women in Libya should have equal rights", she said, true to her usual feminist persona. This was another rich joke, since thanks to the NATO bombing, women in Libya were about to lose the rights they had gained thanks to Gaddafi, not only the right to appear in public unveiled, or to hold significant jobs, but simply to walk down the street in safety, or simply to stay alive....

Perhaps to illustrate American values and interests, Hillary chose the occasion in Tripoli to express her satisfaction at the liberation of Israeli soldier Gilad Shalit. The fact that this much-publicized Franco-Israeli prisoner of Hamas was released in a prisoner exchange can hardly have been of burning interest to the people of Libya.

Before heading off to Oman, Hillary had a final word for Moammar Gaddafi, who, although this was not publicly known, was still fighting to defend his home town of Sirte, alongside his son Mutassim.

"'We hope he can be captured or killed soon so that you don't have to fear him any longer," Hillary told a selected gathering in Tripoli.

Two days later, Gaddafi was both captured and killed. Video footage shows that the Libyan leader and his son were captured alive, atrociously abused and then murdered.

When informed of Gaddafi's death, Hillary had her moment of lasting fame, the moment that will define her in history. Told by her aide Huma Abedin that Gaddafi had been killed, Hillary uttered a girlish, "Wow", before paraphrasing the original imperialist, Julius Caesar: "We came, we saw, he died!", then she broke out into peels of happy laughter.

Thus, the world may see this product of the frantic scramble up the contemporary American power structure for what she really is. Riding the tiger of the military-industrial complex had transformed a near-sighted teacher's pet from the Chicago suburbs, the girl most likely to succeed in her class at Wellesley, into a gloating murderess, lacking even a shadow of the remorse of Lady Macbeth.

Postscript to Murder

When a man taken prisoner is brutally murdered, it doesn't bother Hillary Clinton that the act was cruel, or illegal, or simply embarrassing. It was a success. If the prisoner is a "bad guy", she is as gleeful as a high school cheerleader when her team wins. When the prisoner is a member of her own team, she is devastated. It is a terrible human tragedy, and it might even harm her career. It was a failure, although she doesn't quite admit that it was *her* failure.

In *Hard Choices*, Hillary fails to mention her reaction to the death of Gaddafi, apparently having been warned that it would not make the good impression she anticipated. But she devotes a chapter of over thirty pages to the death of U.S. Ambassador Chris Stevens and two CIA officers, Glen Doherty and Tyrone Woods, in Benghazi on September 11, 2012. "As Secretary I was the one ultimately responsible for my people's safety, and I never felt that responsibility more deeply than I did that day", she wrote.

No doubt. But then the lawyer gets to work, the one who knows that you can talk your way out of anything. Rationalization begins. "Diplomacy, by its very nature, must often be practiced in dangerous places where America's national security hangs in the balance." Wait a minute. America's "national security" hangs in the balance in Benghazi? How is that? And whatever Ambassador Chris Stevens was doing there on September 11, 2014, it was not, strictly speaking, "diplomacy". According to the most plausible accounts, Chris Stevens and his colleagues were in Benghazi to facilitate arms transfers via Turkey to Islamic rebels in Syria. Arms smuggled from Libya, along with Islamic militants, aided by the United States, have gone on to massacre Shi'ites, Alawites and Christians all across the ancient cradle of civilization in Mesopotamia. Stevens was never practicing "diplomacy", he was practicing imperial regime change, an exercise of state rebuilding that has failed completely. He was working in the context of the dream world of Hillary Rodham Clinton, where this world is to be remade to align with America's universal values and interests.

"When America is absent," she argues in her brief for herself, "extremism takes root, our interests suffer, and our security at home is threatened." This, of course, is just diversionary lawyer talk. Extremism has taken root in the Middle East almost entirely because America was all too present, along with its three-billion-dollar-a-year spoiled brat, Israel. Everybody knows this, but retreat, pursues Hillary, is "just not in our country's DNA," since "Americans have always worked harder and smarter." Working harder and smarter is what millions of people do all over the world, but all human virtues must be identified as particularly "American". This is the sort of meaningless rhetoric developed by "the girl most likely to succeed". It is the rhetoric of ambition. In her long explanation of why Chris Stevens, Glenn Doherty and Tryone Woods were killed, she never actually explains anything. She leans toward the results of an investigation by the *New York Times*, which concluded that "Contrary to claims by some members of Congress, it was fueled in large part by anger at an American-made video denigrating Islam." She is not sure of this and ends on a pragmatic note: after all, now that the damage is done, it is "less important" to know *why* they did it than to find them and bring them to justice.

Find them and bring them to justice without knowing *why* they did it?

The United States barged into a country that only a few specialists knew much about, thanks to intelligence gathering. But policy-makers did not really understand it at all, yet were certain it could be made over in their own image – a godlike task, which created an inferno.

It never seems to occur to Hillary that the murder of Stevens, Doherty and Woods was the natural and entirely predictable outcome of a murderous enterprise that should never have been undertaken. Those who put their hand in a hornet's nest will get stung.

Christopher Stevens did know a lot about Libya. His cables to the State Department, published by Wikileaks, show that Stevens knew that Gaddafi was not a "dictator" and that the Colonel had been "at war" with Islamic terrorism and al Qaeda far more vigorously and for far longer than the United States had been. But, like China, Gaddafi was trying to contribute to independent African development. This was bad news for the West which, despite having neglected Africa for decades, still wanted to have privileged access to the continent's resources. In an August 2008 cable to Washington, Christopher Stevens reported that: "Moammar al-Qadhafi recently brokered a widely publicized agreement with Tuareg tribal leaders from Libya, Chad, Niger, Mali and Algeria in which they would abandon separatist aspirations and smuggling (of weapons and trans-national extremists) in exchange for development assistance and financial support." [31]

In short, Gaddafi was using Libya's oil wealth to keep peace in the region. With his death, that peace ended, and war spread to neighboring Mali, while law and order broke down completely in Libya itself. A peaceful and prosperous country descended into chaos.

Perhaps the "over the top rhetoric" and the bizarre costumes, as well as the authoritarianism of the Guide, were useful in the beginning phase of creating a modern nation out of a vast region of sparsely-inhabited desert and its rival tribes. Something original might have evolved out of the Jamahiriya, just as something interesting might have evolved out of Yugoslavia – diverse systems for a diverse world. But for America, there is only one model.

In his masterful, very revealing book, *Slouching Towards Sirte: NATO's War on Libya and Africa* (p.73), Maximilian Forte makes this judgment:

> "Indeed, Gaddafi was a remarkable and unique exception among the whole range of modern Arab leaders, for being doggedly altruistic, for funding development programs in dozens of needy nations, for supporting national liberation struggles that had nothing to do with Islam or the Arab world, for pursuing an ideology that was original and not simply the product of received tradition or mimesis of exogenous sources, and for making Libya a presence on the world stage in a way that was completely out of proportion with its population size (for example most of the larger Caribbean nations have larger populations). One could be a fierce critic of Gaddafi, and still have the honest capability to recognize these objective realities or, if preferring to maintain the narrative of demonization, 'to give the devil his due.'"

Such an "honest capability" to recognize the virtues of one's adversaries is something America's leaders lack entirely, whether it is the half-African Barack Obama, or the all-American Hillary Rodham Clinton. Throughout history, that "peace of the brave" which requires this capability, which calls on the capacity of human beings to see themselves in the distorted mirror of others, has been a mark of nobility of soul. It is totally lacking in today's Western leaders.

The story of Moammer Gaddafi was an epic tragedy. The man was a tragic hero, able to inspire both pity and terror, like one of the protagonists of great literature in times past. He was flawed, like all great heroes. He could be cruel; he could be generous. He was human; he was ridiculous. He had great faults and great virtues, and even comic aspects. His aspirations surpassed his capacity of realization. His final catastrophe was due less to his faults than to his virtues: above all, his "dogged altruism", which cut him off from the critical chorus of his own most prominent people. In his own way, he was as blind as Oedipus. His ghost still needs a future Sophocles, a future Shakespeare.

But is that any longer still possible? The America that aspires to command the world today is killing not only nations; it is killing all nobility of spirit. It is killing tragedy, that ability to grasp the truth of the human condition in its defeat, that ability to bury the dead with honor and to respect the defiance of the brave fool who imagined he could save the world.

In Libya, weighing our "interests", we Americans came; we saw nothing. Our human conscience was already dead.

Chapter 6

Not Understanding Russia

"I sometimes get the feeling that somewhere across that huge pond, in America, people sit in a lab and conduct experiments, as if with rats, without actually understanding the consequences of what they are doing."

–Vladimir Putin, 4 March 2014.

Every nation has its own values and interests. Peaceful international relations should be a matter of respecting values and balancing interests. Looking at U.S.-Russian relations over the past two and a half decades, it is clear that for the Washington foreign policy establishment, such trifles as Russian values and interests are not considered worth respecting, noticing, or understanding at all.

Curiously, to be a Russian expert in Washington today, a prime requirement seems to be an inability to understand the country in question. Autism is the preferred outlook.

Americans seem unable to understand why a nation that in modern times has twice been the object of massive, devastating invasions from the West should mind seeing the United States extend the greatest military machine in history right up to its doorstep. If Russian leaders express objections, the American response is to suggest that they must be paranoid.

U.S. leaders have managed to forget all about the 1990 promise not to extend NATO eastwards in return for allowing a newly-reunited Germany to join the Atlantic Alliance. This promise was accepted by Gorbachev, who did not even demand that it be put in writing, since he naively thought that keeping Germany within U.S.-led NATO would protect Russia by preventing any revival of an aggressive German *Drang nach Osten*. It was the smiling Clinton administration that began the process of violating the spirit of that promise (by joining with Germany in the dismemberment of Yugoslavia), and then the letter (by expanding NATO to the East). The Czech Republic, Hungary and Poland were taken into NATO on the eve of the bombing of Yugoslavia in 1999. The unraveling of the "partnership" that Russian leaders had hoped to establish with Washington had begun.

Rather than respond to multiple Russian overtures for peaceful partnership, the Clinton administration chose to treat Russia as a defeated enemy. The implications of this choice only emerged fully in 2014. The lesson for Russia was that instead of enhancing the prospects for world peace, the dissolution of the Soviet Union and the Warsaw Pact had simply given *carte blanche* to the United States to proceed from the destruction of the USSR to destruction of Russia itself.

Not long after the humiliation of Russia in the Kosovo War, Vladimir Putin succeeded Boris Yeltsin as President of the Russian Federation in 2000, the last year of the Clinton presidency. Russia was in a state of drastic social, economic and demographic decline, largely due to a shock-treatment transition to capitalism that reduced both the living standards and the morale of the population. Putin had spent most of his life as an intelligence officer, and was selected by Yeltsin as an adviser and then successor. Intelligence agencies often provide a superior education in international political and strategic realities. Following the usual rule of double standards, the U.S. propaganda chorus denounced Putin's KGB background as proof of perfidy, conveniently ignoring that President George Bush the First had been head of the CIA. From the start, the West's problem with Putin was doubtless that he knew too much and understood all too well what Washington was up to under the veneer of nice guys and gals just trying to be friendly. The trouble with Putin was that he grasped what was going on much more acutely than the pathetic Boris Yeltsin. Yet Yeltsin may have been vaguely aware of having been hoodwinked by his American "friends". He may even have brought Putin in as his successor for precisely that reason.

Vladimir Putin would not have failed to read the 1997 bible of U.S. Eurasian strategy, *The Grand Chessboard* by Zbigniew Brzezinski. As President Jimmy Carter's National Security Adviser, Brzezinski was the guru behind the strategy that lured the USSR into the Afghan quagmire in 1979. He remained the most prominent strategist linked to the Democratic Party.

Brzezinski claims that the "ultimate objective of American

policy should be benign and visionary: to shape a truly cooperative global community, in keeping with long-range trends and with the fundamental interests of humankind." In short, the United States is supposed to *shape* the whole world, certain that this will "ultimately" be good for humankind. "But in the meantime," he adds, dealing with the here and now, "it is imperative that no Eurasian challenger emerges, capable of dominating Eurasia and thus also of challenging America." This amounts to the preventive weakening of any emerging power, not for what that power does, but simply because it is there. Russia, simply by its size and location, is bound to be seen as a potential "challenger" and thus, an adversary. The conclusion is that the proclaimed Russian hope for revival as a peaceful and prosperous partner of the West is a non-starter for U.S. policy makers.

"To put it in a terminology that harkens back to the more brutal age of ancient empires, the three grand imperatives of imperial geo-strategy are to prevent collusion and maintain security dependence among the vassals, to keep tributaries pliant and protected, and to keep the barbarians from coming together." (*The Grand Chessboard, p.40)* In other words, this means reviving the classical *divide et impera* for our own brutal age. The "vassals" and "tributaries" are our dear European allies: dependent, pliant and protected by NATO, kept in a state of permanent indecisiveness by membership in a Union of 28 highly diverse nations able to veto and paralyze each other. The "barbarians" are, of course, just about everybody else, and not least the Russians. The "collusion" that must be "prevented" is any stable and peaceful relationship between the European Union (especially Germany) and Russia.

The trouble with Putin is that he understood this, considered it unacceptable, and dared to say so.

The Grand Chessboard was published during the second term of the Clinton presidency. It is the most important book on U.S. strategy of the period. It must surely have been read by the President and his wife, perhaps more attentively by Hillary than by Bill.

Indeed, before deciding to run for the Senate, Hillary confided to her good friend Diane Blair that she would "like to be in a think tank". She wanted to be a "policy woman". By that she meant foreign policy, a field in which Bill was weak, but she felt she could be strong.

Carl Bernstein's detailed biography of Hillary, *A Woman in Charge*, written before she became Secretary of State, largely ignores foreign policy. But finally, on page 550, concerning HRC as junior Senator from New York, her transformation is clarified:

"It is clear from conversations with her advisers that Hillary's membership on the Armed Services Committee was intended to be the centerpiece of her new credentials for the presidency. She meant to become a defense intellectual, muscular in her approach, a master of the arcana of policy, weaponry, and strategy that would both serve her if elected, and help her get there by eliminating voters' fears about a woman being commander in chief."

Hillary was keenly aware of Bill Clinton's "weak credentials in this area" and meant to do better. "She assumed from the start that she could count on the liberal wing of the Democratic Party in the pocket of her pants suits", and so her job was to get votes from other constituencies.

Indeed, this is the all too common path of left-liberal politicians. First, she found that in the current system her ambition to enact some great progressive reform, such as health care, was blocked by the nature of the capitalist profit system and the resulting relationship of forces. On the domestic front, almost nothing is possible other than small tweaks. But on the world stage, U.S. military power offers enormous prospects for "doing something": from rousing speeches against "dictators" to bullying whole countries, punishing them with sanctions, overthrowing their governments... all the way to great big wars. History can be made here.

Hillary showed her nationalist colors in 2005 by co-sponsoring a bill to make it a federal crime to burn the U.S. flag, confident that her liberal fans would look the other way at this gesture designed to impress the chauvinist crowd. Once a politician has the helpless left-liberals in her pocket, their feelings and convictions can be safely ignored. They are sure to vote for her as the lesser evil, whatever she does.

For a World of Equals

In February 2007, Vladimir Putin committed an offense far more meaningful than flag burning by speaking truth to power. At the annual international security conference in Munich, Putin spoke out frankly against the model of a "unipolar world", meaning a world with one master, one sovereign, a world that has "nothing in common with democracy". The unipolar model "is not only unacceptable but also impossible in today's world", he said.

Putin's point was that the extreme use of military force in international relations, "plunging the world into an abyss of permanent conflicts", and the "greater and greater disdain for basic principles of international law" by the United States makes everybody feel unsafe and stimulates a dangerous arms race.

In contrast, he said, Russia was in favor of all sorts of peace-promoting measures: conventional disarmament in Europe, reduction of nuclear weapons, initiatives to prevent the use of weapons in outer space, and United Nations authority over the use of force. To solve the Iranian nuclear question, Russia proposed establishing international centers for enriching uranium, under strict IAEA supervision, to enable the legitimate development of civil nuclear energy.

Implicitly responding to U.S. treatment of Russia as "a defeated country", Putin recalled that "the fall of the Berlin Wall was possible thanks to an historic choice – one that was made by our people, the people of Russia – a choice in favor of democracy, freedom, openness and a sincere partnership with all the members of the big European family." Russia was never defeated militarily, but decided freely to end the Cold War and seek partnership with the West. Above all, he concluded, Russia seeks to work together with responsible and independent partners "in constructing a fair and democratic world order that would ensure security and prosperity not only for a select few, but for all."

Putin's speech was met with shock, anger and rejection, and murmurs of a "new Cold War" because he had dared to openly criticize the United States. NATO rallied around Washington, as usual. NATO Secretary General Jaap de Hoop Scheffer echoed the dominant Washington reaction that the speech was "disappointing and not helpful".

Senator John McCain retorted that the world was not unipolar, and at the same time demanded that Russia adopt "Western values" – implying that if it wasn't unipolar, it should be. "Moscow must understand that it cannot enjoy a genuine partnership with the West so long as its actions at home and abroad conflict so fundamentally with the core values of Euro-Atlantic democracies," he said, dismissing Putin's speech as "needless confrontation".

While in the Senate, Hillary had found a foreign policy ally in Senator McCain, the hawkish Republican whom Obama had defeated in the 2008 elections. Senators McCain and Clinton were both particularly eager to unify the world according to "the core values of Euro-Atlantic democracies". As chairman of the International Republican Institute (IRI), a subsidiary of the Congress-funded National Endowment for Democracy (NED), McCain travels around the world lavishing encouragement, advice and U.S. dollars on individuals or discontented minorities eager to bring their countries into the American orbit.

Like McCain, Hillary's language on foreign policy abounds in references to "principles" that essentially concern the internal affairs of other countries, rather than relations between States, especially regarding "democracy" and "human rights". Thus, U.S. foreign policy has increasingly come to mean interference in the domestic policy of countries the United States wants to change and control. Mainstream media act as a reliable agent of this policy, by issuing reports that are often distorted, inaccurate or widely out of context. Constant lecturing confirms the impression that the job of the U.S. State Department is not to smooth relations *between* States, but to interfere in relations *within* foreign States.

In *Hard Choices*, Hillary boasted of having been "a frequent critic of Putin's rule" while in the Senate. She has never ceased to flaunt her antipathy to Putin. At a meeting in January 2015 in Winnipeg, when asked whether she had "decided to be President", she turned the question around and clumsily mimicked Putin "deciding to be President", adding with a gloating self-righteousness that: "*We* have a process" – as if being the second Clinton to run for President, backed by billionaires, was a more virtuous process than Russian elections. While a candidate for the Democratic nomination for President in January 2008, she told a rally in Hampton, Massachusetts that President George W. Bush was mistaken to develop a friendly relationship with Vladimir Putin. Referring to Bush's claim that he had looked into Putin's eyes and seen his soul, Hillary retorted: "I could have told him, he was a KGB agent, by definition he doesn't have a soul."

When Hillary took office in January 2009 as Obama's Secretary of State, Dmitry Medvedev was President. In a superficial gesture designed to get media attention, at her meeting that year with Russia's Foreign Minister Sergey Lavrov (a genuine first-rate diplomat), Hillary pulled out what she described as a "reset" button and got Lavrov to join her in pressing it in front of photographers. "We worked hard to get the right Russian word. Do you think we got it?" She asked proudly. No, came the reply. The gadget actually read "overcharge", rather than "reset". This clumsy photo-op stunt did not, in fact, indicate any real effort to improve mutual understanding. The reset, as Hillary wrote later, was a matter of opportunism. It enabled the United States to "pick off the low-hanging fruit in terms of bilateral cooperation" — another way of saying that Washington bullied Moscow into making some significant concessions, such as granting the Pentagon the right to transport deadly weapons across Russia to Afghanistan, approving heavy sanctions against Iran and North Korea, that sort of thing...

But Russia got no credit for being plucked. Moscow's concessions "masked another agenda", she wrote. "So even as Russia allowed U.S. cargo to move through its territory, it worked to expand its own military footprint across Central Asia ... It was like a modern-day version of the 'Great Game,' the elaborate 19th century diplomatic contest between Russia and Britain for supremacy in Central Asia – except that America had a narrowly focused interest in the region and was not seeking dominance."

What fun to play Great Power games! Oh, but America could not be doing naughty things like seeking dominance! What Russia was actually doing to "expand its military footprint" remains a mystery.

In 2012 Putin was back in the Presidency, and Hillary approached Russia as if she were a therapist treating the "soulless" President. American policy toward Russia had to be based on amateur psychoanalysis, rather than on an understanding of Russia's basic interests and genuine policy aims.

Secretary of State Clinton sent a warning memo to President Obama. He was no longer dealing with the meek Medvedev and needed to be ready to take a harder line. Putin, she said, was "deeply resentful of the U.S. and suspicious of our actions", without noting any reason for such a strange attitude. Putin might call his project of creating a customs union "regional integration", Hillary warned, "but that was code for rebuilding a lost empire." Needless to say, the customs unions that the United States never ceases creating and extending have nothing to do with empire-building, heaven forbid. But a Russian-sponsored customs union might be a first step toward growth of that old Brzezinski taboo: an emerging power in Eurasia.

"Bargain hard," Hillary advised Obama.

In *Hard Choices*, Hillary displays her capacity to read the mind of the Russian President. "Putin's worldview is shaped by his admiration for the powerful czars of Russian history, Russia's long-standing interest in controlling the nations on its borders, and his personal determination that his country never again appears weak or at the mercy of the West, as he believes it was after the collapse of the Soviet Union. He wants to reassert Russia's power by dominating its neighbors and controlling their access to energy. He also wants to play a larger role in the Middle East to increase Moscow's influence in that region and reduce the threat from restive Muslims within and beyond Russia's southern borders. To achieve these goals, he seeks to reduce the influence of the United States in Central and Eastern Europe and other areas that he considers part of Russia's sphere, and to counter or at least mute our efforts in the countries ruled by the Arab Spring."

This supposed "analysis" is nothing but a mixture of projection and groundless supposition. The aspiring "defense intellectual" thinks in stereotypes. Russia's repeated offers to cooperate with the United States on disarmament, on Iran, on combating Islamic terrorism, on economic development, are simply ignored.

"Putin sees geopolitics as a zero-sum game in which, if someone is winning, then someone else has to be losing. That's an outdated but still dangerous concept, one that requires the United States to show both strength and patience."

If Russian advisers also go in for psychoanalysis, they could warn Putin that Hillary's biographer Carl Bernstein stresses her tendency to focus on an "enemy" to demonize. On the international scene, she seems to have chosen Putin for the role.

During the Soviet Union, American commentary on Moscow

policy tended to concentrate on efforts to figure out the mysterious hierarchy of the Russian power elite. This exercise was called Kremlinology. It was quite useless, but always served to distract from genuine issues by reducing everything to obscure power struggles. It upheld the notion of the "enemy" capital as a dark and sinister fortress held by strange creatures motivated solely by power. The focus on Putin's alleged personality is a holdover from Cold War Kremlinology. The fact that Vladimir Putin is very open and frank makes no difference. The "enemy" must be sinister and inscrutable. The Pentagon paid hundreds of thousands of dollars to a group of so-called "movement pattern analysis" experts who concluded in a confidential 2008 report that Vladimir Putin was suffering from Asperger Syndrome, a mild form of autism. There was no evidence for this, but the "experts" had surmised from studying Putin's "movement pattern" that the Russian President's "neurological development was significantly interrupted in infancy". The chief "expert", Brenda Connors, claimed that the "difficulty in getting accurate real-time information about Russia and its leaders made the use of movement pattern analysis critical for U.S. officials". The Pentagon expected to learn more about Putin's "thinking processes" from the "body signature" of his "posture/gesture mergers", than from paying close attention to what he actually said.[32]

This seems to lend support to Putin's suggestion that United States leaders treat the rest of the world as if they were experimenting with laboratory rats.

U.S. policy toward Russia up until the crisis of 2014 was so contradictory that it might seem that there was no clear strategy. It was friendly whenever it came to "plucking the low-hanging fruit" and unfriendly the rest of the time. On the whole, the policy can be summed up as a combination of intimidation and subversion, which is applied not only to Russia, but to just about everybody, in varying degrees and proportions.

During the Cold War, Americans accused Moscow of supporting internal subversion by Communists allegedly seeking to "overthrow the government of the United States by force and violence" – which in reality was far beyond the wildest dreams of the Communist Party, U.S.A. Today Russia does not advocate any alien political doctrine and has adopted a free market economy and multi-party elections, while the United States actively promotes groups eager to overthrow the elected President of Russia. The irony of this reversal of roles goes largely unnoticed.

While gratuitously accusing the extremely popular elected President of Russia of being a "dictator" and treating every eccentric oppositionist as the embodiment of genuine democracy, the United States is also treating Russia as a potential military target. It advances its NATO pawns ever closer, carries out military maneuvers on Russia's borders and is building a missile shield whose only plausible use would be to give the United States a nuclear first-strike capacity against Russia by shielding the West from retaliation. It should be recalled that contrary to Moscow, Washington has always proclaimed its own special "right" to resort first to nuclear weapons. The transparent pretext that the missile shield was intended solely to defend the West from Iran was dropped in 2014, when the Ukrainian crisis gave Washington the reason it needed for an openly hostile military buildup against Russia.

Most Americans are surely unaware of the U.S. military threat to Russia, given that national leaders regularly deny it and pretend that only paranoia could make Russians feel threatened by nice America. To know about the almost daily provocative military exercises held by various combinations of NATO forces and their partners (such as Georgia and Sweden) around Russian borders, one must turn to an internet site such as Rick Rozoff's "Stop NATO". Mass media ignore these martial operations, clearly designed as exercises to prepare for war against Russia. When, eventually, Russia reacts to these constant threats, mainstream media will report this reaction as an unprovoked gesture of paranoid hostility.

The recklessness with which the United States flaunts its military alliance on Russia's doorstep can create the impression that Washington is actually planning to go to war against Russia. In practice, however, since the defeat in Vietnam, the United States has always chosen to attack much weaker countries, with no significant means to defend themselves against the air assaults that are a U.S. specialty. Even so, the results have not been impressive. It is preposterous to think that a United States military, which has been unable to pacify Iraq, Libya or Afghanistan, could do any better than Napoleon's mighty armies or the erstwhile invincible Wehrmacht in conquering Russia.

Historically, the Russians, essentially prudent and defensive, are reluctant to start wars, even though they tend to be good at winning them. It is highly probable that U.S. leaders count on Russian prudence to allow them to get away with their provocations, and to back down rather than risk a nuclear war. Perhaps the military threats and intimidation are intended to have a psychological effect by embarrassing and weakening Russia's current leaders, thus lending support to subversion, the primary weapon in the "smart power" arsenal. However, the evident threat has incited the Russians to take defensive military steps; this now raises the possibility of a fatal incident that will trigger war.

Clearly the United States seeks "regime change" in the form of a movement to overthrow Putin and replace him by more pliable leaders. But to what end? Russia under Putin had already sought to cooperate as a partner with the West. The final aim, if there is one, may be to use conflict on the edges of Russia to destabilize rather than to conquer; in short, to create chaos leading to disintegration, just as in other countries targeted by U.S. aggression. The hope may be that a weaker leader would leave Russia open to stimulated disintegration along ethnic lines, on the model of Yugoslavia. Then this vast territory would be easier to dominate and its vast resources easier to appropriate. In reality, it is likely that any successor would be far more hostile to the West than the essentially liberal Putin. The Western threat is almost certain to strengthen nationalist and authoritarian tendencies.

Russia and the Middle East

Russia is currently the preferred target of two powerful strains in the U.S. foreign policy establishment: the Brzezinski school and the neoconservatives. They come from very different places, but their strategies have recently dovetailed. Born in Warsaw in 1928, Zbigniew Brzezinski's background is traditional Russophobic Polish nationalism. His aristocratic paternal family came from a shifting region that used to be part of Poland and is now part of Ukraine. An outspoken critic of the Israel lobby's influence on Congress, Brzezinski has said that he sees no "implicit obligation for the United

States to follow like a stupid mule whatever the Israelis do." On the other hand, the neocons' attachment to Israel is profound; many of them hold dual U.S.-Israeli citizenship.

What the two strategic schools have in common is a readiness to exploit Sunni Islamic extremism as a lesser evil, against Russia for Brzezinski, against Arab nationalism – or Iran – for Israel. Many neocons harbor an ancestral hostility to Tsarist Russia as the land of pogroms. [33]

Brzezinski has long looked forward to the growth of militant Islam along the "soft underbelly" of the USSR, in the vast region he has called the "Eurasian Balkans", as the perfect way to weaken Russia. "In fact, an Islamic revival – already abetted from the outside not only by Iran but also by Saudi Arabia – is likely to become the mobilizing impulse for the increasingly pervasive new nationalisms, determined to oppose any reintegration under Russian - and hence infidel - control." [34]

As Carter's house strategist, Brzezinski acted as midwife to the birth of Osama bin Laden's al Qaeda. The CIA supported the Islamic Mujahideen as essential allies in Brzezinski's strategy to lure the Soviet Union deeper into Afghanistan in order to drive it out. "The worse things get, the better", could have been the slogan for a policy that began with arming the Mujahideen with Stinger missiles to shoot down Soviet aircraft.

Afghanistan was left far worse off than it would have been under Soviet influence, most notably in an area that was of such primary importance to U.S. leaders that they used it to justify their own Afghan invasion a few years: the rights of women. The Soviets supported education and social liberation for women – one of the main reasons that Brzezinski's local protégés wanted to boot them out. Hillary's feminism has never stretched far enough to appreciate that facet of Soviet policy.

Brzezinski saw Afghanistan as linked to the Muslim "soft underbelly" of the Russian empire, a potential source of chaos that might spread northward and finally destabilize Moscow. When the communist empire collapsed, the target remained the same but had the old label once again: Russia.

For the neoconservatives, on the other hand, the primary task was to merge Israeli and U.S. interests into a single strategy.

Israel's historic enemy was Arab nationalism, which aimed to unite the Arab nations – including Palestine. Originally, Washington was not hostile to Arab nationalism. In May 1948, President Truman recognized the State of Israel, thanks to domestic pressure, but the foreign policy establishment saw good relations with the oil-rich Arab world as far more essential to U.S. interests.[35] It took a long time for Israel's friends in the United States to impose the view that defense of Israel was the top U.S. priority in the region, based largely on cultural and ideological identification. Narratives such as the 1960 movie "Exodus" stressed the implicit parallel between the founding of the United States and of Israel. Alliance with Israel was a matter of "our ideals" outweighing "our interests".

More recently, the neoconservative influence in Washington pretended to unite U.S. and Israeli ideals and interests around the grandiose project of bringing democracy to the world by getting rid of "dictators" – who just happened to be supporters of the Palestinian cause. Veteran neocon Richard Perle's 1996 report for Israeli Prime Minister Benjamin Netanyahu, entitled "A Clean Break", called for getting rid of Saddam Hussein in Iraq as the first in a series of regime changes that would eliminate Israel's perceived main enemies in the Middle East.

Although the neoconservatives are generally associated with the George W. Bush administration because they managed to steer it openly into the invasion of Iraq, the Project for a New American Century (PNAC) launched its program during the Clinton administration with its "Statement of Principles" on June 3, 1997. It called on the United States to "shape a new century favorable to American principles and interests". These "principles" boiled down to an extremely aggressive interpretation of American exceptionalism: "America's unique role in preserving and extending an international order friendly to our security, our prosperity, and our principles". This required increased defense spending, tightened military alliances, and regime change to promote "political and economic freedom abroad". The PNAC followed up in 1998 by calling on President Clinton to remove Saddam Hussein. This amounted to calling on the United States to eliminate Israel's enemies, for they were also portrayed as enemies of the United States and of the whole world.

As Senator, Hillary Clinton adopted the neocon line by voting in favor of the 2003 invasion of Iraq. After the war had become drastically unpopular, she expressed regrets, but these second thoughts have never inspired her to disapprove of subsequent U.S. aggression in the Middle East. On the contrary, after playing a key role in bringing about the destruction of Libya, she boasts of having urged Obama to increase support to rebels trying to overthrow the government of Syria.

The Middle East "regime change" wars have targeted precisely the secular nationalist governments that Israel wanted to get rid of. The only conceivable benefit to the United States of this policy would have been to gain control of those countries' oil resources. This is an explanation favored by various economic determinists. However, the chaos resulting from these wars has made any orderly exploitation of petroleum resources all but impossible. Our supposed "values" have trumped our interests.

The civil war in Syria brought together the pro-Israeli and anti-Russian strains of U.S. foreign policy, since Russia stood in the way of direct U.S. intervention. Russia has a longstanding relationship with Syria, including a naval base, as well as many social and financial ties. After the supposedly defensive "no fly zone" over Libya was used to achieve violent regime change, Russia and China made it clear that when it came to Syria, any attempt to use the R2P pretext to get Security Council approval for U.S. military intervention would be blocked. Their joint veto in February 2012 caused the warrior women to fume and rage in very undiplomatic terms.

U.S. ambassador to the United Nations Susan Rice called the veto "disgusting and shameful". Russia and China, she declared, "chose to align themselves with a dictator who is on his last legs rather than the people of Syria, rather than the people of the Middle East, rather than the principled views of the rest of the international community". She warned that both countries would later regret their actions and that the veto would be remembered by a "democratic Syria".

At a meeting of the Western interventionist "Friends of Syria" In February 2012, Hillary Clinton called the double veto "despicable".

"It's quite distressing to see two permanent members of the Security Council using their veto while people are being murdered – women, children, brave young men – houses are being destroyed. It is just despicable and I ask whose side are they on? They are clearly not on the side of the Syrian people."

Which Syrian people? From the start, the armed rebels that the Syrian government was combating were predominantly Islamists opposed to Assad's secular regime. These forces steadily tightened their control of the rebellion. If Bashar al Assad did not have strong popular support among the Syrian people, he could not have stayed in power so long, given the internationalized war being waged against him with increasingly powerful outside support.

Whose "Zero Sum Game"?

For years, Russian leaders have sought to cooperate with the West against "Islamic terrorism". Such cooperation would have to start with an honest definition of the term and an examination of its real causes and variations. If Washington had accepted such cooperation, it might have prevented the 2013 Boston Marathon bombing: Russia had information on the perpetrators that they were eager to share. Russia has itself been the target of some particularly horrific massacres, such as the 2004 seizure by Chechen terrorists of a school in the Northern Ossetian city of Beslan, which cost the lives of 186 children, as well as 148 adults, most of them parents and teachers. After the United States acknowledged that the armed Syrian opposition organization, al Nusra, was made up of jihadists, Vladimir Putin tried to caution the West against arming such groups. Who knows where arms delivered to the Syrian opposition will end up?, he asked. Or how they will finally be used? "If Assad goes today, a political vacuum emerges – who will fill it? Maybe those terrorist organizations," Putin warned at a June 2013 press conference. "How can it be avoided? After all, they are armed and aggressive."

Far from "seeing everything as a zero sum game", as Hillary claimed, Putin urged the United States to cooperate with Russia in seeking a peaceful solution. A short time later, Russian efforts to bring about a mutually beneficial halt in the killing were so successful that many people in the world believed that they were seeing the beginning of a genuine diplomatic process to end the war that was devastating Syria.

On August 21, 2013, mysterious chemical attacks on the rebel-held suburbs of eastern Damascus caused many deaths among civilians. As usual, Western politicians and media immediately blamed Assad's forces. Over time, a number of serious independent investigations have provided convincing evidence that the Sarin gas attacks were perpetrated by al Nusra rebels, who had both the capability and the motivation to carry out a "false flag" chemical attack that would be blamed on Assad at the very moment when international inspectors were arriving in Damascus. Since Obama had earlier spoken of the use of chemical weapons as a "red line" which Assad must not cross, "or else", attributing the attack to the Syrian government put Obama in a position where he would feel obliged to retaliate. The United States, Britain and France prepared to carry out air strikes to punish the Syrian government.

Mere lack of solid evidence, official denials from Damascus, or even evidence implicating the rebels were not enough to head off the bombing by the Western allies.

However, for once Western public opinion reacted strongly against plans to get into yet another war in the Middle East. On August 30, after a lively debate, the British House of Commons rejected a government motion authorizing air strikes.

When Obama turned to Congress for such authorization, Congress members were flooded with calls and messages from their constituents demanding that they vote no. Obama continued to proclaim that "we know Assad was responsible" and that we must "act" to prevent further chemical attacks. Yet the public reaction indicated that, like British Prime Minister David Cameron, the U.S. President could be heading for a damaging defeat in Congress.

At the time, the office of former Secretary of State Hillary Clinton issued a statement supporting Obama's "effort to enlist the Congress in pursuing a strong and targeted response to the Assad regime's horrific use of chemical weapons." Hillary had quickly forgotten her public statement months earlier that Assad's chemical weapons might easily fall into the hands of rebel groups.

At this point, like the branch a drowning man can clutch to escape from the torrent, the Russians seized on an offhand remark by Hillary's successor, Secretary of State John Kerry. Asked what Bashar al Assad could do to prevent Western air strikes, Kerry replied rhetorically that the Syrian leader could turn over his entire stock of chemical weapons to the international community, adding that "he isn't about to do it and it can't be done".

Russian diplomats rapidly contacted the Syrians who retorted that it could indeed be done. And it was. After rapid and smooth negotiations in the midst of a war, the Syrian government actually handed over its entire arsenal of chemical weapons to international inspectors in record time. This showed what could be done by Russian-American cooperation.

The U.S. decision to join Russia in ridding Syria of chemical weapons, instead of bombing the country's government as "punishment" for allegedly having used them, raised hopes that the worst was over and peace was on the horizon.

Vladimir Putin took advantage of this happy moment to indulge in his habit of speaking rather too honestly about U.S. power. Perhaps he believed that this time he would be understood.

On September 11, 2013, the *New York Times* published a Putin Op-ed under the title, "A Plea for Caution from Russia". The Russian President warned that "Syria is not witnessing a battle for democracy, but an armed conflict between government and opposition in a multi-religious country. There are few champions of democracy in Syria."

"Mercenaries from Arab countries fighting there, and hundreds of militants from Western countries and even Russia, are an issue of our deep concern. Might they not return to our countries with experience acquired in Syria? After all, after fighting in Libya, extremists moved on to Mali. This threatens us all." By the time Putin's warning was verified by the emergence of the decapitation-loving "Islamic State" in Iraq and Syria, or the January 7, 2015 terrorist murder of *Charlie Hebdo* cartoonists in Paris, it had been forgotten and Putin was being demonized more ferociously than Assad.

Putin insisted that Russia was not protecting a particular Syrian government, but international law. "It is alarming that military intervention in internal conflicts in foreign countries has become commonplace for the United States. Is it in America's long-term interest? I doubt it. Millions around the world increasingly see America not as a model of democracy but as relying solely on brute force, cobbling coalitions together under the slogan 'you're either with us or against us'." Countries react by seeking to acquire weapons of mass destruction in self-defense. To strengthen non-proliferation, it would be necessary to "stop using the language of force and return to the path of civilized diplomatic and political settlement."

Putin predicted that a "shared success" on the chemical weapons issue could open the door to cooperation for other critical issues. He welcomed what he felt was "growing trust" in his relationship with President Obama, but then dared to differ with Obama's statement that U.S. policy is "what makes America different. It's what makes us exceptional."

"It is extremely dangerous to encourage people to see themselves as exceptional, whatever the motivation", the Russian President concluded. "There are big countries and small countries, rich and poor, those with long democratic traditions and those still finding their way to democracy. Their policies differ, too. We are all different, but when we ask for the Lord's blessings, we must not forget that God created us equal."

This plea for equality was greeted with outrage in the U.S. political class.

Putin was much too optimistic. The Russian proposal to eliminate Syria's chemical weapons was a total success. It prevented Western bombing of Syria in 2013. It had indeed opened the door to real international cooperation to end the bloodshed in Syria. But nobody among Western leaders chose to go through that door. On the contrary....

The Norwegian Nobel Committee awarded the 2013 Nobel Peace Prize to the intergovernmental Organization for the Prohibition of Chemical Weapons, for having "defined the use of chemical weapons as a taboo under international law". This was a neat way to avoid giving Russian diplomacy credit for what it had accomplished in Syria.

In September 2013, as Russia saved Obama from potential political defeat in Congress and showed the way to fruitful diplomacy, the Western elite was planning a major blow against Russia itself. *The Economist* wrote that the future of Ukraine and Europe today "was being decided in real time" at a meeting being held in the very Palace in Yalta, Crimea, where Roosevelt, Stalin and Churchill met to decide the future of Europe in 1945. Bill and Hillary Clinton, former CIA head General David Petraeus, former U.S. Treasury secretary Lawrence Summers, former World Bank head Robert Zoellick, Swedish foreign minister Carl Bildt, Shimon Peres, Tony Blair, Gerhard Schröder, Dominique Strauss-Kahn, Mario Monti, and Poland's influential foreign minister Radek Sikorski were among the attending dignitaries. On September 20, their host Viktor Pinchuk, considered Ukraine's second richest man and founder of the Yalta European Strategy (YES) conference, introduced Hillary for her dinner speech on "leadership" by telling Bill Clinton: "Mr. President, you are really a super star, but Secretary Clinton, she is a real, real mega star." Hillary used the occasion to claim that "Ukraine's products, including its wonderful chocolate, will find ready markets anywhere in the world". This was a nod toward the candy oligarch and future U.S.-backed President Petro Poroshenko, who was attending along with Viktor Yanukovych. Yanukovich, President of Ukraine at the time, could not know that this conference was part of a process that would force him from office five months later.

Of particular significance was the presence of former U.S. energy secretary Bill Richardson, who was there to talk about the shale-gas revolution which the United States hoped to use to weaken Russia by substituting fracking for Russia's natural gas reserves.

The center of discussion was the "Deep and Comprehensive Free Trade Agreement" (DCFTA) between Ukraine and the European Union, and the prospect of Ukraine's integration with the West. The general tone was euphoria over the prospect of breaking Ukraine's ties with Russia in favor of the West.

However, Putin adviser Sergei Glazyev was also present, warning that the projected Trade Agreement would have a negative impact on the Ukrainian economy. Glazyev noted that Ukraine was running an enormous foreign accounts deficit, funded with foreign borrowing, and that the substantial increase in Western imports resulting from the DCFTA could only swell this deficit. Ukraine "will either default on its debts or require a sizable bailout", he observed. The *Forbes* reporter concluded that "the Russian position is far closer to the truth than the happy talk coming from Brussels and Kiev."

Glazyev also warned of the internal political consequences

of Western integration. The Russian-speaking population of the Donbass (Donetsk River basin) region in Eastern Ukraine, the industrial heartland of the country, owed its ongoing prosperity to trade with Russia. Since this trade would be threatened by DCFTA terms, the Donbas population might move to secede, rather than cutting its particularly close ties with Russia.

American interventionists knew full well that their plans to integrate Ukraine into the West would cause trouble, but trouble was evidently exactly what they wanted – trouble for Vladimir Putin. Carl Gershman, whose role as president of the NED is ostensibly to "promote democracy" around the world, rejoiced that absorbing Ukraine into the Western camp would be a blow to Russia's elected President. In a September 26, 2013 Op-ed piece in the *Washington Post*, Gershman wrote that "Ukraine's choice to join Europe will accelerate the demise of the ideology of Russian imperialism that Putin represents. ... Putin may find himself on the losing end not just in the near abroad, but within Russia itself," implying that the loss of Ukraine would undermine Putin's domestic standing and political popularity.

Yanukovych's prime minister Mycola Azarov described Ukraine as a "battering ram" to be used against Russia. The Brzezinski doctrine holds that Russia cannot be a significant empire without Ukraine. Detaching it from Russian influence has been a long-term goal; it could then be brought into NATO, in order to gain control of Russia's Black Sea naval base in Sebastopol, Crimea. Traditional hostility to Russia in Western Ukraine had been a political asset used by U.S. agencies since the Cold War.

Understanding Ukraine

Ukraine, a term meaning borderland, is a country without clearly fixed historical border, stretched too far to the East and too far to the West.

It was extended too far East, incorporating territory that had been Russian, apparently in order to distinguish the USSR from the Tsarist empire and demonstrate that the Soviet Union was really a union among equal socialist republics. As long as the whole Soviet Union was under Communist leadership, these borders didn't matter too much.

Ukraine was extended too far West at the end of World War II. The victorious Soviet Union extended Ukraine's border to include the western regions, dominated by the city which has been variously named Lviv, Lwow, Lemberg or Lvov, depending on whether it belonged to Lithuania, Poland, the Habsburg Empire or the USSR. The region was a hotbed of anti-Russian sentiment, markedly expressed in the religious rivalry between the Uniate Church, which recognizes the authority of the Vatican, and the Eastern Orthodox Church, which does not. No doubt conceived as a defensive move to neutralize hostile elements, this extension created a fundamentally divided nation that constitutes such perfect troubled waters for hostile fishing today.

Ukraine "is a cleft country with two distinct cultures. The civilizational fault line between the West and Orthodoxy runs through its heart and has done so for centuries." This deep cultural divide between Eastern and Western Ukraine can hardly have been a secret to U.S. policy-makers. It was spelled out in those terms by top foreign policy advisor Samuel P. Huntington in *The Clash of Civilizations and the Remaking of World Order*, his 1996 "landmark" book, considered absolute required reading in the Washington policy establishment. Ukraine's east-west split was "dramatically evident in the July 1994 presidential elections", Huntington wrote. At that time, Ukraine had been independent of the Soviet Union for only two and a half years. Leonid Kravchuk, a self-styled Ukrainian nationalist, carried the thirteen provinces of Western Ukraine with majorities ranging up to over 90 percent. His opponent Leonid Kuchma carried the thirteen Eastern provinces with similarly lopsided majorities. Kuchma won by a deceptively-balanced margin of an overall 52 percent of a drastically divided country. This has been the situation of Ukraine ever since.

Particularly significant is what Huntington wrote about Crimea. In May 1992, only months after Ukraine's independence from the Soviet Union, the Crimean parliament "voted to declare independence from Ukraine and then, under Ukrainian pressure, rescinded that vote." Meanwhile, the Russian parliament voted to cancel the 1954 cession of Crimea from Russia to Ukraine, ordered by Khrushchev without consulting the people of Crimea.

In short, the question of Crimea leaving Ukraine and returning to Russia had come up repeatedly ever since Ukraine gained its independence. That Crimea would go ahead with its long-contemplated plan to leave Ukraine and return to Russia once an anti-Russian putsch seized power in Kiev could not have been a surprise to anyone with even a rudimentary knowledge of the region.

Huntington went on to make some interesting predictions. He believed that "violence between Ukrainians and Russians is unlikely" since these are two Slavic, primarily Orthodox peoples who have had close relationships for centuries and between whom intermarriage is common. He was wrong about that. However, Huntington thought it "somewhat more likely" that Ukraine could "split along its fault line into two separate entities, the eastern of which would merge with Russia". He evidently imagined this happening peacefully.

In the light of these well-known facts, it is preposterous to claim that Crimea's 2014 referendum on returning to Russia was the first step in a master plan by Vladimir Putin to invade Russia's Western neighbors, Poland and the Baltic States. Yet this is the wild tale that NATO has been telling, and it claims that its military build-up in those countries is to "defend" them from Russian "aggression". All those within the Western power structure who repeat this tale are either bald-faced liars or too ignorant to qualify for their present positions.

As soon as Ukraine gained independence with the 1991 dissolution of the USSR, the East-West division of the country showed up in electoral results. Presidential elections inevitably became contests between the candidate of the East and the candidate of the West. In late 2004, the results of the Presidential election between Viktor Yushchenko, whose votes were concentrated in the West, and Viktor Yanukovych, whose votes were concentrated in the East, was so close that a second vote was held. When Yanukovych was declared winner, accusations of electoral fraud led to demonstrations calling for a third vote, which was won by Yushchenko. The United States invested heavily in these demonstrations, known as the "Orange Revolution" because of the color of equipment furnished by American agencies. The presidency of Yushchenko was disappointing, marked by conflict with his political ally, Yulia Tymoshenko, a corrupt businesswoman famous for her folkloric artificial blond braid, later convicted and jailed for embezzlement and abuse of power. Yushchenko's popularity plummeted while he was in office, and in 2010 his rival Yanukovych was elected President by a comfortable majority.

What is significant is that U.S. intervention in the "Orange Revolution" was never on behalf of democracy against dictatorship. Whoever was elected, Ukraine was essentially run by "oligarchs", the hugely rich businessmen who took over main chunks of the country's economy when state ownership collapsed. The U.S. intervention was always, and remains today, on behalf of the West end of the country against the East end. Precisely because Ukraine is fundamentally so divided, the Ukrainian nationalists in the West insist vehemently on forcing an artificial unification that demonizes and excludes the Russian part of the population. Ukrainian nationalists glorify the Ukrainian language and promote a mythical anti-Russian version of history that feeds antagonism.

In the last few years, Ukrainian nationalists have vigorously constructed a new myth on the basis of the tragic famine that struck the rural population in the Soviet Union in 1932-33 as a result of forced requisitions of crops to feed rapid industrialization. Historians consider that about two million Ukrainians perished in this brutal campaign directed against successful small farmers (*kulaks*), which also affected Russian agricultural regions. In recent years Ukrainian nationalists have asserted that the deaths were part of a deliberate plan to exterminate the Ukrainian nation, commemorated as the "Holomodor". In open competition with the Holocaust, Ukrainian nationalists claim that up to ten million victims were deliberately starved in the Holomodor, which would make Ukraine the victim of "the greatest genocide in history". The large Ukrainian diaspora in Canada numbers about 1.2 million, making it the largest Ukrainian population outside Ukraine and Russia, and is particularly zealous in commemorating this "genocide". It is able to put political pressure on the government in Ottawa to join the anti-Putin campaign (although Putin obviously had nothing to do with the famine).

A man of modest origins whose votes mostly came from the predominantly Russian industrial East, Yanukovych was branded a

Moscow puppet in the West. In reality, the deal with the European Union confronted Ukraine with a genuine dilemma. Yanukovych seemed to want both the trade deal with the European Union and the existing trade deals with Russia, but this would require negotiating trade terms and standards with Russia, which the Europeans refused to do. Russia could not allow the Europeans to export their goods and services duty-free into Russia "by the back gate" (as Putin later put it) via Ukraine. Yanukovych was also obliged to take into account the worries of his Eastern constituents, especially since the Party of Regions, his main political support, rejected a half dozen pieces of legislation demanded by the E.U., including permission for Yulia Tymoshenko to leave prison and move to Germany. Moreover, the IMF was demanding austerity measures so unpopular that Yanukovych would surely lose the scheduled 2015 elections if he complied.

In late November 2013, Prime Minister Mycola Azarov concluded that the country needed more time to deal with the conflicting economic pressures. President Yanukovych abruptly suspended the DCFTA, to the great disappointment of Ukrainians who aspired to be "part of Europe". The protests in Kiev's Independence Square, labeled "Euro-Maidan", grew throughout the winter, feeding on a range of grievances in a country where bad government is chronic. U.S. officials openly encouraged the movement's anti-Yanukovych and anti-Russian potential. U.S. Assistant Secretary of State for European and Eurasian Affairs Victoria Nuland, IRI sugar-daddy Senator John McCain and French agitator Bernard-Henri Lévy all visited the Maidan scene to exhort the Ukrainians to defy Vladimir Putin.

As stated earlier, Victoria Nuland had been a close member of Hillary's team at the State Department. "Toria Nuland, my intrepid spokeswoman", as Hillary called her, wrote the "talking points" email memo which had blamed the Benghazi attack that killed U. S. Ambassador Chris Stevens on a mob angered by an American-made movie insulting the Prophet Mohammed. Ambassador to the United Nations Susan Rice took the heat for expressing this rather evasive explanation on television.

Victoria Nuland's promotion to take charge of Washington's aggressive Ukraine operation is proof of the durable role of the neoconservatives in U.S. foreign policy. From July 2003 to May 2005, "Toria" had served as deputy national security advisor to Vice President Dick Cheney. In his memoir, *Duty*, former Defense Secretary Robert Gates described Cheney's view of Russia, which could well be that of Nuland, then and now: "When the Soviet Union was collapsing in late 1991, Dick wanted to see the dismantlement not only of the Soviet Union and the Russian empire but of Russia itself, so it could never again be a threat to the rest of the world."

Victoria Nuland is the wife of Robert Kagan, who is probably the most active and influential neoconservative today. Kagan was a founder both of PNAC and of its current successor, the Foreign Policy Initiative. He began his mischief in the State Department Policy Planning staff in the mid-1980s, when he was, according to the *New York Times,* "deeply involved in the Reagan Administration's policy on the rebels in Nicaragua". In case there is any doubt about the bipartisan nature of America's neoconservative foreign policy, Kagan also served as foreign policy advisor to John McCain when McCain ran as the Republican candidate for President in 2008, before being taken onto the State Department Foreign Affairs Policy Board by Hillary Clinton.

Robert Kagan has made the now-famous comparison: "Americans are from Mars and Europeans are from Venus", alluding to the fact that Europeans, after suffering through devastating recent wars on their own territory, have lost enthusiasm for the martial exercise, in contrast to Americans, who are used to waging wars on other people's territory.

Her husband's assessment of trans-Atlantic relations seems to be reflected in the three words that brought Victoria Nuland to public attention: "Fuck the E.U." The context was her February 6, 2014 telephone call to the U.S. ambassador to Ukraine, Geoffrey Pyatt, during a discussion of who should be put in power in Kiev. German Chancellor Angela Merkel's political party had been promoting former boxer Vitaly Klitschko as its candidate. Nuland's remark meant that the United States, not Germany or the E.U., was to choose the next leader, who was not to be Klitschko but the man she called "Yats", Arseniy Yatsenyuk. Indeed, Yats was soon to get the job of Prime Minister. With a sinister lack of charisma, the American-trained Yats was clearly chosen for his devotion to IMF austerity policies, his desire to join NATO, and an almost pathological hatred of Russia, reflected in his astonishing statement on January 7, 2015, that: "All of us still clearly remember the Soviet invasion of Ukraine and Germany". Born in 1974, Yats obviously does not remember any such thing, but apparently belongs to a school of Ukrainian nationalists whose hatred of Russians leads them to overlook the massive invasion of the Soviet Union by the Wehrmacht in June of 1941, which devastated Ukraine, and to blame the war on those who fought back and finally won: the Red Army.

A significant detail of the Nuland-Pyatt conversation was her mention of the fact that she had just spoken to Ban-Ki Moon's Under Secretary General for Political Affairs, Jeffrey Feltman, who was taking steps to bring the United Nations into the game, obviously on the side of the United States. She thought this would "help glue this thing and to have the U.N. help glue it and, you know, fuck the E.U." Feltman had recently been Nuland's colleague in Hillary Clinton's State Department team. As Assistant Secretary of State for Near Eastern Affairs, he had worked with Hillary, twisting appropriate arms to put together a "coalition of the willing" Arabs to smash Libya's Gaddafi. On July 2, 2012, Jeffrey Feltman went on to become the U.N. Secretary General's main political adviser, after a thirty-year career in the United States Foreign Service. This meant that a United States official was henceforth in charge of analyzing crises, advising Ban-Ki Moon and briefing the U.N. Security Council on Syria, Israel and Palestine, and, of course, Ukraine. So everything was put in place to steer international reaction to events in Ukraine and isolate Russia.

Fabricating the Russian Enemy

For an outsider, it is impossible to say precisely when, how and by whom the decision was made to use the Ukrainian battering ram to destabilize Putin and Russia. Back from her multiple visits to Kiev, Victoria Nuland told an international business conference sponsored by the U.S.-Ukraine Foundation in Washington on December 13, 2013, that since the dissolution of the Soviet Union, the United States had invested over five billion dollars to ensure Ukraine "the future it deserves". That meant pulling it into the Western camp. The hefty sum no doubt included the expenses of the "Orange Revolution," as well as other less conspicuous operations. The relentless pursuit of the 2014 regime change operation, the unanimity of the NATO-land chorus (notably in diffusing a wildly biased version of events), makes it clear that some sort of a game plan was being pursued. The whole operation was prepared for public opinion by months of anti-Putin propaganda centered on sexy topics such as Pussy Riot and gay rights.

The American approach all along was to ignore the economic problems posed by the DCFTA, which might be the object of negotiations and compromise, and instead to interpret the conflict as a clash between the "good" West and the "bad" Russian leader, Vladimir Putin. By February 2014, the pro-European demonstrations in Kiev, cheered on with snacks handed out to the protestors by Victoria Nuland, support from John McCain and oratory from Bernard-Henri Lévy, were joined by the militant fascistic and even outright neo-Nazi groups that flourish in Western Ukraine to demand regime change.

Throughout the winter, the Maidan protests had been increasingly militarized by far right groups. Andriy Parubiy of the Svoboda party, disciples of the fascist hero Stepan Bandera, became the "commander" of Maidan, responsible for security. Violence grew and on February 18, rightists attacked and set fire to the office of the Party of Regions, causing two deaths.

On February 20, all hell broke loose in central Kiev, bringing the crisis to a head. The morning began with shots fired between advancing "protesters" and members of the Interior Ministry security unit, Berkut. Finding themselves the target of hidden snipers, with three dead and several wounded, the Berkut police withdrew. Ordered by the Maidan command to continue advancing down a broad street just off Maidan square, protesters carrying shields and sticks were shot one after the other by unidentified snipers firing from surrounding buildings, mainly the Hotel Ukraina, used as a headquarters by the Maidan protest movement itself. According to conflicting claims, between fifty and a hundred protesters were killed, and many more wounded, in this weird massacre. Opposition leaders hastened to accuse President Yanukovych of having ordered his security forces to fire on the protesters. This accusation was the basis for his overthrow within hours.

The next day, in the resulting atmosphere of hysteria, the foreign ministers of three E.U. countries, Germany, France and Poland, with Russian agreement, sponsored a deal with opposition leaders whereby Yanukovych, destabilized by the violence, agreed to step down for early elections in 2014, following constitutional changes.

But the next day, February 22, Yanukovych fled for his life, no doubt for good reason. As he left, he ordered police to withdraw, which enabled the fascist militia, Right Sector and Svoboda, to take control of key buildings. Many members of the pro-government parties either disappeared or were "persuaded" to join the opposition. Far right nationalist groups violently attacked members of the Communist Party. Those who remained in the parliament divested Yanukovych of the presidency and proclaimed a transitional government, headed by Washington's choice for Prime Minister, Arseniy Yatsenyuk. From then on, Washington's protégés were in charge of organizing "free and fair" elections that the West was bound to win, given that the heavily populated Donbass region in the East went into open revolt when the government they had helped to elect was overthrown.

This was a perfectly executed regime change. The crowds of protesters, whose precise demands were never clarified and so could not be met, provided the "democratic" excuse for overthrowing an elected government, while the mysterious snipers provided the veil of confusion needed to enable an illegal, unconstitutional coup d'état to take place.

The February 20 sniper attack that set the stage for overthrowing Yanukovych has subsequently been shown to have been a clear "false flag" operation, organized by far right militias precisely in order to accuse the hapless Yanukovych of having ordered the killings. The truth first emerged a few days after the attack, in a leaked telephone conversation between Estonian Foreign Minister Urmas Paet and EU foreign policy chief Catherine Ashton. Paet told Ashton that he had learned from reliable sources in Kiev that the snipers had not been sent by Yanukovych's government but by groups active in the Maidan protests. On April 10, this was confirmed by the German documentary program "Monitor", which found that the snipers did not fire from government buildings, as the putschists alleged, but from the Hotel Ukraina, which was fully under the control of the Svoboda fascist party and the Right Sector militia. The first detailed academic study of the incident, by Ivan Katchanovski of the University of Ottawa, concluded that certain elements of the Maidan opposition, notably Dmytro Yarosh's the Right Sector militia, organized the massacre in order to seize power.[36]

False flag operations are especially successful when the public they are meant to impress refuse to believe that such operations even exist. Although "false flag" operations have been a standard facet of warfare throughout the ages, many people seem loath to believe that anybody could be so wicked as to target their own people. However, especially when outside powers act as mediators, a false flag operation can break a deadlock by giving one's own side the moral advantage of "victim" status. False flags seem to have been used more than once by Ukrainian nationalists.

Many eye-witnesses corroborated Katchanovski's conclusions, notably Ina Kirsch, a German Social Democrat who from 2011 to 2014 was the director of the European Center for a Modern Ukraine, set up to smooth rapprochement between Ukraine and the E.U. In a February 19, 2015 interview with the Austrian newspaper *Wiener Zeitung* [37], Ina Kirsch implied that the Maidan commander, Andriy Parubiy, was involved in organizing the massacre. Ms Kirsch claimed that U.S. billionaire George Soros who "supported Maidan, paid people there – in two weeks on Maidan they earned more than in four work weeks in West Ukraine." Ms Kirsch said she knew of people who were paid to take part in both pro- and anti-Maidan demonstrations. "That's nothing unusual in Ukraine", she observed. Ukrainian oligarchs pay militia to protect their property and harass their competitors, she noted.

Russian-speaking Eastern Ukraine had remained calm during the Maidan uproar. But the region rebelled at the unconstitutional change of government in Kiev that brought to power individuals and groups whose hatred of Russians is pathological. Speakers at rallies or on television in Western Ukraine could be heard calling for war to "kill all Russians", or to drive the Russians out of Eastern Ukraine and take its resources, or to ban the Russian language. The latter measure was actually undertaken by the new government, but was rapidly rescinded under pressure from their E.U. sponsors.

A modern art gallery in Kiev mounted a bizarre exhibit displaying two drunk and degenerate "Russians" (played by actors) in a cage as in a zoo, hung with signs such as "keep away", and "do not feed".

The Eastern Ukraine rebels demanded constitutional changes that provided for local self-government; they were instantly stigmatized as "terrorists" by the new authorities in Kiev. This was to lead to civil war.

The historic Russian-speaking, multicultural Black Sea port city of Odessa was a center of federalist demands. In the spring, activists set up tents in a square opposite the trade union building to collect signatures for a referendum calling for a constitution that would allow regions to elect their own governments. On May 2, Right Sector militia violently attacked the federalists, who fled into the building which was then set on fire by their assailants. Some perished in the flames; others, who managed to jump out of windows, were beaten to death by nationalist militants. There were forty-eight confirmed dead, yet Kiev has tended to blame the victims. The Odessa massacre was played down by Western media. It aroused only mild concern among those Western human rights organizations that had previously gone all-out in their campaign to defend Pussy Riot.

On May 25, the American-backed oligarch Petro Poroshenko, with a fortune made in chocolate and funeral parlors, was elected President. With Eastern Ukraine under siege, the victory of the anti-Russian West was assured. The American sponsors were happy: the people (at least those who mattered) had voted, so the new Ukraine was "democratic". Many observers think Poroshenko a transitional figure who has more fanatical successors waiting in the wings.

Crimea Goes Home

The February coup turned the government in Kiev over to right-wing Ukrainian nationalists eager to take Ukraine into NATO. This posed an immediate strategic threat to Russia, whose warm-water fleet was based in the Crimean port of Sebastopol. When Khrushchev arbitrarily gave Crimea to Ukraine in 1954, this purely administrative decision didn't seem to matter, since Russia and Ukraine were both part of the Soviet Union. When they split,

Ukraine leased the Sebastopol port to Russia, but this would become a vulnerable position should Ukraine join NATO. The U.S. Navy was already patrolling the Black Sea and it is notorious for its appetite for military bases in foreign lands. By supporting the takeover of Ukraine by virulent anti-Russians, the United States and European leaders were consciously provoking Russia to react defensively, one way or another. This was not a mere matter of a "sphere of influence" in Russia's "near abroad", but a matter of life and death for the Russian Navy as well as a grave national security threat right on Russia's border.

They could not be sure exactly how President Putin would react, but he was certain to respond somehow. A trap was thereby set for Putin: he was damned if he did and damned if he didn't. He could underreact, betraying Russia's basic national interests by allowing NATO to advance its hostile forces to an ideal position for attack. This would destroy his prestige at home and perhaps lead to his early downfall. Or he could overreact, sending Russian forces to invade Ukraine. The West was ready for this and would scream out that Putin was "the new Hitler", poised to overrun poor, helpless Europe, which could only be saved (again) by the intervention of generous Americans.

In reality, the Russian defensive move was a very reasonable middle course. But the West screamed as loudly as if Russia had treated Ukraine in the way the United States had, not so long ago, treated Panama or the tiny island of Grenada – by armed invasion.

Thanks to the fact that the overwhelming majority of Crimeans had always considered themselves Russian and felt threatened by the anti-Russian putsch in Kiev, a peaceful and democratic solution was rapidly found. The Crimean Parliament called for a referendum to leave Ukraine and return to Russia. This was a project that had been in the air ever since the Soviet Union disintegrated, severing Crimea from Russia. However, the Western powers refused to recognize the referendum, but volunteer international observers found the proceedings free and fair. On March 16, with 82% turnout, 96% of Crimeans voted to return to Russia.

As part of its Sebastopol lease, Russia already had troops stationed in Crimea. As a protective measure, Russia sent in reinforcements, without, however, exceeding the legal level of

25,000 troops. Not a shot was fired, nor was the vote marred by any violence.

Nevertheless, the West denounced this democratic process as a "Russian invasion". U.S. Secretary of State John Kerry led the chorus of self-righteous indignation, accusing Russia of the sort of thing his own government is in the habit of doing: "You just don't invade another country on phony pretexts in order to assert your interests. This is an act of aggression that is completely trumped up in terms of its pretext", Kerry pontificated. "It's really 19th century behavior in the 21st century". Instead of laughing at this hypocrisy, U.S. media, politicians and punditry zealously took up the theme of Putin's unacceptable expansionist aggression. The Europeans followed with an obedient echo.

To justify Crimea's secession from Ukraine, Russia cited the July 2010 ruling by the International Court of Justice that "general international law contains no applicable prohibition of declarations of independence". This was ironic, considering that the ruling was in response to a complaint by Serbia, which hoped for a ruling against Kosovo's unilateral declaration, but had lost. Speaking in Brussels on March 26, President Obama took it upon himself to refute the Russian argument by declaring that: "Kosovo only left Serbia after a referendum was organized, not outside the boundaries of international law, but in careful cooperation with the United Nations and with Kosovo's neighbors. None of that even came close to happening in Crimea." In reality, none of what he mentioned even came close to happening in Kosovo. The breakaway Serbian province declared independence with no referendum and no cooperation with anybody else – except probably, confidentially, with Washington. It owed its independence to NATO bombing and occupation, whereas Crimea's change of status was peaceful.

Crimea's decision to secede from Ukraine apparently did violate the Ukrainian constitution – yet the constitution itself had just been violated by the putsch in Kiev, which created an entirely new situation. But there is no legal basis for the accusation that the Crimean referendum violated *international* law.

From the sidelines, Hillary Clinton had already resorted to the indispensable Hitler analogy. "Now if this sounds familiar, it's what Hitler did back in the thirties", she claimed, likening the Russian leader's concern for ethnic Russians in Ukraine to Hitler's bellicose claims on Germany's eastern neighbors. This was only the start of a crescendo of vituperation using the Hitler analogy that was soon to rival even what was said about the Nazi Führer himself in his lifetime.

President Putin, in his March 18 speech to the Russian Duma justifying the Crimean referendum, came up with another analogy. Putin hoped Germans would recall that Moscow had fully endorsed the 1990 reunification of East and West Germany, and would see Crimea's choice as a comparable reunification. He insisted that things would stop there: "We do not want to divide Ukraine; we do not need that." While politically obliged to support the Russophone rebels in Donetsk and Luhansk, Putin's constant position has been to urge both sides to hold Ukraine together by agreeing to a federal system which provides for various measures of local government. When neither side agrees to this, Putin gets the blame.

As a matter of fact, so many people in Germany do indeed understand the Russian point of view that "*Putinversteher*" ("Putin-understander") has become a common semi-ironic term in political arguments. Many Germans, including leading businessmen, consider the anti-Russian policy being imposed on Europe by the United States to be unrealistic, unjustified and contrary to German interests. But to the evident surprise and disappointment of Russian leaders, the German political class and media have almost unanimously adopted the hostile NATO line set by Washington. Foreign Minister Sergei Lavrov has admitted that Russia overestimated Europe's independence from the United States.

The New Iron Curtain

In 1945, the Soviet Union liberated Eastern Europe. It stayed there too long, but finally left voluntarily nearly fifty years later. The United States liberated Western Europe and never left. At some point, a permanent "liberation" needs to be renamed as a conquest.

To justify the endless presence of U.S. military bases, not to mention NSA spying and the control of Europe's defense forces by NATO, it is a good idea for Washington to keep reminding Europeans that they need to be protected.

At the same time, the European Union is in growing need of an emotional element to enforce its internal cohesion. Common enemies might do the trick: Islamic terrorists on one side, the Russian bear on the other.

Ukraine is not the only entity that has been overextended. So has the European Union. With 28 members of diverse language, culture, history and mentality, the E.U. is unable to agree on any foreign policy other than the one imposed upon it by Washington. Meanwhile, the great unifier, the Euro, and the austerity policies mandated by Brussels have caused economic hardship and dissension. The May 25, 2014 European Parliament elections revealed a large measure of disaffection with the European Union among voters. The eastward extension of the Union to former Soviet satellites has totally broken whatever deep consensus might have been possible among the countries of the original Economic Community: France, Germany, Italy and the Benelux states. Poland and the Baltic States see E.U. membership as useful, but their hearts are in America – where many of their most influential leaders have been educated and trained.

Washington is able to exploit the anti-communist, anti-Russian and even pro-Nazi nostalgia of northeastern Europe to raise the old cry of "the Russians are coming!" in order to obstruct the growing economic partnership between Russia and the old E.U., most importantly Germany. Encouraged by the United States and NATO, this endemic hostility rooted in the new northeastern edge of the E.U. provides the psychological impetus for the new "iron curtain" designed to achieve the aim spelled out in 1997 by Zbigniew Brzezinski in *The Grand Chessboard*: keeping the Eurasian continent divided in order to perpetuate U.S. world hegemony. The old Cold War served that purpose, cementing U.S. military presence and political influence in Western Europe. A new Cold War can prevent U.S. influence from being diluted by good relations between Western Europe and Russia.

The United States has forced its European allies to impose economic sanctions on Russia that are costly for both Russia and the European allies themselves. European farmers, already in difficulty, were the first to be punished by counter-measures taken by Russia banning E.U. agricultural products. French and German manufacturers are losing profitable markets. The first Iron Curtain was accompanied by an economic reward for Western Europe in the form of Marshall Plan investments. This time, Western Europe shares the punishment, with no reward.

For months, financier George Soros has argued that the European Union can save itself by saving Ukraine. [38] Soros criticizes Europeans for failing to recognize that "the Russian attack on Ukraine is indirectly an attack on the European Union and its principles of governance". Thus the European Union itself is "indirectly at war", which makes a policy of fiscal austerity "inappropriate". Instead: "All available resources ought to be put to work in the war effort even if that involves running up budget deficits".

By this proposal, Soros is attempting to play, for the European Union, the same role Paul Nitze played for the United States in 1950: initiating a Keynesian "Cold War" to boost the economy on the pretext of responding to the "Russian threat".

"Sanctions against Russia are necessary but they are a necessary evil", inasmuch as they have a "depressive effect not only on Russia but also on the European economies, including Germany." On the contrary, he argued, "assisting Ukraine in defending itself against Russian aggression would have a stimulative effect not only on Ukraine but also on Europe." The parallel with Nitze's NSC-68 policy paper is remarkable. Just as Nitze's Soviet scare justified dropping Rooseveltian New Deal Keynesianism, which favored social projects such as rural electrification over military spending, Soros' proposal would justify the ongoing reduction of European social spending by shifting deficit spending to pay for a Ukrainian war against Russia.

Just as Nitze exaggerated the Soviet military threat to Western Europe, Soros goes overboard when he asserts that: "it is unrealistic to expect that Putin will stop pushing beyond Ukraine when the division of Europe and its domination by Russia is in sight. Not only the survival of the new Ukraine but the future of NATO and the European Union itself is at risk..."

There is method in such madness, since an official war scare gives big investors something to invest in, with guaranteed profits.

The Fog of War

The majority Russian-speaking population in Southeastern Ukraine was as disturbed by the regime change in Kiev as the Crimeans, but for them there was no easy solution. Or rather, there could have been an easy solution, if the new authorities in Kiev had been willing. Despite its sharp regional differences, Ukraine is governed in a highly centralized way, with local governors named in Kiev. The Southeast, in particular the Donbass industrial center, had one clear demand: a constitutional change which would allow regions to elect their own governments. From the start, this demand for federalism was described by Western media as "pro-Russian separatism", while Kiev dismissed the federalists as "terrorists". In mid-April, Kiev sent armed forces to repress the Donbass; this violence effectively made the federalists much more separatist. Hundreds of thousands of citizens of Donbass, especially women and children, fled to Russia – a form of "ethnic cleansing" which may have been one of the objectives of the Western assault.

Especially in Germany, the *Putinversteher* were hoping that behind the scenes, Angela Merkel and Vladimir Putin were working out a peaceful settlement to the crisis. There was even hope that the newly-elected President Poroshenko would be amenable to a peaceful solution and would agree to a federal system similar to that which exists in other countries (Germany itself is an example).

Then, on July 17, Malaysian Airlines flight 17 (MH17) from Amsterdam to Kuala Lumpur crashed in southeastern Ukraine near Donetsk, killing all 298 passengers and crew. It was assumed that the aircraft had been shot down by a Russian-made radar-guided "Buk" surface-to-air missile. Kiev immediately accused the separatist rebels. It was reported, and then denied, that the rebels had stolen a Buk system from the Ukrainian Army. Later, evidence emerged that the airliner had been approached by one or more fighter jets and holes in the cabin suggested that one of them might have shot it down. Although the culprit remained a mystery, this event succeeded in destroying all prospects of peace negotiations. U.S. opposition to negotiations now enjoyed moral support, fueled by indignation against the Russians who had allegedly shot down a passenger airliner in cold blood.

To err is human, and no environment is more favorable to terrible mistakes than war. War is also the perfect environment for propaganda and false accusations. Who, if anybody, could have a motive to shoot down a passenger jet over Eastern Ukraine?

That question was scarcely asked by U.S. leaders who knew automatically where to place the blame.

That very evening, Hillary Clinton implied that Russia was to blame. In an hour-long interview on the "Charlie Rose Show," she went so far as to give marching orders to Europeans as to how they must make Russia "pay the price".

"If there is evidence linking Russia to this, that should inspire the Europeans to do much more on three counts.

"One, toughen their own sanctions. Make it very clear there has to be a price to pay.

"Number two, [...] find alternatives to Gazprom.

"And thirdly, do more in concert with us to support the Ukrainians."

With no hesitation, HRC seized on a tragedy (there was no conclusive evidence yet as to the perpetrator) as a sort of Gulf of Tonkin incident to justify European reprisals against Russia. "There should be outrage in European capitals" over Russian aggression, she added, without missing the standard cliché that "the only language [Putin] understands" is toughness. HRC declared that Putin is "pushing the envelope as far as he thinks he can", implying that the Russian President deliberately shot down an airliner in order to test Western resolve.

By an odd coincidence, Putin himself was flying across that part of Ukraine at about the same time that MH17 was shot down. He was returning to Moscow from Brazil, where his efforts on behalf of equality among nations were supported by fellow BRICS leaders Dilma Rousseff, Narendra Modi of India, China's Xi Jinping and Jacob Zuma of South Africa. A wild but neglected hypothesis was that Ukrainian nationalists might have shot down the Malaysian airline by mistake, thinking it was Putin's flight.

The day after the tragedy, Jeffrey Feltman, the American State Department official on loan to the United Nations as Deputy Secretary General for Political Affairs, expressed Ban-Ki Moon's strong condemnation of "this apparently deliberate downing of a civilian aircraft".

If it was "apparently deliberate", there must have been a motive. But what could that be? For example, why would the Eastern rebels deliberately shoot down a civilian airliner? It is easier to imagine a provocative motive on the part of the anti-Russian Ukrainian nationalists, yet another false flag operation of monstrous proportions, but that too must remain mere speculation.

Fatal accidents happen in wars.

An example: on July 3, 1988, the USS Vincennes, a guided missile cruiser patrolling the Persian Gulf during the war between Iran and Iraq, shot down an Iranian civilian airliner on a regularly scheduled flight from Teheran to Dubai, killing all 290 people aboard, including 66 children. Although ostensibly neutral, the United States was then supporting Iraq. The guided missile shot down Iran Air flight 655 in Iranian airspace, over Iran's territorial waters.

The comparison with Malaysian Airlines Flight 17 is instructive. There was no international outcry demanding that the United States "pay the price" for this "apparently deliberate downing of a civilian aircraft". The United States never apologized, and George H.W. Bush, Vice President at the time, even boasted at a presidential campaign rally a month later that he would "never apologize for the United States. I don't care what the facts are... I'm not an apologize-for-America kind of guy." Although there was never any doubt about their responsibility, the captain and crew of the Vincennes were all awarded medals for their service.

Exceptionalism means: some can get away with murder; others can't even get away with innocence.

Ten days after the Malaysian airline disaster, Hillary returned to the charge on CNN: "I think if there were any doubt it should be gone by now, that Vladimir Putin, certainly indirectly – through his support of the insurgents in eastern Ukraine and the supply of advanced weapons and, frankly, the presence of Russian Special Forces and intelligence agents – bears responsibility for what happened."

"We have to up the sanctions that are required. The United States has continued to move forward on that, Europe has been reluctant," she insisted. "They need to understand they must stand up to Vladimir Putin." Nagging the Europeans to "do more" was the main point.

The chorus of unsubstantiated accusations distracted from the indiscriminate military attacks on Eastern Ukraine. Far more people were killed in those ongoing attacks than in the tragically doomed airliner, but it is naturally much easier for anyone in the West to identify with an innocent Dutch airline passenger than with a Russian-speaking Ukrainian grandmother hiding in her cellar.

Cui bono? is a question that does not lead to all the answers in a world full of mistakes and incompetence. We are all free to imagine more or less probable hypotheses, false flags included, and we might even guess correctly. However, real knowledge depends on expert forensic investigation. Unfortunately, there is reason to believe that after months of unsubstantiated accusations, conflicting evidence and above all, lengthy delays, no final explanation will ever be totally convincing.

From the start, Western reaction to the disaster was so biased that doubts must persist about whether the truth will ever be known, especially since Western governments close to the United States took control of the official inquiry early on.

Although the airliner was Malaysian, Malaysia was somehow excluded from the initial inquiry. On grounds that the flight had taken off from Amsterdam and that the greatest number of victims were Dutch, the Netherlands took charge at the start of the investigation, along with Ukraine, Belgium and Australia – two NATO Member States, plus two fiercely anti-Russian governments.

On August 8, 2014, those four governments reportedly signed a secret agreement stipulating that results would not be published unless all four countries were in agreement. "This gave one of the prime suspects in the atrocity, Ukraine, an effective veto over any investigation results that attributed blame to them. This is an astonishing situation and probably without precedent in modern air crash investigations," observed Australian lawyer James O'Neill, who has attempted in vain to procure a copy of the agreement.[39]

It is interesting that Malaysia's semi-official English language newspaper, the *New Straits Times*, credits the theory that the airliner was shot down by a Kiev government jet fighter. Does this relate to the fact that Malaysia was only belatedly invited to take part in the Joint Inquiry, in December 2014?

It is odd indeed that not only was the Russian denial of involvement ignored by the West, but also the Russian military's disclosure to the press of its own radar and satellite data which showed that MH17 had been diverted from its scheduled route and was being shadowed by two fighter jets as it flew over the war zone. The Russians stated that an American spy satellite was directly over the scene at the time and asked the Americans to share their data – in vain. Above all, the Russian request to take part in a genuinely impartial international investigation was ignored. It is also odd that the content of the downed aircraft's black boxes was kept secret by Western governments, and that Western spokesmen, who gradually dropped the whole subject after the black boxes were found, began to issue statements suggesting that unfortunately, the truth may never be known. However, the anti-Russian accusations and the punishing sanctions persist.

On September 5, the prominent Russia expert Stephen Cohen observed that the British and Dutch had had plenty of time to interpret the information in the black boxes, but that there "seems to be have been an agreement among the major powers not to tell us who did it".

For these reasons, the final results of the investigation are almost certain to encounter skepticism, whatever its conclusions. In any case, the U.S. treatment of the MH17 tragedy is a lesson in itself. Once Washington has focused on an "enemy", any incident may be seized upon as a pretext for denunciation, sanctions, or war. Whatever the truth of the catastrophe, neither Hillary Clinton nor the rest of the anti-Putin chorus *knew* that truth, nor could they possibly have known it, when they hastened to accuse Russian President Putin. Yet they not only rushed to claim to know who was guilty, they also used these unproved assumptions to demand punishment and to force their "allies" to do the same.

This is exactly the sort of premature judgment, Gulf of Tonkin-style, which leads to major wars.

In the Mood For War

The MH17 tragedy was used to create a mood in which no kind word could be uttered about Russia or its President.

Former U.S. ambassador to Ukraine William Taylor told CNN that: "Mr. Putin is clearly responsible for the problems we're seeing in Ukraine and for the shooting down of this airliner". Putin "is a pariah at this point", he said. The pro-Russian rebels "are thugs, murderers, these are people that shot down this aircraft".

U.S. deputy national security adviser Antony Blinken said that: "We expect the European Union to take significant additional steps this week, including in key sectors of the Russian economy". Blinken claimed that sanctions were intended "not to punish Russia but to make clear that it must cease its support for the separatists and stop destabilizing Ukraine".

The situation was actually clear enough. United States and the European Union had excluded the heavily-populated Donbass provinces from the political process by insisting that Ukraine as a whole join the Atlantic alliance against Russia and by supporting a coup in Kiev that brought anti-Russophone nationalists to power. The Donbass revolt was initially democratic: the demand was for self-government within a federal Ukraine. When Kiev refused, called them "terrorists", and responded with armed force, a civil war broke out over control of the Eastern region. This local conflict is drawing in support from outside on both sides: Russia is surely supporting the Donbass fighters, not by "invading" as the West alleges, but with equipment and volunteers, while NATO is supporting Kiev. For example, there are Serb volunteers fighting for Donbass and Croat volunteers on the Kiev/NATO side, in a disturbing echo of the Yugoslav conflict.

The Western propaganda line is to blame this conflict entirely on "Russian aggression", and even to assert that this "aggression" in Donbass is symptomatic of a larger "Russian aggression" which threatens European members of NATO and the European Union itself – a totally preposterous assertion that is echoed without challenge by Western media. Since Russia alone is to blame, the only solution is for Russia to stop its "aggression". As long as Ukraine is destabilized, Putin is to blame and Russia must be punished.

Watching Western media sometimes gives the impression that commentators are competing to win a prize for the most utterly ridiculous attack on Putin. So far, the imaginary prize – let's call it "The Soros Prize" – should go to CNN aviation analyst Jeff Wise. Wise actually wrote a book claiming that Malaysian Airlines flight MH370, which went missing on March 8, 2014 on a flight from Kuala Lumpur to Beijing, was actually whisked off to Kazakhstan by Vladimir Putin...perhaps in a "show of strength". But the contest is still on...

Not so long ago, Libya was destroyed as a functioning society supposedly to protect a rebellion in Benghazi from theoretical government repression. Later, the United States urged the Kiev government to continue using its armed forces to suppress a rebellion in Donbass. Ukrainian President Petro Poroshenko is not being accused of "bombing his own people" – although that is exactly what is happening.

A main purpose of the torrent of abuse leveled at Putin was to bully European leaders into taking sanctions against Russia. The longer the sanctions are maintained, the likelier they are to create a lasting barrier between America's Western European satellites and Russia. Meanwhile, secret negotiations are underway to complete the Trans-Atlantic Free Trade Area (TAFTA), which will cement U.S. domination of Europe, with the consent and complicity of major European corporations primarily interested in access to the U.S. market.

This domination has already been demonstrated by Europe's reluctant acceptance of sanctions against Russia. United States trade with Russia is minimal, and sanctioning Russia costs America virtually nothing. The same is not true for Europe.

It took heavy pressure from President Obama and British Prime Minister David Cameron to persuade French president François Hollande to refuse delivery to Russia of a Mistral helicopter carrier. The Russians had already paid 1.2 billion euros for the ship, and had ordered another. Cancellation of the order not only obliges France to return the payment and pay fines, it also means the loss of hundreds of jobs at the Saint Nazaire shipyard and damage to French industry's reputation for reliability.

Many German industrialists have openly protested against the loss of markets resulting from anti-Russia sanctions. Labor unions, farmers and businessmen complain of these blows to the economy, but the political class pays more attention to Washington than to their own citizens.

Referring to the blocked Mistral delivery, U.S. Vice President Joe Biden told an audience at Harvard: "It is true - they did not want to do that but again it was America's leadership and the President of the United States insisting, oftentimes almost having to embarrass Europe to stand up and take economic hits..."

Oddly enough, European leaders are praised for their "courage" for having given in to U.S. pressure at the expense of their own economies.

Victoria Nuland declared: "Implementing sanctions isn't easy and many countries are paying a steep price. We know that. But history shows that the cost of inaction and disunity in the face of a determined aggressor will be higher."

History shows that "history shows" whatever you want it to show – especially if you are the one rewriting it. Today, it is being rewritten as it happens, in real time. This instant rewriting of contemporary history is full of contradictions: Russia is simultaneously accused of being the equivalent of Hitler's mighty German war machine and of being too insignificant to be worthy of our attention...

According to Senator McCain, Russia is "a gas station posing as a country". He is so proud of that description that he enjoys repeating it.

Russia is a declining nation, Obama told *The Economist.* "Russia doesn't make anything. Immigrants aren't rushing to Moscow in search of opportunity."

In his annual presidential speech to the United Nations, Obama listed Russia as number two of the three main threats to the world, in between the Ebola virus and the "Islamic State" fanatics in Iraq and Syria.

In another speech, Obama attributed to Putin "a vision of the world in which might makes right -- a world in which one nation's borders can be redrawn by another, and civilized people are not allowed to recover the remains of their loved ones because of the truth that might be revealed. America stands for something different. We believe that right makes might -- that bigger nations should not be able to bully smaller ones, and that people should be able to choose their own future."

On January 21, Obama gloated to Congress that: "Last year, as we were doing the hard work of imposing sanctions along with our allies, some suggested that Mr. Putin's aggression was a masterful display of strategy and strength. Well, today, it is America that stands strong and united with our allies, while Russia is isolated, with its economy in tatters."

U.S. leaders emphasize repeatedly that, unlike Russia and old-time colonialists, we Americans do not invade countries "for territory or resources". For example, Obama has recalled that when invading Iraq the United States had "sought to work within the international system and did not grab Iraqi territory or resources." It ended the war and "left Iraq to its people."

If Iraq is an inspiring example of unselfish American generosity, then Ukraine must be another. In May 2014, Hunter Biden, son of the particularly belligerent U.S. Vice President Joe Biden, joined the Board of Directors of Ukraine's largest gas producer, Burisma Holdings. Ukraine is believed to have considerable shale oil reserves. It also has the richest soil outside of Iowa. The U.S. agribusiness giant Cargill is particularly active in Ukraine, investing in grain elevators, animal feed, egg production and agribusiness, as well as the Black Sea port at Novorossiysk. The very active U.S.-Ukraine Business Council includes executives of Monsanto, John Deere, DuPont, Eli Lilly and others. Monsanto plans to build a big non-GMO corn seed plant in Ukraine, perhaps targeting the GMO-shy European market, as well as GMO products. Now that the new Ukraine has signed the deal with the European Union which allows free entry to E.U. markets, low Ukrainian labor costs should make these Ukraine-based U.S. enterprises highly competitive against European grain producers.

Since they are in virtual control of the government in Kiev, the Americans are in a good position to provide a favorable environment for U.S. business in Ukraine. In December 2014, President Poroshenko swore in three foreigners as cabinet ministers, all favorable to deregulation and privatization measures. An American, Natalie Jaresko, is the new Finance Minister; a Lithuanian, Aikvaras Abromavicius (who speaks Russian but not Ukrainian), is Economy

Minister and U.S.-educated Georgian Aleksandr Kvitashvili, who also does not speak Ukrainian, is Health Minister. Another Georgian, Ekaterina Zguladze was appointed a few days later to a senior role in the Interior Ministry.

Even stranger, in February 2015, Poroshenko named Georgia's disgraced ex-President Mikheil Saakashvili as his top foreign advisor. Educated in the United States on State Department fellowships, Saakashvili was elected president thanks to the U.S.-sponsored "Rose Revolution" in Georgia in 2003. But after provoking an unsuccessful war with Russia over South Ossetia in 2008, his popularity plummeted. While dodging demands by Georgian prosecutors for his extradition to answer charges on a whole range of criminal offenses, most notably embezzlement of government funds and abuse of power, Saakashvili began a new career as chairman of Poroshenko's International Consulting Council for Reforms. Media speculated that Saakashvili could use his position as Senator McCain's pet protégé to negotiate the transfer of U.S. weapons to Ukraine. He remains best-known to millions of Youtube viewers for chewing his red necktie while being filmed by the BBC during the South Ossetia crisis.

Three months later, on May 30, 2015, Poroshenko gave his "old friend" Saakashvili an even more astonishing assignment: governor of the troubled Odessa region. Nothing could better illustrate the reasons behind Odessans' demand for a federal system than this arbitrary imposition of a disgraced foreign autocrat as their Governor. Poroshenko granted Saakashvili Ukrainian citizenship minutes before he took up his new job. Anonymous protesters posted red neckties "for Misha" (Mikhail) on trees and monuments in Odessa.

While accusing Putin of nefariously seeking to "restore the Soviet Union", U.S. officials and their local puppets sometimes behave as though the Soviet Union in some way still exists, but is now run by Washington. One way or another, the United States is constructing its own little empire on the corrupt Western edge of the defunct Soviet bloc.

Meanwhile, according to Ina Kirsch, corruption in Ukraine is far worse than under Yanukovych. "I don't know anyone who now wants to invest in Ukraine. The planned big Ukraine investors' conference keeps being postponed [...] Logical: there are no investors. And frankly not only because there is war in Ukraine, but because the system in Ukraine has become even more corrupt and unreliable. Any potential investor will say, without credible guarantees we won't invest there." This may cause Europeans to hesitate, but the Americans don't seem to mind.

From a free market perspective, Russian gas exports to Western Europe could be seen as an excellent example of supply meeting demand. However, according to that great champion of free trade, the United States, Russian gas exports are nothing but a sinister "political weapon" being wielded by Putin for sinister, unspecified purposes. America proposes to rescue Europe from this potential tyranny by substituting the products of the U.S. hydraulic fracturing process. Well, not directly... Rather, the idea is that American fracking, by meeting domestic U.S. needs, will free up alternative resources to heat European homes in the winter. If this pig in the poke doesn't do the trick, Europeans will be exhorted to "sacrifice" for the greater good of punishing Russia for its alleged crimes.

While the United States was taking over Ukraine, U.S. representatives were putting pressure on European countries to back out of the South Stream gas pipeline project. The deal was signed in 2007 between Gazprom and the Italian petrochemical company ENI, in order to ensure Russian gas deliveries to the Balkans, Austria and Italy by bypassing Ukraine, whose unreliability as a transit country had been demonstrated by repeated failure to pay its bills and by siphoning off gas intended for Europe. Major German and French energy companies were also investors.

The pipeline was destined to traverse the Black Sea and reach European markets through Bulgaria. However, during the Ukrainian crisis, the Americans started putting pressure on Bulgaria. The U.S. ambassador to Sofia, Marcie Ries, warned Bulgarian businessmen that they could suffer from doing business with Russian companies under sanctions. The retiring president of the European Commission, José Manuel Barroso from Portugal, who used to be a "Maoist" back when "Maoism" was the cover for opposition to Soviet-backed liberation movements in Portugal's African colonies, threatened Bulgaria with E.U. proceedings for alleged irregularities in South Stream contracts. Finally, John McCain flew into Sofia to browbeat

Bulgarian Prime Minister Plamen Oresharski into pulling out of the deal. The pressure succeeded. This is a serious blow to countries that were counting on reliable natural gas provisions. But never mind: anything is good that hurts Russia.

A major step toward all-out war against Russia was taken on December 4, 2014, when the U.S. House of Representatives adopted a resolution condemning Russia for imaginary "armed aggression against United States allies and partner countries". Resolution 758 combines a long list of blatant lies with calls to arm Ukraine against alleged Russian aggression. It amounts to a potential declaration of war against Russia. The text was adopted without debate by an overwhelming majority of 411 apparently indifferent representatives who were leaving the chamber at the time, with only ten voting against it. It is dismaying to observe that the most vigorous denunciation of this shameful document came from two courageous men who are no longer in Congress, Dennis Kucinich and Ron Paul. [40]

The reckless adoption of a resolution that could be used to justify going to war against a major nuclear power is alarming evidence of the failure of the intelligence, honesty and sense of responsibility of the political system that Washington is trying to force on the entire world. Far from playing its constitutional role as the place where policy can be seriously debated, where foreign entanglements can be untangled and wars can be prevented, the U.S. Congress has degenerated into an echo chamber for lobbies and special interests, thoughtlessly endorsing the possibility of nuclear war with no more reflection that a sports star endorsing a soft drink. This frivolity indicates that the problem of Hillary Rodham Clinton goes far beyond a single individual and reveals a far deeper crisis in the American political system.

Russian Reality

The combination of enormous military, economic and ideological power with a profound disinterest in the rest of the world has led American leaders to assume that their own illusions can erase the reality of others. You can swat a bee thinking it is a giant poison mosquito, or crush a frog thinking it's a tarantula, and afterwards no one can tell the difference. Don Quixote's windmills were only a mild illusion compared to the enemies that the United States perpetually conjures up for itself.

As Washington proceeds on its endless crusade to eradicate Evil, it is treated by its subservient allies like the Mad King whose fantasies must be taken seriously. European leaders pretend to believe it all and hope that the damage can be kept within bounds. Opportunists and con men from around the globe, whether religious fanatics, fascists or just plain gangsters, approach the deranged monarch with pledges of fealty and oaths of devotion to "democracy", and are rewarded with modern weapons and an appropriate U.N. Security Council Resolution.

Ignoring the evidence, Washington has managed to go on claiming that it fought to save medical students in Grenada, bombed a chemical weapons factory in Sudan, prevented genocide in Kosovo, freed the women of Afghanistan, eliminated weapons of mass destruction in Iraq and saved the people of Libya from being eaten alive by a pitiless tyrant.

In choosing Vladimir Putin as the latest embodiment of Evil, however, the United States has run up against a Russian reality that cannot so easily be denied.

For many years, ever since Mikhail Gorbachev ended the Cold War, Russian leaders treated the United States with the deference required within the respectable confines of the "international community". The response was rude disdain. This might have gone on indefinitely, if the United States had not pushed farther and farther, and finally, in Ukraine, too far. The provocation, intended to isolate and weaken a great nation wounded by its past, has awakened Russia to its reality and its future. Essentially slow and defensive, Russia is always at its best when under attack. To use the common image, the United States has awakened the Bear from its hibernation.

Vladimir Putin, the contemporary personification of the little boy who shouts that the Emperor has no clothes, made this particularly clear during an informal speech on October 24, 2014 at the Valdai International Discussion Club in Sochi, attended by such diverse personalities as former French Prime Minister Dominique de Villepin and former Federal Chancellor of Austria Wolfgang

Schuessel. In regard to sanctions, Putin observed that they were interfering with the free trade that the West itself had promoted to its own advantage. "I think that our America friends are quite simply cutting off the branch they are sitting on," he said, stressing that: "Russia is not going to get all worked up, get offended or come begging at anyone's door. Russia is a self-sufficient country. We shall work within the foreign economic environment that has taken shape, develop our domestic production and technology and act more decisively to carry out necessary transformations. Pressure from outside, as has been the case on past occasions, will only consolidate our society, keep us alert and make us concentrate on our main development goals."

In international affairs, despite provocations, Russia would continue to seek measures to prevent global anarchy, and to counter the risks that result when other powers stimulate multiple arms races and endless ethnic, religious and social conflicts. For Putin the key word is "Respect": a stable world must be based on mutual respect, something that is lacking in the United States' approach to others. The United States, he observed, having declared itself the winner of the Cold War, saw no need to construct a stable system. "Pardon the analogy, but this is the way *nouveaux riches* behave when they suddenly end up with a great fortune, in this case in the form of world leadership and domination. Instead of managing their wealth wisely, for the benefit of themselves and others, I think they have committed many follies." The effort by the United States to impose its own models leads to the escalation of conflicts, "instead of sovereign and stable states we see the growing spread of chaos", and instead of democracy there is support for dubious elements ranging from open neo-fascists to Islamic radicals.

The Bear, said Putin, is "the master of the taiga, and I know for sure that he does not intend to move to any other climate zone – he would not be comfortable there. However, he will not let anyone else take his taiga either." Or in other words: "We don't need to be a superpower; that would only be an extra burden for us. I have already mentioned the taiga. It is immense, limitless, and simply to develop our territories we need plenty of time, energy and resources. We have no need to get involved in others' business, to order others around, but we want others to stay out of our affairs and to stop pretending that they rule the world. That is all. If there is an area where Russia could be a leader, it is in asserting the norms of international law."

U.S. mainstream media have been engaged in a massive propaganda campaign to erase Russian reality by imposing a fictional version of the Ukrainian crisis upon it, blaming the conflict on a hypothetic drive by Putin to reconstitute the Soviet Union or the Tsarist Empire, or something even more sinister. However, the Russian leader's plain talk is getting through to the rest of the world and it is making sense. Even Washington's European satellites are going to find it harder and harder to ignore the Russian reality.

United States leaders, Hillary Clinton in the forefront, are setting out to "isolate" the largest nation on the planet. Perhaps next on its fantasy agenda would be to "isolate" the most populous, China. But in reality, who is isolated? The big question is: can anything but devastating violence, such as nuclear war, awaken America from its fantasy of being the unique and exceptional nation that can and must lay down the law for all others?

Chapter 7

The War Party

"Leadership in this world can be assured not by persuading oneself of one's exclusiveness and God-given duty to be responsible for everyone, but only by the ability and craft in forming a consensus."

– *Sergei Lavrov, November 22, 2014*

The American people are prisoners of the illusion of being "the exceptional nation" called upon to "shape" the world. This illusion is maintained by the political branch of the entertainment industry: politicians, mass media news coverage, defense intellectuals, commentators. The show is brought to us by their sponsors.

To know who those sponsors are, take a look at the list of Clinton Foundation donors who have contributed millions of dollars, supposedly for charity – the sort of charity that begins at home. These are philanthropists who give in order to get. Eight digit donors include: Saudi Arabia, the pro-Israel Ukrainian oligarch Victor Pinchuk, and the Saban family. Pinchuk has pledged millions to a branch of the Foundation, the Clinton Global Initiative, for a program to train future Ukrainian leaders according to "European values". Seven digit donors include: Kuwait, Exxon Mobil, "Friends of Saudi Arabia", James Murdoch, Qatar, Boeing, Dow, Goldman Sachs, Walmart and the United Arab Emirates. Cheapskates paying their dues to the Clintons with contributions above only half a million include: the Bank of America, Chevron, Monsanto, Citigroup and the inevitable Soros Foundation. What is it about the Clintons that makes them so popular, particularly with Saudi Arabia?

With friends like that, you need enemies. And Hillary knows where to find them – in countries these friendly donors don't like.

In her driving ambition to be the First Woman President of the United States, Hillary Rodham Clinton has made herself a figment of the collective imagination by fitting herself into the role of top salesperson for the ruling oligarchy:

- She has shifted her interest from children's rights, a field with no big money backers, to promotion of military power (also known as "the only language *they* understand").

- She has spread the message that U.S. interference in other countries is motivated by the generous impulse to spread "our ideals" to the dark corners of elsewhere.
- She readily treats foreign heads of state with dehumanizing contempt, declaring that they have "no soul", or "no conscience", and dismissing them as lowly creatures that "must go".
- She "misspeaks", but sees nothing wrong with that. In politics, who doesn't "misspeak"? She is not there to tell the truth, but to tell her story.
- She can still pose as a woman whose only aspiration is to "break the glass ceiling" for the benefit of all women, who will now be able to fill all the top jobs in the country... thanks to Hillary!

In short, she has used all the stereotypical clichés of the "exceptional America" narrative as rungs in her ladder to the top.

Hillary Clinton's performance as Secretary of State was a great success in one respect: it has made her the favorite candidate of the War Party. This appears to have been her primary objective.

But Hillary Clinton is far from being the whole problem. The fundamental problem is the War Party and its tight grip on U.S. policy.

One reason there is so little public resistance is that the wars started by the War Party hardly feel like real wars to the American people. Americans are not seeing their homes blown up. The drone armada is removing the inconvenience of "boots on the ground" veterans coming home with post-traumatic stress syndrome. War from the air is increasingly safe, distant, invisible. For most Americans, U.S. wars are simply a branch of the entertainment industry, something to hear about on television but rarely seen. These wars give you a bit of serious entertainment in return for your tax dollars. But they are not *really* a matter of life and death...

In fact, it hardly seems to matter what happens in these wars. The United States no longer even makes war in order to win, but rather to make sure that the other side loses. Hillary Clinton accused Vladimir Putin, quite falsely, of adhering to a "zero-sum game in which, if someone is winning, then someone else has to be losing". The United States is playing something even worse: a "no win", or a "lose-lose", game in which the other side may lose, yet the United States cannot be called the winner. These are essentially spoiler wars, fought to get rid of real or imagined rivals; everyone is poorer as a result. Americans are being taught to grow accustomed to these negative wars, whose declared purpose is to get rid of something – a dictator, or terrorism, or human rights violations.

The United States is out to dominate the world by knocking out the other players.

"Our ideals" are part of the collateral damage. With its wartime crackdown on internal enemies and its Homeland Security and Patriot Acts, the United States is not only sacrificing its own freedom, it is undermining the very belief in progressive values: in democracy, in progress, in science and technology, in reason itself. By loudly identifying itself with these values, the United States is actually promoting their rejection. Such ideals increasingly resemble a mere camouflage for aggression. What is the use of democratic and liberal ideals when they are reduced to serving as pretexts for war?

And yet, opposition to the War Party is certainly shared by countless Americans. It is probably much greater than the pro-war establishment realizes. But those who are increasingly alarmed by the danger feel helpless to do anything about it. This is because the War Party is firmly in control of the two-party political system.

In February 2015, Paul Craig Roberts wrote:

> Jobs offshoring destroyed the American industrial and manufacturing unions. Their demise and the current attack on the public employee unions has left the Democratic Party financially dependent on the same organized private interest groups as the Republicans. Both parties now report to the same interest groups. Wall Street, the military/security complex, the Israel Lobby, agribusiness, and the extractive industries (oil, mining, timber) control the government regardless of the party in power. These powerful interests all have a stake in American hegemony. The message is that the constellation of forces precludes internal political change.

And he concluded that: "Hegemony's Achilles' heel is the US

economy."

If Roberts is right, and it is hard to see where he is wrong, the only thing that can liberate Americans from their warlike fiction would be economic collapse. This is not a cheerful prospect. It is hard to hope for an economic catastrophe as the only way to avoid nuclear annihilation. Whatever the odds, one cannot help wishing that the American people would come to their senses and figure out a way to end this policy of war and thus find a constructive way of dealing with the world. This happy ending is theoretically possible, but looks extremely unlikely because of the American political system.

The U.S. Presidential election is essentially a popular entertainment event. Billionaire sponsors send two carefully-vetted contenders into the arena, sure to win either way. The intellectual level of Republican-Democrat confrontation increasingly recalls that of the parties that divided the early Byzantine Empire, based on blue and green chariot racing teams. In the 2016 presidential election, the Good Cop party and the Bad Cop party will disagree about domestic policy issues before everything gets stalled in Congress. But the most significant issue of all is the choice of war.

Since the War Party dominates both branches of the Two-Party-System, the recent track record suggests that the Republicans will nominate a candidate bad enough to make Hillary look good.

But let us suppose that a miracle happens, and that thanks to a genuine popular revolt, one of the parties actually nominates a "peace candidate". That would be a good sign, but it is not enough. We remember that Obama promised "change" and was so convincing that some (falsely) naïve Norwegians awarded him the Nobel Peace Prize. He went on to outdo even his predecessors in useless aggressive war-making – with moments of hesitation, however, which we cannot expect from Hillary.

Even a sincere peace candidate needs to have a peace team to take over from the War Party in the White House and the State Department. Despite the upbeat talk, Obama had no peace team and essentially let the same old War Party take over.

It might still not be too late to radically reverse the direction of U.S. policy. There are numerous qualified individuals in the United States to form a peace team. To mention just a few, we could start with Stephen Cohen as Ambassador to Moscow, backed up in the State Department by John Mearsheimer, Stephen Walt, Chas Freeman, and many others. Ron Paul would be an excellent budget-cutting Secretary of Defense. Dennis Kucinich could head a newly formed Department of Peace Transformation, to seek ways to promote both peaceful relations abroad and a culture of peace at home – no small task. Let Cynthia McKinney be the new Ambassador to the United Nations. Former FBI whistle-blower Coleen Rowley is well qualified to be in charge of the security agencies. William R. Polk, a descendant of the family of the eleventh President of the United States, would make a fine National Security Advisor for the new President in this dream administration.

And it is indeed a dream.

None of these honorable personalities could be confirmed by a Senate whose members are not only beholden to AIPAC for campaign contributions, but is largely convinced by the rhetoric of major newspapers. The Senate then regurgitates this same rhetoric as part of the great national chorus of an exceptional nation which stands up to threats from the Evil Ones.

A last-minute peace candidate would be a divine surprise. But a real alternative to the War Party must be built up over time, for institutional blockage also exists in Congress.

Anti-war movements have declined drastically in the United States, perhaps because people feel, with justification, that they are useless. Indeed, the type of anti-war movement that flourished in the Vietnam War is inappropriate today. A war fought by a conscription army, as in Vietnam, can be effectively opposed by a popular anti-war movement remote from power, because it threatens the loyalty of the cannon fodder. But the War Machine has learned to make war without unwilling boots on the ground. By trying to repeat the movement opposing the Vietnam War, surviving anti-war movements tend to be almost deliberately marginal. They are able only to rally unofficial representatives of identity groups that feel more or less alienated, justifiably or not, because they are more tied to the theme of identity politics than to stopping war. Such movements have no strategy or ambition for taking power and influencing policy. Mere street protests will be repressed without making any impression on Washington.

Wars fought at a distance by mercenaries and drones must be stopped at the top, or finally defeated either by foreign forces or by domestic collapse.

A peace party must have a strategy for stopping war at the top. The rise of Hillary Clinton should make clear the total failure of clinging to the Democratic Party as the "lesser evil". A Peace Party needs to be non-partisan and cross-partisan, rallying people who are fed up with a War Party composed of neocons and humanitarian hypocrites. People can honestly disagree on domestic policy and still understand that war is a matter of life and death.

What should be done? People may figure out what to do once they are aware of what is at stake. That hasn't happened yet.

The United States cannot go on dominating the world. The question is: can the United States dominate itself?

Basic wisdom is ancient and simple. *Pride goeth before destruction, and a haughty spirit before a fall.* That is a lesson almost anyone should be able to understand.

Endnotes

1   Nikolas Kozloff, "Obama's Real Message to Latin America? The Coup in Honduras", CounterPunch, June 29, 2009. Eva Golinger, "Washington behind the Honduras coup: Here is the evidence", Global Research, July 15, 2009

2   Dana Frank, "Dinner With Obama: Repression's Reward in Honduras?" CounterPunch, September 23, 2010.

3   Dana Frank, A High Stakes Election in Honduras, The Nation, November 25, 2013 http://www.thenation.com/article/177028/high-stakes-election-honduras#

4   Dana Frank, "Who's Responsible for the Flight of Honduran Children?" Huffington Post, http://www.huffingtonpost.com/dana-frank/whos-responsible-for-the-honduras_b_5530518.html

5   It is relevant to note that according to a recent study by the Free University in Berlin, 60 percent of East Germans consider socialism or communism a good idea, compared to 37 percent of West Germans. http://www.fu-berlin.de/presse/informationen/fup/2015/fup_15_044-studie-linksextremismus/index.html

6   Plus Richard Armitage, John Bolton, Stephen Bryen, Douglas Feith, Frank Gaffney, Fred Ikle, Zalmay Khalilzad, William Kristol, Michael Ledeen, Bernard Lewis, Peter Rodman, Gary Schmitt, Max Singer, Casper Weinberger, David Wurmser and Dov Zakheim.

7   "The Influencer" by Connie Bruck, The New Yorker, May 10, 2010.

8   Ibid.

9   [Jason Horowitz, "Can Liberal Zionists Count On Hillary Clinton?", The New York Times, December 17, 2014.]

10 Secret negotiations are proceeding rapidly to conclude the Trans-Atlantic Free Trade Area (TAFTA), enthusiastically supported by great corporations and the political ruling class on both sides of the Atlantic, despite growing popular opposition.

11 [http://www.theguardian.com/world/2014/jul/04/edward-snowden-legal-defence-hillary-clinton-interview]

12 [July 9, 2014 interview with Amy Goodman on "Democracy Now".]

13 [Hard Choices, pp.552-555.]

14 Kathryn Joyce and Jeff Sharlet, "Hillary's Prayer: Hillary Clinton's Religion and Politics", Mother Jones, September 1, 2007.

15 "Ghosts of Rwanda", FRONTLINE: PBS, http://www.pbs.org/wgbh/pages/frontline/shows/ghosts/interviews/ghali.html

16 Charles Onana, Les Secrets de la Justice Internationale, Editions Duboiris, 2005; pp.367-370.

17 Samantha Power, A Problem From Hell, p.326.

18 Richard Holbrooke's, "To End a War", Random House, 1998. On page 202, he recounts that it was "Kofi Annan's strength on the bombing in August" that had "made him the private favorite" of American officials to replace Boutros Boutros-Ghali. "Although the American campaign against Boutros-Ghali, in which all our key allies opposed us, was long and difficult [...] the decision was correct, and may well have saved America's role in the United Nations." The key event was the August 30, 1995 bombing. On page 99, Holbrooke recounts the eve of that bombing. "In New York, Ambassador Albright continued her vigorous campaign with those United Nations officials she could round up; fortunately, Secretary-General Boutros-Ghali was unreachable on a commercial aircraft, so she dealt instead with his best deputy, Kofi Annan, who was in charge of peacekeeping operations. At 11:45 a.m., New York time, came a big break: Annan informed Talbott and Albright that he had instructed the U.N.'s civilian officials and military commanders to relinquish for a limited period of time their authority to veto air strikes in Bosnia. For the first time in the war, the decision on the air strikes was solely in the hands of NATO -- primarily two American officers [...]" To sum it up, page 103: "Annan's gutsy performance in those twenty-four hours was to play a central role in Washington's strong support for him a year later as the successor to Boutros Boutros-Ghali as Secretary General of the United Nations. Indeed, in a sense Annan won the job on that day."

19 David S. Cloud, "How James Rubin Shaped Pact With Hashim Thaci of the KLA", *The Wall Street Journal*, June 29, 1999.

20 Seth Ackerman, 'What Reporters Knew About Kosovo Talks - But Didn't Tell. Was Rambouillet Another Tonkin Gulf?' *FAIR Media Advisory*, 2 June 1999.

21 This focus on the State Department ignores such a glass ceiling breaker as CIA agent Alfreda Frances Bikowsky, the champion of torture who served as model for Maya in the film "Zero Dark Thirty" – made by a woman.

22 See John Ashton & Ian Ferguson, *Cover-Up of Convenience: the Hidden Scandal of Lockerbie*, Mainstream, 2001; Report by Trial Observer Dr. Hans Koechler http://i-p-o.org/lockerbie-report.htm

23 The European Community was then in the process of transforming itself into the European Union.

24 See my book *Fools' Crusade : Yugoslavia, NATO and Western Delusions*, Pluto Press (London), Monthly Review Press (USA), 2002.

25 "Kouchner rit": https://www.youtube.com/watch?v=PSYOIV7bto4

26 In March 2014, an Iranian defector confirmed that Iran and not Libya was responsible for bringing down PanAm flight 103 over Lockerbie. http://www.telegraph.co.uk/news/uknews/terrorism-in-the-uk/10688067/Lockerbie-bombing-was-work-of-Iran-not-Libya-says-former-spy.html

27 See John Ashton & Ian Ferguson, *Cover-Up of Convenience: the Hidden Scandal of Lockerbie*, Mainstream, 2001; Report by Trial Observer Dr. Hans Koechler http://i-p-o.org/lockerbie-report.htm

28 http://www.youtube.com/watch?v=VZZvPlGCt_8&feature=em-share_video_user.

29 http://www.informationclearinghouse.info/article40843.htm

30 http://townhall.com/columnists/dianawest/2014/04/25/did-the-us-choose-war-in-libya-over-qaddafis-abdication-n1829075/page/full

31 Maximilian Forte, *Slouching Towards Sirte: NATO's War on Libya and Africa*, Baraka Books, Montreal, 2012, p.295.

32 Ray Locker, "Pentagon 2008 study claims Putin has Asperger's syndrome", USA Today, February 4, 2015, http://www.usatoday.com/story/news/politics/2015/02/04/putin-aspergers-syndrome-study-pentagon/22855927/ .

33 "I regret to say what we are seeing here in the Unites States are the ascendancy of two factions in this country who are against Russia and the Russians. First is Brzezinski, who was Obama's mentor when Obama was a college student in Columbia, and Brzezinski in 2008 ran all the foreign affairs and defence policies of the Obama presidential campaign and has stacked his administration with advisor on Russia at the National Security Council comes from the Brzezinski's outpoll CSIS there in Washington D.C. I graduated from the same Ph.D. programme at Harvard that produced Brzezinski before me.

"He is a die-hard Russian hater, he hates Russia, he hates the Russian, and he wants to break Russia up into its constituent units, and, unfortunately, he has his people, his protégés in the Democratic Party and in this Administration. Second faction lining against Russia are the neo-conservatives, for e.g. this latest Brookings Institute report calling for arming the Ukrainian military in these Nazi formations which is now reflected in this latest bill just introduced into the Congress yesterday, and the neoconservatives feel exactly the same way against Russia and the Russians.

"I went to school with large numbers of these neoconservatives at the University of Chicago, Wolfowitz and all the rest of them. Many of them are grandchildren of Jewish people, who fled the pogroms against Jews, and they have been brainwashed against Russia and the Russians. So you have two very powerful factions here in the United States against Russia and the Russians who are driving this policy, and I regret to report there are very few voices opposing this." Francis Boyle: Brzezinski wants to break Russia up into constituent units - English pravda.ru, http://english.pravda.ru/news/world/16-02-2015/129834-brzezinski_russia-0/

34 *The Grand Chessboard*, p. 133.

35 0See *Against Our Better Judgment*, by Alison Weir.

36 "The 'Snipers' Massacre' on the Maidan in Ukraine" by Ivan Katchanovski, Ph.D., University of Ottawa. https://www.academia.edu/8776021/The_Snipers_Massacre_on_the_Maidan_in_Ukraine]

37 http://www.wienerzeitung.at/_em_cms/globals/print.php?em_ssc=LCwsLA==&em_cnt=736123&em_loc=530&em_ref=/nachrichten/europa/europastaaten/&em_ivw=RedCont/Politik/

Ausland&em_absatz_bold=0

38 "Wake Up Europe" by George Soros http://www.nybooks.com/articles/archives/2014/nov/20/ wake-up-europe/ and "A New Policy to Rescue Ukraine" by George Soros http://www.nybooks.com/ articles/archives/2015/feb/05/new-policy-rescue-ukraine/.

39 James O'Neill, "Why the Secrecy on the MH17 Investigation", CounterPunch, December 19-21, 2014.

40 See the commentary by Ron Paul: http://www.ronpaulinstitute.org/archives/featured-articles/2014/December/04/reckless-congress-declares-war-on-russia/ and http://original.antiwar.com/paul/2014/12/05/reckless-congress-declares-war-on-russia/#.VILpR1Ost4l.gmail .

Index